Worker Injury Third Party Cases

Recognizing and Proving Liability

Vincent A. Gallagher

Bernan Press
Lanham • Boulder • New York • London

Published by Bernan Press
An imprint of The Rowman & Littlefield Publishing Group, Inc.
4501 Forbes Boulevard, Suite 200, Lanham, Maryland 20706
www.rowman.com
800-865-3457; info@bernan.com

Unit A, Whitacre Mews, 26-34 Stannary Street, London SE11 4AB

British Library Cataloguing in Publication Information Available

Library of Congress Cataloging-in-Publication Data

Names: Gallagher, Vincent A., author.
Title: Worker injury third party cases : recognizing and proving liability / Vincent A. Gallagher.
Description: Lanham, Maryland : Bernan Press, [2017] | Includes index.
Identifiers: LCCN 2017001534 (print) | LCCN 2017001700 (ebook) | ISBN 9781598889086 (pbk. : alk. paper) | ISBN 9781598889093 (electronic)
Subjects: LCSH: Industrial safety—Law and legislation—United States. | Industrial hygiene—Law and legislation—United States. | Employers' liability—United States. | United States. Occupational Safety and Health Administration. | Product safety—Law and legislation—United States.
Classification: LCC KF3570 .G35 2017 (print) | LCC KF3570 (ebook) | DDC 344.7304/65—dc23
LC record available at https://lccn.loc.gov/2017001534

∞™ The paper used in this publication meets the minimum requirements of American National Standard for Information Sciences—Permanence of Paper for Printed Library Materials, ANSI/NISO Z39.48-1992.

Printed in the United States of America

Worker Injury
Third Party Cases

Contents

Acknowledgments

First of all, I would like to thank Michele Szachewicz for all of her work, which not only made this book possible but also helped me in all of my work. It is a blessing to have such a good administrative assistant.

Thanks to the many lawyers, especially Joe Lurie and Marty Brigham, who always had time and patience to help me understand the broader picture so I could see how a safety professional can help lawyers. Thanks also to the hundreds of workers who taught me to identify and control hazards. I learned much more from workers than from anything I learned in graduate school.

I am also most grateful to the hundreds of workers whose injuries and deaths I have investigated, which have taught me ways to prevent recurrences. I pray that I never forget the lessons learned from their tragedies, and that this book provides some insight for others who serve workers to do a better job.

Introduction

A workers' comp attorney called to see if he had a likely third party case. His client fell from a roof on a construction site. The damages were significant. But because the workers left their fall protection in their van, he thought that their negligence and their employer's negligence was so clear that liability was unlikely.

On a scale of one to ten, his case was a ten. Liability doesn't get much better. The general contractor, as Controlling Employer under OSHA's Multi-Employer Citation Policy, violated OSHA standards by permitting the contractor's workers to work for several days in violation of OSHA standards. The essential question is "why" did the general contractor/construction manager (GC/CM) allow the employer to violate OSHA standards? The answer is often because it can save time and money, that is, if an injury does not result in a lawsuit.

Another call was from a seasoned personal injury lawyer. His client was a sole proprietor hired by a contractor to perform siding work at a residence. His client had fallen from a pump jack scaffold.

The two poles were each attached to the building at the roof only. There was no attachment at the bottom. His client removed the attachment point of the pole on the top right. When he did, the work platform fell and he was injured. The attorney also thought he had no case because of the conduct of his client.

I told him that there was likely a viable theory of liability against the contractor who hired his client due to:

- Failure to hire a safe contractor
- Failure to verify that his client received the OSHA required safety training for building and disassembling scaffolds

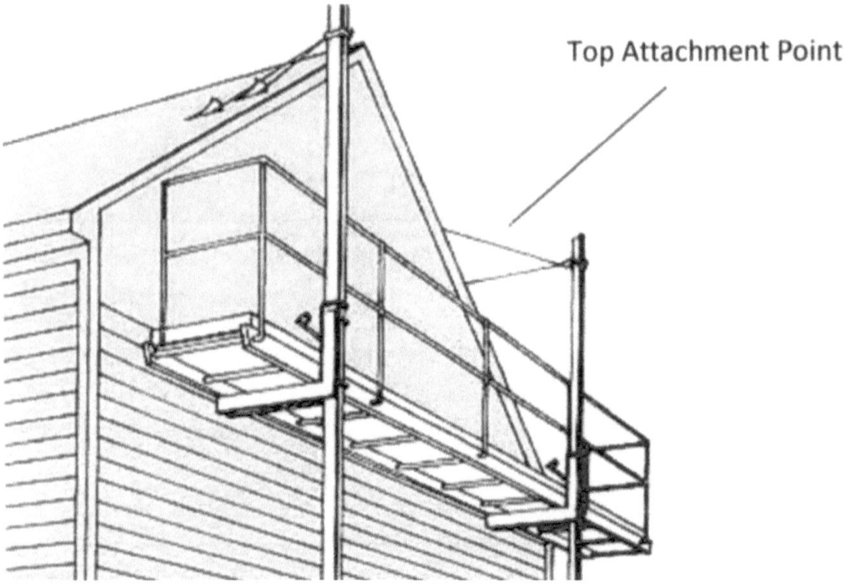

Figure I.1. Pump Jack Scaffold

- Failure to ensure that each pole was attached at the top and bottom both as required by OSHA

It may seem counterintuitive, but the more negligence on the part of the employer, the more negligence on the part of the construction project owner, general contractor or construction manager who permitted the work to be done unsafely. These two calls led me to question: If a seasoned worker's comp and personal injury lawyer failed to see what appeared to me to be clear cases of liability, how many others overlooked theories of liability that were not so obvious? So I decided to write this book to help attorneys and others answer two important questions:

- Is there a third party theory of liability that is likely to be successful?
- What are the facts needed to prove liability, and how do you get them?

COMMON MYTHS WHICH CAN BLIND

Safety Is Common Sense

One mental block is the failure to understand the Standard of Care relative to worker injury prevention. Attorneys recognize in medical malpractice cases that there is a standard of care or recognized body of knowledge established by medical authorities relative to standard methods to diagnose, evaluate and treat various illnesses and injuries and perform various procedures. So they consult a specialist to get advice before pursuing liability. Attorneys representing injured workers often have little understanding that in worker injury cases, there is an established body of knowledge relative to standard methods to identify, evaluate and control hazards to prevent injury and death. There are also industry and government safety standards and customary procedures to manage safety. So the attorney performs a cursory evaluation thinking that safety is "common sense" and that they understand what should be done.

Most Accidents Are Caused by the Unsafe Acts of Workers

Another block to seeing liability is that the attorney thinks the "employee misconduct" was too significant to warrant a lawsuit. The fact that a worker's behavior led to injury does not mean that the worker's conduct was a cause of injury.

If the worker was trained and instructed to comply with OSHA standards and the GC/CM had taken reasonable steps to implement a safety program, there is likely no basis to sue the GC/CM. However, if the exposure to the hazard was not an "isolated incident" and the defendant GC/CM had knowledge of the hazard (actual or constructive), there is likely a viable case. In my experience in plaintiff cases, more often than not, the worker and other workers had been performing the dangerous task for several days prior to this incident. Quite often, the worker did not violate safety instructions, was not trained about hazard and risk, and was required to work in an unreasonably dangerous environment where the safety management systems at all levels failed in many ways.

Construction Work Involves Inherent Hazards

Another mental block is the notion that some work is inherently dangerous and we must accept some hazards. There are no hazards that are "inherent" in work. There are only hazards that are controlled or uncontrolled. When a worker is injured, it is because of exposure to an uncontrolled hazard. The answer to "why" the hazard was not controlled will likely lie within the management system of the defendant GC/CM, construction project owner (CPO), premise owner or product manufacturer. To understand causation, safety professionals ask questions relative to "why" the defendant's management system permitted the hazard to evolve and to continue to exist. The root cause of the injury is the defendant's failure to implement or require the implementation of a safety program or product safety management program which would have eliminated or controlled the hazard.

THE HAZARD IS A CAUSE OF INJURY

Another mental block results from viewing causation "mechanistically" rather than "systematically." A "mechanistic evaluation" of causation performed by an engineer would conclude that the injury was caused by the unsafe condition such as an unprotected floor opening or an exposed electrical conductor. It focuses on who created the hazard and who should have controlled it. A "systematic evaluation" performed by a safety professional sees the hazard as a "symptom" not as a "cause." The uncontrolled hazard should never have been permitted to exist in the first place. To understand causation, system safety analysis asks "why" the management system failed to plan, monitor and ensure that the hazard was eliminated or controlled by reasonable means. The root cause of the injury is the defendant's failure to manage safety.

STANDARD OF CARE VS. THE LAW

While testifying in court, a judge instructed me: "You should know that in the state of New Jersey, the landlord or property owner does not have a duty regarding the safety of contractor workers when it hires a contractor to perform work on its premise. The owner has the responsibility for the safety of the structure of the building but has no responsibility for the safety of the work performed by contractors that it hires, do you understand?"

I was tempted to ask: "Do you mean, Your Honor, that in the state of New Jersey, there is no relationship between the law and the standard of care of a corporation or business owner such as the defendant regarding what industry safety authorities say are reasonable steps the business owner or corporation (defendant) should take to prevent contractor worker injury?"

Many times in other cases in New Jersey, I was able to tell the jury about the standard of care of the corporation/business owner who hires a contractor to work on their premise. In New Jersey, decisions support both arguments. Decisions which conclude that a corporation/business owner has no responsibility to oversee and manage the safety of contractors and other non-employees who work on its premise are contrary to the standard of care or customary safe practice in industry. There should not be a distinction between the standard of care and the law. The standard of care is simply what is customarily accepted as reasonable. Industry standards and OSHA establish what is reasonable.

I remember one day listening to a recording of the late Harry Philo, a prominent plaintiff attorney, instructing lawyers on what to do when the law grants privilege to some at the expense of others. He said in no uncertain terms: "The law is not the law until the law is **fair**. The law is not the law until the law is **just**." If the law and the standard of care are at odds, that is not reasonable. If a worker was injured because a defendant violated the standard of care, from a safety expert's point of view, that is not fair or just. Some attorneys readily accept the fact that the law grants unjust privilege to some. Some attorneys with greater imagination and zeal argue and convince judges to open doors of unjust privilege. I have found that judges are not likely to prevent an expert from explaining the "standard of care" or the "customary safe practice" of the defendant to the jury.

The decision for an attorney to sue someone for causing serious injury or death should not be taken lightly. It is a serious matter to file a complaint that essentially accuses a person or entity of negligently causing harm to another person. It is also a serious matter for a disabled worker or surviving spouse and his/her family to be able to survive economically after a serious, catastrophic injury or death occurs. Plaintiff attorneys should do everything possible to avoid barking up the wrong tree. They should also know how to perform evaluations to identify all possible viable theories of liability. They should know how to effectively investigate the question of whether or not there was a violation of the standard of care. No one has all of the answers. My hope is that this book will be of value to plaintiffs' attorneys to better know when to hold them and when to fold them. I hope it is of value to defense attorneys so that they know when the plaintiff's attorney has a solid case and when he/she is barking up the wrong tree.

HOW TO USE THIS BOOK

It is important to have an overall understanding of the principles and practices of safety management to understand when and why failures in safety management occur, that is, to understand causation. Part I should be helpful in understanding what should be done to implement the overall job site safety program. Parts II and III should be helpful in identifying and preparing injury cases related to construction and premise cases. Part IV should be helpful in products cases. Part V includes chapters which should be of general interest and hopefully helpful in depositions and cross examination of defendant representatives and experts.

Many attorneys do not like to simply read questions during depositions and trial. So they prepare by organizing the key issues and ask questions in ways which make them appear spontaneous. In my experience, the results are inevitably better when the attorney simply reads the prepared questions. Experts are usually very good at listening. They recognize a good question no matter how spontaneous it appears to be asked. They are also likely to be experts at "dancing." But they know they cannot dance too far away from a good question without it being apparent. My experience is that the attorneys who read well-crafted questions and insist on an answer invariably provide me with a good factual basis to perform my evaluation. Attorneys who paraphrase my proposed questions often change it in ways that give the deponent a way to wiggle out.

Many chapters include lists of questions which can be used in deposition or cross examination of defendants and experts. They are designed to get the key facts. In new construction cases, the most important facts will likely come from the superintendent of the GC or CM. The answers will give your expert a list of facts which he/she could list in the expert report as the basis for his/her opinion. For example, the expert report could include in the Hazard Analysis section the following:

DEPOSITION OF MR. _____, THE SUPERINTENDENT OF ABC GENERAL CONTRACTING COMPANY

The following is the most important deposition testimony of Mr. __________:

- He has been a superintendent for this company for 20 years (6-4).
- He scheduled contractors, coordinated contractors, held weekly meetings, inspected the work of contractors, authorized payments, and ran the job (7-20).
- He has had no OSHA or safety training (9-15).
- He did not require contractors to attend a pre-job safety meeting (12-8).
- He did not hold weekly safety meetings with contractors (15-22).
- He did not perform daily inspections (22-1).
- No one from his company performed daily safety inspections (23-7).
- He did not require any workers exposed to falls to have the OSHA required safety training (29-12).
- He never did anything to verify if forklift operators had the OSHA required safety training (31-6).
- He never did anything to verify that workers on scaffolds received the OSHA required scaffold safety training (32-4).
- He never verified that any workers received any OSHA required training (33-10).
- He never evaluated the safety performance of any contractor (41-5).

- His safety performance was never evaluated by anyone in his company (43-1).
- He has no written assigned safety management tasks (44-2).
- He does take reasonable steps to make sure that the contract is implemented with regard to quality of work or specification compliance (47-8).
- He does not do anything to ensure that contractors comply with OSHA as required by his company's contract with them (49-13).
- If he had seen the plaintiff exposed to this hazard prior to this incident, he would have told him to stop working (54-3).
- The plaintiff and co-workers had been performing their work in the same way for several days prior to this incident (59-9).
- The exposure of the plaintiff and co-workers to the fall hazard was conspicuous, that is, was easy to identify.

For trial, you could make a PowerPoint presentation with a list of all of the key facts for presentation to the jury by your expert. You could show the list of facts during cross examination of the opposing expert and ask him/her to tell the jury if those facts were important for his/her evaluation and to explain why. The facts are the currency of the expert.

Full disclosure: I have worked for the plaintiff's attorney in about 90 percent of my cases—10 percent for the defendant. However, I don't think I am biased. I believe that the facts alone lead to reasonable opinions and conclusions. I believe the facts alone determine if "somebody done somebody wrong."

My intention is to provide information to help both plaintiff and defense attorneys so that both are better able to recognize the strengths and weaknesses of their case. I hope this book reinforces the notion that litigation is truly a search for truth and justice. If the defendant knew or should have known of the hazard which led to injury of the worker and failed to act reasonably to prevent injury, the plaintiff's attorney should be successful. If the defendant was conscientiously managing safety or did not know or could not reasonably be expected to know of the existence of the hazard that led to injury, the defense attorney should be successful. The facts are everything!

Part I

PRINCIPLES AND PRACTICES OF SAFETY MANAGEMENT

Chapter One

Common Theories of Liability

CONSTRUCTION CASES

In new construction cases, the theory of liability will likely be that the GC/CM who was running the job failed to comply with the standard of care, that is, the industry and government standards which establish the customary safe practices for the GC/CM to follow to manage safety. The customary safe practice is for the GC/CM to plan, monitor and ensure that contractors and subcontractors work safely and in compliance with OSHA standards.

The following are types of incidents that have resulted in lawsuits in construction cases:

~ ~ ~ ~

Description of Incident: **Worker hammering nail struck in eye by nail.**
Failure: Failure of GC/CM to require framers/carpenters to use eye protection.

~ ~ ~ ~

Description of Incident: **Worker electrocuted when crane boom contacts overhead power line.**
Failure: Failure of GC/CM to require the power company to deenergize or cover exposed power lines.

~ ~ ~ ~

Description of Incident: **Scaffold plank cracks causing worker to fall.**
Failure: Failure of GC/CM to require contractor to use scaffold grade lumber.

~ ~ ~ ~

Description of Incident: **Employee working from ladder falls.**
Failure: Failure of GC to require work to be done safely from scissors lift or scaffold when work involved the use of two hands and/or the manipulation of tools.

~ ~ ~ ~

Description of Incident: **Trip and fall over construction debris.**
Failure: Failure of GC/CM to require the implementation of a housekeeping program.

~ ~ ~ ~

Description of Incident: **Worker falls in hole of sump pump in basement.**
Failure: Failure of GC/CM to require a cover over hole—failure of GC/CM to require sufficient lighting.

~ ~ ~ ~

Description of Incident: **Worker descending steps slips and falls on mud.**
Failure: Failure of GC/CM to require safe walkways through areas with heavy mud.

~ ~ ~ ~

Description of Incident: **Worker struck by bucket of backhoe.**
Failure: Failure of GC/CM to prevent operation of backhoe with worker within swing radius of the bucket.

~ ~ ~ ~

Description of Incident: **On weekend, a child falls into unprotected stairway opening of new home being constructed.**
Failure: Failure of GC/CM to require a guardrail or cover over opening.

~ ~ ~ ~

Description of Incident: **Aluminum ladder strikes overhead power line.**
Failure: Failure of GC/CM to ensure that the power company deenergized or covered exposed conductors.

~ ~ ~ ~

Description of Incident: **Worker struck by falling object.**
Failure: Failure of GC/CM to require a canopy at entrance to construction site. Failure of GC/CM to require hardhats.

~ ~ ~ ~

Description of Incident: **Worker struck by high pressure water in face when attempting to cut high pressure water line.**

Failure: Failure of GC/CM to require line to be bled or deenergized.

~ ~ ~ ~

Description of Incident: **Painter overcome by gases and vapors in confined space.**
Failure: Failure of GC/CM to hire safe contractors and require implementation of confined space entry program.

~ ~ ~ ~

Description of Incident: **Fall from telecommunications tower while free climbing.**
Failure: Failure of GC/CM to require lifeline to use as fall protection while climbing.

~ ~ ~ ~

Description of Incident: **Worker buried when trench collapses.**
Failure: Failure of GC/CM to require sloping to angle of repose, shoring or use of trench box.

~ ~ ~ ~

Description of Incident: **Masonry wall blown over by wind, crushing worker.**
Failure: Failure of GC/CM to require bracing of the wall.

~ ~ ~ ~

Description of Incident: **Worker falls from pump jack scaffold.**
Failure: Failure of GC/CM to require guardrails.

~ ~ ~ ~

Description of Incident: **Scissors lift wheel goes in hole causing lift to tip over.**
Failure: Failure of GC/CM to require floor holes to be covered.

~ ~ ~ ~

Description of Incident: **Worker on scaffold makes contact with overhead power line.**
Failure: Failure of GC/CM to ensure scaffolds were located at least ten feet away from overhead power lines or require power company to cover power lines.

~ ~ ~ ~

Description of Incident: **Worker using nail gun without eye protection—struck by nail.**

Failure: Failure of GC/CM to require framer/carpenter to use eye protection.

~ ~ ~ ~

PREMISE CASES

In premise cases, the theory of liability is likely to be that the corporation which hired a contractor or other non-employee to work on its premise failed to comply with the standard of care by taking reasonable steps to ensure that the contractor and other non-employees on its premise worked safely. The customary safe practice is for the premise owner/host employer to plan, monitor and ensure that all non-employees on its premise are provided with a safe work environment and perform their work safely and in compliance with OSHA standards.

The following are types of incidents that have resulted in lawsuits in PO/HE cases:

~ ~ ~ ~

Description of Incident: **Truck driver falls from tank truck while securing hatch cover.**

Failure: Failure of premise owner to provide a catwalk or safe platform for truck drivers to gain access to the top of tank trucks.

~ ~ ~ ~

Description of Incident: **Contract worker is overcome by toxic vapors while cleaning chemical tank.**

Failure: Failure of premise owner to ensure contractor implemented a confined space entry program.

~ ~ ~ ~

Description of Incident: **Contractor worker performing electrical work is electrocuted while removing equipment.**

Failure: Failure of premise owner to require electrical contractor to de-energize before working.

~ ~ ~ ~

Description of Incident: **Contractor installing rack handled material unsafely causing a worker to be struck by falling material.**

Failure: Failure of premise owner to require forklift operator to be trained and to handle loads safely.

~ ~ ~ ~

Description of Incident: **Contractor painter performed spraying from ladder—slips and falls.**

Failure: Failure of premise owner to require work to be done from safe work platform such as scissors lift, scaffold, or other personnel lift.

~ ~ ~ ~

Description of Incident: **Contractor HVAC worker trips and falls through unprotected skylight on roof.**

Failure: Failure of premise owner to provide guard to prevent falls through skylight.

~ ~ ~ ~

Description of Incident: **Roofer falls through roof opening while repairing roof.**

Failure: Failure of premise owner to require roofers to use fall protection.

~ ~ ~ ~

Description of Incident: **Contractor plumber crushed when trench collapses.**

Failure: Failure of premise owner to require contractor to protect trench from collapse.

~ ~ ~ ~

Description of Incident: **Wall falls and crushes worker when contractor performs demolition.**

Failure: Failure of premise owner to require contractor to perform engineering survey to identify unforeseen collapse of walls.

~ ~ ~ ~

Description of Incident: **Contractor worker falls when scaffold plank breaks.**

Failure: Failure of premise owner to require contractor to comply with OSHA and use scaffold grade lumber.

~ ~ ~ ~

Description of Incident: **Truck driver falls while tarping load of flatbed truck.**

Failure: Failure of premise owner to construct facility so truck drivers could use a personal fall arrest system while securing tarp.

~ ~ ~ ~

Description of Incident: **Construction worker in petrochemical plant exposed to fire suffers burn injury.**

Failure: Failure of premise owner to require contractors to wear flame resistant clothing.

~ ~ ~ ~

Description of Incident: **Truck driver struck in face by hot asphalt while removing hose from standpipe of premise owner.**

Failure: Failure of premise owner to require truck drivers to wear face shield while making connections.

~ ~ ~ ~

PRODUCTS CASES

In products cases, the theory of liability will be related to either a manufacturing or design defect. Manufacturing defects are relatively rare. The theory of liability in design defect cases is related to the lack of a safe design technique or safety device which would have prevented injury. Safe design includes warnings related to foreseeable uses and misuses as well as instructions regarding safe use.

Common theories of liability are related to the failure of the manufacturer to provide safe design such as:

- Interlocks
- Pressure sensing devices
- Presence sensing devices
- Automatic visual alarms
- Audible alarms
- Deadman controls
- Two-hand control
- Fail safe devices
- Monitors
- Pressure relief devices
- Barriers
- Restraints
- Break-away devices
- Tamper proof designs
- Retention cables

If a product lacks a safety device or design method that is economically and technologically feasible and would likely have prevented injury, there is a theory of liability that is likely to be successful. There may also be a viable theory of liability related to a failure to warn or failure to provide safe instructions related to assembly and/or use of the product.

A viable theory of liability in products cases is sometimes not obvious to even seasoned experts. For example, a product may have included an interlock which would have prevented an injury, however it was not maintained by the employer. Or perhaps the interlock was removed by a worker or a foreman who wanted to increase production. Many evaluators would conclude that there is no basis for a lawsuit because the manufacturer's safe design was altered by the user. However, it is highly foreseeable that some types of interlocks will be removed, especially if by doing so production can be significantly increased. In such cases, the manufacturer should design interlocks that cannot be easily defeated. An example of an interlock that cannot be easily defeated is on a microwave oven door. You would destroy the microwave oven if you attempted to defeat the interlock.

There is criterion that designers can use to select the safest and most reliable interlocks for various applications. It is not a simple matter to select the proper interlock.

Safety technology is advancing rapidly. There are a wide variety of sensors, monitors, interlocks and automatic alarms that can be applied to industrial equipment. The rapidly advancing safety technology applied to automobiles gives one an idea of the many opportunities to apply similar technology to industrial equipment. As time passes, the cost of safety devices goes down significantly. Soon all cars will be equipped with the safety technology used in the more expensive cars. Hopefully, industrial equipment manufacturers will enhance the safety of their products by including more and more safety devices as better and less expensive technology is developed.

OTHER THIRD PARTY THEORIES

- **Lessors of construction equipment** (scissors lifts, forklift trucks, telescoping and articulating boom lifts, etc.) for failing to verify and ensure that users were trained to safely use the equipment. The customary safe practice is for the lessor to verify that users have been trained as required by the manufacturer.
- **Suppliers of work clothing**—for failure to supply flame resistant clothing to workers exposed to ignition sources. The customary practice is for the supplier of the work clothing to take reasonable steps to ensure that the clothing supplied is safe for the environment of use.
- **Temporary labor agency** for failing to comply with contract to supply trained workers.
- **Host employer** who hired temporary workers for failure to provide a reasonably safe work environment.
- **Safety consultant** hired by the employer failed to provide appropriate safety training to workers as specified by OSHA.

- **Safety consultant** hired by the employer to perform safety inspections failed to identify a hazard that led to injury.
- **Scaffold erector** hired to build and inspect scaffolds failed to ensure the scaffold was safe.
- **Homeowner** acting as general contractor performed all of the functions of a general contractor to build his or her house but did nothing regarding contractor safety.
- **Architect** who assumed functions of general contractor but did not manage safety nor require any entity to manage safety.
- **Architect** designed contracts between owner and contractors and failed to assign safety management responsibilities regarding implementation of the job site safety program.

Chapter Two

Principles of Safety Management

In order to understand if the defendant's failure to manage safety was a cause of injury, it is important to have a framework for understanding the process of managing safety. That philosophical framework is the Principles of Safety Management.

Principles are fundamental beliefs or truths. Certain principles of safety management permeate the industrial safety literature of the National Safety Council, the American Society of Safety Engineers, the Occupational Safety and Health Administration, the American National Standards Institute and others. An understanding of these principles is important to understanding how safety should be managed and why safety management failures occur. The first principle is:

SAFETY BEGINS AT THE TOP

The construction project owner, premise owner, general contractor or construction manager is the Top. His/her role is to ensure implementation of policy. If those at the top do not require the implementation of a safety program, contractor and subcontractor managers, supervisors and workers at all levels will know that they can cut corners to save time and money. Whether or not top management is serious about safety quickly becomes apparent to everyone on the site. On some jobs you could be in trouble if caught without a hardhat. On other jobs, almost everyone is without a hardhat. It is usually easy to tell if the "Top" is serious about safety.

SAFETY PAYS

Safety professionals believe in the long run that it is not only ethical to control hazards, it is also good business. The principle will be abundantly clear after serious injury or death has resulted. However, we also know that "safety costs." It takes time and money to control hazards. There is a perennial conflict between getting the job done quickly and getting the job done safely. That is why Congress passed the Occupational Safety and Health Act.

ASSIGNMENT OF RESPONSIBILITY AND ACCOUNTABILITY

Managers should be assigned specific management tasks and held accountable for their safety performance by those at the top. If not, the written program will be simply a paper tiger. In order to hold foremen, construction managers and superintendents accountable, their safety performance must be evaluated by their superiors.

PLANNING IS OF THE ESSENCE

Planning should take place so that hazards associated with particular tasks are identified and specific hazard controls are determined before work begins.

SAFETY IS A SHARED RESPONSIBILITY

All levels of management and all workers have safety responsibility. On multi-employer construction sites, contract documents should be designed to require oversight by all levels of management. One entity should be assigned the responsibility to ensure overall safety and implementation of the job site safety and health program. The entity is usually the general contractor or construction manager. Sometimes lawyers, architects or consultants hired by the CPO design contract documents which do not specify one entity to have overall safety management responsibility. Sometimes they simply design documents with indemnification clauses or save harmless clauses which protect the economic interests of the potential defendant and say nothing with regard to who has responsibility to implement a safety program. Sometimes they design contract documents to say each contractor or subcontractor is "solely responsible" for safety. This creates the relationship where no entity is managing and coordinating the safety of contractors and subcontractors. Contract documents should clearly assign safety responsibility to all tiers of management.

A PROACTIVE RATHER THAN REACTIVE APPROACH IS BEST

To be proactive means to act beforehand to prevent the evolution of a hazard by planning, foreseeing, identifying potential hazards, specifying control measures and then monitoring to ensure that controls are in place. To be reactive is simply to rely upon safety inspection to hopefully identify the hazard before someone gets injured.

ACCIDENTS ARE FORESEEABLE AND PREDICTABLE

We believe, as a matter of principle, that all of the ways that workers can be injured can be identified before work begins. While we know that humans will never be perfect, we nevertheless strive to create an environment that does not accept the notion that some jobs are "inherently dangerous." We do not accept the notion that "accidents will happen." Safety professionals try to avoid the use of the word "accident." We believe there are simply hazards which the management system controls or fails to identify, evaluate and control.

During trial, it might be helpful for the jury to hear your safety expert explain some of the principles of safety management listed in his/her report which were important for his/her evaluation. For example, you could ask the safety expert the following questions.

SAFETY EXPERT DIRECT TESTIMONY—PRINCIPLES OF SAFETY MANAGEMENT

- Were there any principles of safety management that were important for your evaluation?
- What are principles?
  Answer: Fundamental beliefs held by people of a particular discipline.
- Tell the jury which principles of safety management were important for your evaluation and why they were important.
  Answer: A fundamental principle is "**safety begins at the top**." The organization at the top is the general contractor or construction manager. The

top manager has more power, control and authority than anyone else. They run the job and control the work. They set the stage and communicate with contractors about whether or not safety will actually be managed. Everyone quickly learns whether or not the superintendent or construction manager is serious about safety or whether they will allow you to cut corners to save time and money.

- Were there any other principles that were important for your evaluation? Answer: Another principle is "**safety pays**." As a matter of principle, we believe that in the long run, it is good business to control hazards. There are tremendous costs associated with exposures to hazards that lead to serious injury. There are direct medical costs, lost wages and significant costs related to litigation. Research has also shown that there are other indirect costs which are even more than direct costs. While we believe safety pays in the long run, we also know that in the short run, it takes time and costs money to control hazards. But as a matter of principle, safety professionals believe that it is not only morally and ethically responsible to spend the time and money to control hazards, it is good business because it saves money.
- Were there any other principles that were important for your evaluation? Answer: **Planning is essential**. This means that we should have a pre-job safety conference before work begins to anticipate hazards associated with the work so that controls can be put in place before work begins. It is irresponsible to allow hazards to develop and hope that safety inspections identify the hazard before injury occurs.

The safety expert could demonstrate through the facts obtained in deposition that the defendant general contractor/construction manager violated the principles of safety management. That is, they failed to plan, monitor and ensure that the money was spent to control the hazard.

Chapter Three

Fundamental Elements of an Occupational Safety and Health Program

The hazard that led to injury is a symptom, not a cause of the injury. For example, the hazard may be an unguarded stairway opening, a truck reversing without a backup alarm or an exposed electrical conductor. The cause of the injury is the general contractor/construction manager's failure to implement and/or require contractors and subcontractors to implement an occupational safety and health program. This chapter explains what a safety program is and why safety programs are important to prevent injury.

OSHA has found that injury and illness prevention programs are effective in reducing injuries, illnesses and fatalities; lowering workers' compensation and other costs; improving morale and communication; improving processes, products and services.[1] OSHA examined the injury and illness prevention programs in eight states where either the state had required a program or provided incentives or requirements through its workers' compensation programs. These programs lowered injury and illness incidents by 9 to more than 60 percent.

- **Alaska** had an injury and illness plan requirement for over 20 years (1973 to 1995). Five years after the program was implemented, the net decrease in injuries and illnesses (i.e., the statewide reduction in injuries and illnesses over and above the national decrease during the same time period) for Alaska was **17.4 percent**.
- **California** began to require an injury and illness prevention program in 1991. Five years after this requirement began, California had a net decrease in injuries and illnesses of **19 percent**.
- **Colorado** has a program that allows firms to adopt basic injury and illness prevention program components in return for a workers' compensation premium reduction. The cumulative annual reduction in accidents was 23

percent and the cumulative reduction in accident costs was **between 58 and 62 percent**.
- **Hawaii** began to require employers to have injury and illness prevention programs in 1985. The net reduction in injuries and illnesses was **20.7 percent**.
- **Massachusetts** Workers' Compensation program firms receive a premium credit for enrolling in a loss management program. In the first year of this program, firms participating in the program had a **20.8 percent** improvement in their loss ratios.
- **North Dakota** has a program under its workers' compensation program for employers who have a risk management program. The incentive is a 5 percent discount on annual workers' compensation premiums. These risk management programs contain many of the elements of an injury and illness prevention program. They resulted in a cumulative decline for serious injuries of **38 percent** over a four-year period.
- **Texas** had a program under its workers' compensation commission from 1991 to 2005 which identified the most hazardous workplaces. Those employers were required to develop and implement injury and illness prevention programs. The reduction in injuries, over a four-year period (1992–1995), averaged **63 percent each year**.
- **Washington** began requiring establishments to have injury and illness prevention programs in 1973. Five years later the net decrease in injuries and illnesses was **9.4 percent**.

The research is clear. Implementation of occupational safety and health programs prevent worker injury and death. Currently 34 U.S. states have established laws and regulations designed to require or encourage injury and illness prevention programs, including 15 states with mandatory regulations for all or some employers.[2] All 27 members of the European Union require employers to implement occupational safety and health programs.

ELEMENTS OF AN OCCUPATIONAL SAFETY AND HEALTH PROGRAM

A safety program is a proactive process to help employers find and fix workplace hazards before workers are hurt. The basic elements of an occupational safety and health program are:[3]

- Management Leadership
- Worker Participation
- Hazard Identification and Assessment

- Hazard Prevention and Control
- Education and Training
- Program Evaluation and Improvement

OSHA has summarized these major elements in their Fact Sheet—Injury and Illness Prevention Program.

Management Leadership

- Establish clear safety and health goals for the program and define the actions needed to achieve those goals.
- Designate one or more individuals with overall responsibility for implementing and maintaining the program.
- Provide sufficient resources to ensure effective program implementation.

Worker Participation

- Consult with workers in developing and implementing the program and involve them in updating and evaluating the program.
- Include workers in workplace inspections and incident investigations.
- Encourage workers to report concerns, such as hazards, injuries, illnesses and near misses.
- Protect the rights of workers who participate in the program.

Hazard Identification and Assessment

- Identify, assess and document workplace hazards by soliciting input from workers, inspecting the workplace and reviewing available information on hazards.
- Investigate injuries and illnesses to identify hazards that may have caused them.
- Inform workers of the hazards in the workplace.

Hazard Prevention and Control

- Establish and implement a plan to prioritize and control hazards identified in the workplace.
- Provide interim controls to protect workers from any hazards that cannot be controlled immediately.
- Verify that all control measures are implemented and are effective.
- Discuss the hazard control plan with affected workers.

Education and Training

- Provide education and training to workers in a language and vocabulary they can understand to ensure that they know:
    - Procedures for reporting injuries, illnesses and safety and health concerns.
    - How to recognize hazards.
    - Ways to eliminate, control or reduce hazards.
    - Elements of the program.
    - How to participate in the program.
- Conduct refresher education and training programs periodically.

Program Evaluation and Improvement

- Conduct a periodic review of the program to determine if it has been implemented as designed and is making progress towards achieving its goals.
- Modify the program, as necessary, to correct deficiencies.
- Continuously look for ways to improve the program.

There is no specific regulation that requires a safety program in 29CFR1910—the OSHA General Industry Standards. However, there are specific safety management standards in 29CFR1926 for the Construction Industry. See Appendix A—Safety Management Standards in Construction.

For an example of a Safety and Health Program for Small Business, see Appendix B.

INDUSTRY CONSENSUS STANDARDS—SAFETY AND HEALTH MANAGEMENT PROGRAMS

There are two industry consensus standards that give the requirements for an occupational safety and health program, sometimes called an injury or illness prevention program.

- The American National Standards Institute (ANSI) and American Industrial Hygiene Association (AIHA) have published a voluntary consensus standard, ANSI/AIHA Z10—2005 *Occupational Safety and Health Management Systems* (ANSI/AIHA, 2005).
- The Occupational Health and Safety Assessment Series (OHSAS) Project Group, a consortium of selected Registrars, national standards bodies, professional associations and research institutes, has produced a similar docu-

ment, OHSAS 18001—2007 *Occupational Health and Safety Management Systems* (OHSAS Project Group, 2007).

The above consensus-based standards have been widely accepted in the world of commerce and adopted by many businesses on a voluntary basis.

Essentially the methodology of evaluation of a GC/CM is to determine if it has implemented the job site safety program and required contractors to comply with OSHA, that is, to see if the GC/CM planned, monitored and ensured that the contractor's work was done safely and in compliance with OSHA. Did it perform the functions of hazard identification, evaluation and control? Did it hold a pre-job safety conference with contractors, a weekly safety meeting, and did it perform daily safety inspections? Did it have a management system to hold its foremen, supervisors and managers accountable for their safety performance?

NOTES

1. U.S. Department of Labor, Occupational Safety and Health Administration, "Injury and Illness Prevention Program White Paper," January 2012, p. 5.
2. The 15 states are: Arkansas, California, Hawaii, Louisiana, Michigan, Minnesota, Mississippi, Montana, North Carolina, New Hampshire, Nevada, New York, Oregon, Utah, and Washington.
3. U.S. Department of Labor, Occupational Safety and Health Administration, "Injury and Illness Prevention Program White Paper," January 2012, p. 1.

Part II

CONSTRUCTION INJURY CASES

Chapter Four

Understanding Causation in Construction Cases

System Safety Analysis, sometimes called Root Cause Analysis, is a method used by safety professionals to understand causation. It sees the hazard or dangerous condition/procedure as a "symptom," not a cause. To understand causation, we ask questions related to "why" the management system of the general contractor/construction manager (GC/CM) or construction project owner (CPO) permitted the hazard to be created and why it permitted it to continue to exist. It should not have been created if there was planning to identify and control the hazard **before work began**. It should not have been able to continue to exist because periodic monitoring by the GC/CM should have identified and required it to be controlled.

System safety analysis looks at the management system to identify specific management failures that led to the existence of the hazard that resulted in injury. The facts show specifically how the management system failed. The following are key questions to ask to reveal the facts and to determine if there was a violation of the standard of care. These are facts which the expert will be able to use to support his or her opinions.

- Did the GC/CM evaluate the safety performance of bidders as part of the bid review and contractor selection process? (See chapter 17)
- Did the GC/CM select safe contractors?
- Did the GC/CM have a written safety program?
- Did the GC/CM require contractors and subcontractors to have a written safety program?
- Did the GC/CM review the safety program of contractors and subcontractors?
- Did the GC/CM require the contractor to have an OSHA competent person on site?[1]

- Did the GC/CM's safety policy require a pre-job safety conference where plans were made to control hazards?
- Were minutes retained?
- Did the GC/CM hold weekly safety meetings where representatives of all contractors were required to attend?
- Were minutes retained?
- Did the GC/CM perform daily safety inspections?
- Were reports retained?
- Did the construction manager or superintendent of the GC/CM have a written job description which included specific safety tasks?
- Was the performance of the construction manager/superintendent evaluated?
- Was the superintendent/construction manager trained in safety?
- Did the GC/CM's policy require contractors and subcontractors to verify that their workers were trained as required by OSHA?

Some examples of hazards are:

- A stairway opening without guardrail or cover
- An electrical tool without an effective ground
- A crane boom operating near an energized overhead power line
- An unprotected trench
- A scaffold without a guardrail
- A floor hole
- A worker without a hardhat

Essential to proving negligence is showing that the defendant knew or should have known of the hazard that led to injury. It is unfair to fault a defendant for injury resulting from a hazard that they did not know about or could not reasonably be expected to have known about. Sometimes the exposure to the hazard is of such short term duration or it is essentially an "isolated incident" that the GC/CM could not reasonably be expected to have known. Sometimes the worker's behavior is a violation of safety instruction that the defendant had been enforcing with reasonable diligence and would not have permitted had he/she known of it.

Planning in the pre-job safety conference should identify and foresee hazards associated with the proposed work. Controls should be agreed upon by the superintendent of the GC/CM and the foreman of the particular craft. Monitoring should then take place periodically to ensure that the work is done safely as planned. Monitoring or safety inspection should be performed at least once a shift.

The first step is to identify the type of hazard that led to injury. Hazards which result in injury can be classified as:

- Falls from elevation
- Falls to the same level
- Electrocution
- Struck by falling object
- Caught between two objects
- Burns—chemical/heat
- Repetitive motion/cumulative trauma
- Musculoskeletal injury from over-lifting
- Asphyxia in confined space

Key questions for hazard analysis are:

- What was the hazard?
- Who created it?
- How long did it exist?
- Were there other instances of exposure to the same hazard at this site prior to this incident?
- How long did they exist?

If other workers were exposed to the same hazard on prior days or if this exposure existed more than a shift, constructive knowledge is easily imputed. If the exposure was only for a few moments, it may not be possible to impute knowledge to the general contractor or construction manager. It might be an "isolated incident" which the GC/CM could not be expected to be aware of. It depends on the facts.

EVALUATION OF KNOWLEDGE ON PART OF GC/CM

Key questions to ask are:

- What specific task was the plaintiff performing at the time?
- Did the GC/CM hold a pre-job safety conference with the plaintiff's employer to foresee the potential hazard associated with this task?
- Were plans made to identify the appropriate hazard control?
- What was the duration of exposure? That is, how long did it take to perform the task that the plaintiff was performing at the time of the incident (minutes, hours or days)?

- What was the frequency of the exposure by the plaintiff? One time per day? Six times per day? Ten times a day for three weeks?
- What was the duration and frequency of exposures by the plaintiff and others to similar hazards at this job site? For example, the plaintiff may have been injured due to a fall hazard exposure from an unprotected stairway opening but other workers were also exposed to fall hazards while working on the roof. You should look for broad exposures to the same hazards in order to prove constructive knowledge. Another example may be a worker who was injured due to failure to use safety glasses while using a nail gun and other workers were not required to wear hardhats. This is further evidence of the GC/CM failing to require appropriate personal protective equipment.
- What was the frequency and duration of other workers' exposures to the hazard which injured the plaintiff? That is, were others doing the same type work that the plaintiff was doing and were they exposed to the same hazard?
- What was the duration and frequency of other workers' exposures to similar hazards at this job site?
- How conspicuous was this hazard, that is, was it easily seen by the GC/CM?
- Were any workers at this site exposed to other hazards? There may have been many examples of this GC/CM permitting many workers to be exposed to many hazards in violation of OSHA standards.

The answers to these questions will show whether or not the defendant was managing safety. They will also show whether or not it should have known of the hazard that led to injury. Once knowledge is established, we can begin to investigate specifically how the management system failed to control the hazard. The deposition of the general contractor's superintendent or construction manager is key.

TRAINING TO PREVENT INJURY—FALL HAZARDS

You may have a viable theory of liability even though knowledge of the exposure to the hazard that led to injury cannot be established. One way is to show that the GC failed to ensure that construction workers received the OSHA required training relative to the incident hazard. The defendant should take reasonable steps to verify whether or not contractors' and subcontractors' employees have received safety training when it is required by a particular OSHA standard. If the GC/CM did not verify whether or not the injured worker had been trained as required by OSHA, you could reasonably argue that the injury would not have occurred if the worker had been trained and instructed not to work in violation of the OSHA standards.

The OSHA standard 29CFR1926.21(b)(2) requires the employer to instruct each employee in the recognition and avoidance of unsafe conditions and the regulations applicable to his work environment to control or eliminate any hazards or other exposures to illness or injury. OSHA also has specific training requirements for various hazards including the following fall protection requirements. You will see that with regard to fall hazards the instructor must be a competent person and the content of the training is quite specific.

> 29CFR1926.503. Training requirements for workers who work at elevation. The following requirements supplement and clarify 1926.21(b)(2) which requires workers to be instructed about how to avoid exposure to fall hazards.
>
> 29CFR1926.503(a)(1). Training program. The employer shall provide a training program for each employee who might be exposed to fall hazards. The program shall enable each employee to recognize the hazard of falling and shall train each employee in the procedures to be followed in order to minimize these hazards.
>
> 29CFR1926.503(a)(2). The employer shall assure that each employee has been trained, as necessary, by a **competent person** qualified in the following areas:
>
> (i) The nature of fall hazards in the work area;
> (ii) The correct procedures for erecting, maintaining, disassembling, and inspecting the fall protection systems to be used;
> (iii) The use and operation of guardrail systems, personal fall arrest systems, safety net systems, warning line systems, safety monitoring systems, controlled access zones, and other protection to be used;
> (iv) The role of each employee in the safety monitoring system when this system is used;
> (v) The limitations on the use of mechanical equipment during the performance of roofing work on low-sloped roofs;
> (vi) The correct procedure for handling and storage of equipment and materials and the erection of overhead protection;
> (vii) The role of employees in fall protection plans;
> (viii) The standards contained in this Subpart.
>
> 29CFR1926.503(b)(1). Certification of Training. The employer shall verify compliance with paragraph (a) of this section by preparing a written certification record. The written certification record shall contain the name or other identity of the employee trained, the dates of the training, and the signature of the person who conducted the training or signature of the employer.
>
> 29CFR1926.503(b)(2). The latest training certification shall be maintained.

FORKLIFT OPERATOR TRAINING—OSHA STANDARDS

OSHA standard 1926.602(d) which references 1910.178(l) requires forklift operators in the construction industry to receive training in safe operation. It also requires certification in standard 1910.178(l)(6). The GC/CM should verify that all forklift operators had training to comply with OSHA standards. Verification can be by email, fax or by asking the operator to show evidence of the card received during training. According to OSHA standards, the documentation should indicate the name of the operator, date of training and the identity of the person who performed the training.

An example of how a failure to verify training by the GC/CM can be linked to proximate cause relative to forklift operation is one where a worker falls from a box made of two by fours and plywood which is raised on the forks of the forklift by the operator. It is not unusual for the box to be makeshift and not designed to be secured to the forks as required by OSHA. It is likely that the forklift truck manufacturer's operating instructions warn against the use of makeshift boxes to raise workers. If the operator was properly trained and instructed, he/she would have known not to use the makeshift box. If the operator had been trained and instructed, he/she would have inspected the box to ensure that it was safely secure before raising it. He/she should have been instructed not to participate in any work where a worker entered the box to offload material without reliable fall protection.

SCAFFOLD SAFETY TRAINING

OSHA has scaffold safety training standards for workers who use, build and disassemble scaffolds. The GC/CM should take reasonable steps to determine whether or not the contractors' and subcontractors' workers have been trained by a competent trainer as required by OSHA. Training should include the **instruction** to workers not to expose themselves to a hazard likely to lead to serious injury or death in violation of OSHA standards. They should be instructed to refuse to work in such an environment. That is the intent of Congress. It should also be the intent of all levels of construction management. It should be the policy of the GC/CM that workers have the right to refuse to work in violation of OSHA standards.

Your analysis may find that the defendant failed to verify that workers had received the OSHA-required scaffold safety training and instruction. Any expert would have to agree that workers should be trained as required by OSHA. They have to agree that training should include instruction not to expose oneself or others to a hazard likely to lead to serious injury or death in violation of OSHA standards. They also have to agree that had the worker been properly trained and instructed to never work in violation of the OSHA standard that it is likely that the injury would not have occurred.

The defense expert might argue that the GC/CM has no responsibility to verify if contractor and subcontractor workers have been trained. That would be inconsistent with the American Society of Safety Engineers and other safety authorities.

The American Society of Safety Engineers in their book entitled CONSTRUCTION SAFETY MANAGEMENT AND ENGINEERING has the following to say with regard to the GC/CM making sure that subcontractor employees are properly trained:

> Making sure that subcontractor employees are trained before they are allowed to work on the job site is the best way that the general contractor has of ensuring that all employees on the site have received at least the minimum training required.[2]

See appendix C for a list of all the OSHA standards which require training.

THE ROLE OF SAFETY INSPECTION

Constructive knowledge can be established when the duration of the exposure was such that periodic safety inspection or monitoring should have identified it. The Associated General Contractors of America in their ACCIDENT PREVENTION MANUAL states the following:

> Day-by-day, hour-by-hour, job inspections should be made and a list of violations noted for use and discussion at the next safety meeting of supervisors after correction has been made. Along with their normal daily surveys of supervisors, a safety committee should tour the job site to confirm or add to the list of unsafe acts already noted.[3]

Likewise, the Occupational Safety and Health Administration standard 29CFR1926.20(b)(2) states:

> Such programs (accident prevention programs) shall provide for frequent and regular inspections of the job sites, materials, and equipment to be made by **competent persons**[4] designated by the employers.

On some jobs at some times it is reasonable to expect the GC/CM to make hour-by-hour inspections. Other jobs may be so large that a walkthrough of the entire job site would be expected only once a shift. Sometimes a superintendent may be responsible for two or three very small jobs being done at the same time and cannot be expected to be at all jobs at the same time. The key question is whether or not the representative of the GC/CM took reasonable steps to plan, monitor and ensure that the work was done safely as planned.

CONSTRUCTIVE KNOWLEDGE

Sometimes the hazard is so conspicuous that it is easy to establish constructive knowledge. For example, the GC/CM should be on the job during steel erection. At that time, it is very easy to see if fall protection is being used because there is relatively little other work taking place. It is easy to just look up from anywhere on the job site and see how the work is being performed and whether or not fall protection is in place.

In residential construction, fall hazard exposure of roofers and framers is also usually very conspicuous. The GC/CM just has to pass by and look up to see if fall protection is being used. In both steel erection and residential construction, the GC/CM may be able to see how work is done simply by looking out the window of the job trailer.

One sure way to establish constructive knowledge is when the hazard had existed for more than one shift. The customary safe practice is for safety inspections to be performed by a competent person at least once per shift.

"AFTER HOUR" INJURIES AND "MONDAY MORNING" INCIDENTS

In cases where there is no actual knowledge of the hazard that led to injury, it may be possible to impute knowledge of the hazard to the GC/CM because they failed to ensure that the work site was safe before work was completed on the day before the incident. The GC/CM should have ensured that the work site was free of hazards at the end of the day because the public is potentially exposed to hazards on the job site. You could argue that, although the defendant was unaware of the exposure to the hazard which occurred at 7:30 a.m., it had constructive knowledge of the floor opening which led to injury because he/she should have ensured that there was no fall hazard at the end of work on the day before. Chapter 13 gives further guidance related to construction hazards to which the public may be exposed.

During residential construction for example, there is potential exposure to delivery personnel, children, realtors, potential buyers, their family and friends who would enter the job site after hours or on the weekend. Safety authorities agree that the GC/CM has a responsibility to take reasonable steps to prevent the public from hazards associated with the construction activity. The GC/CM should ensure that all floor openings and other hazards are controlled at the end of the day because it is foreseeable that the public may come onto the job site after hours.

PLANNING

Another way to establish constructive knowledge is through planning. During the pre-job safety conference, plans should be made to foresee hazards involving the work so that specific hazard controls can be agreed upon. For some construction activity, the hazard should be identified before bid documents are sent out. Sometimes the cost of hazard controls are significant, for example, with trenching and excavation and fall protection in steel erection. Conscientious GC/CMs will require bidders to show the costs for hazard control in their bid so they can be sure the bids include the costs for safety. That way they will be able to make realistic evaluations of bids. Otherwise, some bidders will cut safety costs in order to submit the lowest bid in order to get work.

If the GC/CM argues that he/she did not know that the trench was unsafe, constructive knowledge could be imputed by showing that they should have known because they should have planned with the excavation contractor before work began about the specific ways the trench/excavation was to be made safe. The plans would have resulted in instructions to the excavator contractor and excavator operator to control the hazard and therefore prevent the injury.

SIGNIFICANT SAFETY MANAGEMENT FAILURES

Another way to show negligence as a proximate cause of injury when actual knowledge cannot be directly shown is when there is a significant failure in the management system of the defendant. For instance, sometimes you will find that the defendant:

- Had no written safety program and policy
- Did nothing to evaluate the safety performance of bidders
- Did not hold a pre-job safety conference
- Did not hold safety meetings

- Did not perform safety monitoring inspections
- Did not assign safety responsibility to any personnel in the organization
- Did not evaluate safety performance of anyone on the job site
- Did not have an OSHA competent person on site
- Did nothing to manage safety of the contractors and subcontractors

When there is an almost complete abdication of safety management responsibility on the part of the defendant, you could reasonably argue that a "de facto" policy of permitting work to be done unsafely was established. This failure in safety management was in essence a policy which taught contractors and subcontractors that they do not have to work safely and can get away with cutting corners in violation of OSHA standards. As we have seen, the "root cause" of injury is not the exposure to the hazard. The root cause lies within the management system which permits the work to be done unsafely. The cause is the defendant's failure to manage safety. Sometimes the evidence of a management failure regarding safety is abundantly clear and essentially gives the message to all that you could work very unsafely and in violation of OSHA standards and get away with it.

In every construction environment, time is money. When the GC/CM creates an environment where all learn that safety is being ignored, this increases the likelihood that workers' safety will be compromised in a variety of ways. The proximate cause argument is simply—workers should have been trained to recognize the hazard and to not work while exposed to the danger. If they were trained and did not perform the work dangerously, there would have been no injury. If the management system was functioning as it should, the superintendent, construction manager, foremen and supervisors would have known that they could not get away with allowing their workers to be exposed to hazards. The workers then would have learned that they would be in trouble if they got caught working unsafely and would therefore likely perform the work safely. At some construction sites, there is a culture where everyone knows if they get caught violating a safety rule, they will be in trouble. On some sites, almost everyone is allowed to work without hardhats and unsafely and no one is ever called on it.

The following are general questions regarding safety management for the deposition of the GC/CM rep. In other chapters there will be other lists of questions related to hazards and subjects which may also be relevant for the GC/CM rep. These questions should be helpful to both defense and plaintiff attorneys. Hopefully, the answers will reveal the most important facts related to failures in safety management. If the safety management system was being implemented, the answers will show the strength of the defense case.

GENERAL QUESTIONS FOR THE DEPOSITION OF THE GC/CM REPRESENTATIVE

1. How long have you been with this company as a superintendent or construction manager?
2. What positions have you held?
3. List all of the safety responsibilities that you had in each position.
4. Have you worked for other companies in a construction management position? What companies? What positions have you held with each company?
5. List all of the safety responsibilities that you had in each position.
6. Can you describe some of the types of jobs that you ran as construction manager or superintendent prior to this job?
7. What are your job duties? (Note: You want to show that this rep performed the tasks which show that he/she controlled the job site. Superintendents and construction managers coordinate, sequence and control the work. They tell the contractor what work is to be done, decide when work is done and where it is done. They determine if it is done correctly and whether or not they are going to pay. He/she does not usually control the means and methods. However, he/she makes sure that the contractors do what the contract says and he/she will not authorize money to be paid unless it is done in a timely manner and done correctly.)
8. Did you hold meetings at this job site?
9. Did you schedule contractors when they should work?
10. Did you coordinate the work among contractors?
11. Did you schedule deliveries?
12. Did you walk through the site to evaluate progress?
13. Did you monitor and inspect to see that the work was done according to contract specifications?
14. Did you ensure that the job was done on schedule?
15. Did you authorize payment if the work was done according to specifications?
16. What percentage of the time do you work in the field as opposed to working in the office?
17. Does the company that you work for now have a written occupational safety and health program?
18. Did you ever work for other companies that had written safety and health programs? Which?
19. Have you ever received training related to OSHA standards?
20. Tell me everything that you can about the training that you received relative to construction safety: dates, places, instructors, length of classes, topics.

21. Does your company require the contractors and subcontractors to have written safety and health programs?
22. Do you know what an OSHA competent person is? (Answer: A competent person is one who is familiar with OSHA standards and has the authority to require compliance.)
23. Do you know who the OSHA competent person was for your company at this job site?
24. Does your company require contractors and subcontractors to employ an OSHA competent person?
25. Did your company require contractors and subcontractors on this job to have a written safety program?
26. Do you have a written job description? If so, would you supply me with a copy of your written job description?
27. Does your job description specify any safety duties?
28. If so, tell me specifically what your job description says with regard to your safety duties.
29. Is your safety performance evaluated by your superiors?
30. If so, how often is it evaluated?
31. Do you ever get written performance evaluations relative to your safety performance?
32. List for me all of your safety responsibilities on this job. NOTE: This is an important question. You could make a list as an exhibit. You could use it during your opening statement and cross examination of the opposing expert. It should include the requirements for him/her to:
    - Hold a pre-job safety conference with contractors
    - Hold weekly safety meetings with contractors
    - Perform daily safety inspections
    - Verify that contractors received OSHA required training
33. Is it your company's policy to hold a pre-job safety conference with contractor representatives?
34. Is it your company's policy to maintain minutes of the pre-job safety conference?
35. Have you ever attended a pre-job safety conference?
36. Does your company have a written agenda to be followed during pre-job safety conferences?
37. When you worked for other companies, did you ever hold pre-job safety conferences?
38. Have you ever seen minutes of meetings of any pre-job safety conference that you ran? That anybody ran?

39. Was there a pre-job safety conference held at this job site?
40. If so, what was discussed?
41. List all hazards that were discussed.
42. List all hazard controls that were anticipated.
43. Is it your company's policy to plan and foresee the evolution of hazards before work begins so that controls can be decided upon before exposure takes place?
44. Is it your company's policy to monitor the work of contractors and subcontractors to ensure it is done according to the contract?
45. If so, who is required to monitor the work of contractors and subcontractors?
46. How long has that been your policy?
47. According to your company policy, how frequently should monitoring take place?
48. Is it your company's policy to monitor the work of contractors and subcontractors to see that their work is done according to OSHA's requirements?
49. How long has that been your policy?
50. How frequently is a representative of your company required to monitor regarding safety?
51. Is it your company's policy to maintain written reports of inspections or monitoring of contractors' work relative to OSHA compliance or contract compliance?
52. Is it your company's policy to hold periodic safety meetings attended by contractors and subcontractors?
53. Is that written anywhere?
54. Are reports of periodic safety meetings kept by your company?
55. Did you perform periodic safety inspections at this site?
56. How frequently were they done?
57. Were reports kept?
58. Did anyone from your company perform safety inspections at this job site?
59. How frequently were they done?
60. Were reports required to be kept?
61. If you see a danger on the job where someone might be seriously injured or killed, according to your company's safety policy, are you supposed to do anything to respond?
62. What are you supposed to do?
63. Have you ever seen any dangerous condition on a site when you were superintendent/construction manager where a contractor or subcontractor's employee was exposed to a risk of serious injury?
64. Did you ever see a worker exposed to a hazard and do nothing?

65. Do you ever see workers without hardhats?
66. Have you ever seen workers on scaffolds without guardrails?
67. Have you ever seen floor openings or floor perimeters without guardrails?
68. Have you ever seen workers exposed to other falls from elevation? Explain.
69. What did you do when you saw workers exposed to those dangers?
70. Are you familiar with the OSHA regulations as they relate to construction environments?
71. Do you have your own personal copy?
72. Do you keep one on every job that you are on?
73. Have you referred to the OSHA regulations in the past?
74. What were some of the questions that you looked up in the OSHA regulations?
75. If you had seen the plaintiff working in the place where he or she was working just moments before this incident occurred, would you have recognized this as being a dangerous situation?
76. What was the hazard to which the plaintiff was exposed?
77. Have you ever seen a worker exposed to a hazard similar to the exposure of the plaintiff before on any other job? What did you do?
78. If you had seen the plaintiff just before this incident working in the manner that he or she was working just prior to this occurrence, what would you have been required to do according to your company's safety policy?
79. Is it your company's policy to investigate injuries to learn how to prevent recurrences?
80. Did you or anyone in your company give any thought to how to prevent a recurrence of this type of incident?
81. In retrospect, is there anything that any foreman, supervisor, or superintendent of your company could have done before this incident to prevent it?
82. In retrospect, is there anything that anyone could have done to prevent it?
83. Have you thought about whether or not you could have done anything to prevent it?
84. Could you have done anything to prevent it?
85. Did you do any planning to foresee this hazard before it evolved?
86. Did you foresee exposure to this hazard before the plaintiff was exposed to this hazard?
87. Was it possible for you to have foreseen exposure to this hazard beforehand?
88. Are you aware of any other workers on any other jobs that you have worked on in the past who were exposed to a similar hazard as the plaintiff? What did you do?
89. Do you know of any way that those exposures could have been prevented?

DISCOVERY DOCUMENTS

The following are documents that should be requested from the GC/CM:

- The defendant's written safety and health program.
- Copy of the pre-job safety conference minutes.
- Copy of all safety inspection reports.
- Copy of all weekly safety meeting minutes.
- Written job description of the superintendent.
- Contract of GC/CM with construction project owner.
- Contracts of GC/CM with others.
- Incident investigation report performed by GC/CM.
- Incident investigation report performed by employer of injured employer.
- Safety inspection reports performed by insurance company loss control representatives.
- Inspection reports performed by consultant or others.

DEPOSITION OF EXPERT IN NEW CONSTRUCTION CASES WHERE GC/CM IS DEFENDANT—METHODOLOGY OF EVALUATION

The following are questions for an expert in cases where a defendant GC/CM runs a project for a Construction Project Owner (CPO):

1. Do you know what I mean by the term "authoritative"? (Answer: Able to be trusted as accurate or true, reliable, valid, dependable.)
2. Are there any industry organizations which you consider to be authoritative regarding guidance of the steps that GC/CMs should take to prevent contractor and subcontractor worker injury?
3. Are there any safety journals that you consider to be authoritative in the field of construction safety management?
4. Are there any books that you consider to be authoritative in the field of construction safety management?
5. Are there any authors that you consider to be authoritative when they write on the field of construction safety management?
6. Who are some of the most respected construction safety professionals in the United States?
7. Do you know of any construction industry authorities that give guidance to GC/CMs regarding reasonable steps that the GC/CM should take to prevent contractor worker injury?

8. If so, list them and for each, tell me what steps they say a GC/CM should take to prevent contractor and subcontractor worker injury.
9. Do you know what the National Safety Council says with regard to a GC/CM's role in preventing contractor worker injury? If so, explain.
10. Do you know what the Associated General Contractors of America says with regard to a GC/CM's role in preventing contractor worker injury? If so, explain.
11. Do you know what the American Society of Safety Engineers says with regard to a GC/CM's role in preventing contractor worker injury? If so, explain.
12. Do you know what the Construction Industry Institute says with regard to a GC/CM's role in preventing contractor worker injury? If so, explain.
13. Do you know what the National Safety Management Society says with regard to a GC/CM's role in preventing contractor worker injury? If so, explain.
14. Do you know if there are any American National Standards Institute standards that give guidance to GC/CMs relative to reasonable steps it should take to prevent contractor worker injury? If so, explain.

    NOTE: The ANSI construction standards that give guidance to GCs/CMs are:

    - A10.33—Safety and Health Program Requirements for Multi-Employer Projects
    - A10.1—Pre-Project and Pre-Task Safety and Health Planning
    - A10.38—Basic Elements of Employer Program to Provide a Safe and Healthful Work Environment

15. Did you ever perform an evaluation of a GC/CM by evaluating whether or not the GC/CM complied with the steps that the National Safety Council says a GC/CM should take to prevent contractor worker injury?
16. Did you ever perform an evaluation of a GC/CM by evaluating whether or not the GC/CM complied with the steps that the Associated General Contractors of America says a GC/CM should take to prevent contractor worker injury?
17. Did you ever perform an evaluation of a GC/CM by evaluating whether or not the GC/CM complied with the steps that the American Society of Safety Engineers says a GC/CM should take to prevent contractor worker injury?
18. Did you ever perform an evaluation of a GC/CM by evaluating whether or not the GC/CM complied with the steps that the Construction Industry Institute says a GC/CM should take to prevent contractor worker injury?

19. Did you ever perform an evaluation of a GC/CM by evaluating whether or not the GC/CM complied with the steps that the National Safety Management Society says a GC/CM should take to prevent contractor worker injury?
20. Did you ever perform an evaluation of a GC/CM by evaluating whether or not the GC/CM complied with the steps that the American National Standards Institute standard A10.33—Safety and Health Program Requirements for Multi-Employer Projects—says a GC/CM should take to prevent contractor worker injury?
21. Did you ever perform an evaluation of a GC/CM by evaluating whether or not the GC/CM complied with the steps that the American National Standards Institute standard A10.1—Pre-Project and Pre-Task Safety and Health Planning—says a GC/CM should take to prevent contractor worker injury?
22. Did you ever perform an evaluation of a GC/CM by evaluating whether or not the GC/CM complied with the steps that the American National Standards Institute standard A10.38—Basic Elements of Employer Program to Provide a Safe and Healthful Work Environment—says a GC/CM should take to prevent contractor worker injury?
23. In this case, did you perform your evaluation by considering whether or not the GC/CM took the steps that the National Safety Council says a GC/CM should take to prevent construction worker injury?
24. In this case, did you perform your evaluation by considering whether or not the defendant did what the Associated General Contractors of America says a GC/CM should do regarding injury prevention of contractor workers?
25. In this case, did you perform your evaluation by considering whether or not the defendant did what the American Society of Safety Engineers says a GC/CM should do regarding injury prevention of contractor workers?
26. In this case, did you perform your evaluation by considering whether or not the defendant did what the Construction Industry Institute says a GC/CM should do regarding injury prevention of contractor workers?
27. In this case, did you perform your evaluation by considering whether or not the defendant did what the National Safety Management Society says a GC/CM should do regarding injury prevention of contractor workers?
28. In this case, did you perform your evaluation by considering whether or not the defendant did what the American National Standards Institute says a GC/CM should do regarding injury prevention of contractor workers?
29. Have you ever heard of any "principles of construction safety management?"

30. Do you know what principles are?

    Answer: Principles are fundamental beliefs within a particular society. The following are some construction safety management principles. The industry safety literature is permeated with fundamental agreement with these principles.

    - *Safety begins at the top.*
    - *A proactive rather than a reactive approach is best.*
    - *Assigning specific responsibility and holding people accountable are key to successful management.*
    - *Planning is of the essence.*
    - *Accidents are foreseeable and predictable.*
    - *Safety pays.*

31. You could ask the expert to explain each principle and ask if he/she agrees with those principles and practices.
32. Did you apply any of those principles in your evaluation of the defendant's conduct in this case? How? Explain each.
33. In your opinion, should a company such as the defendant GC/CM have a written policy regarding safety management oversight when it hires contractors to perform work?
34. In your experience, have you ever come across a GC/CM that implemented a construction safety program?
35. In your experience, do GC/CMs normally require contractors to implement construction safety programs?
36. In your experience, do GC/CMs customarily take steps to see that the contract is complied with?
37. Please list for me all of the steps that GC/CMs customarily take to prevent contractor worker injury in your experience.
38. In this case, can you list for me all of the steps that the record shows that the GC/CM took to ensure that the contractor performed their work safely?
39. In your opinion, should a GC take reasonable steps to hire safe contractors?
40. Are you familiar with any industry authorities that give guidance to GC/CMs relative to steps that a GC/CM should take to hire safe contractors?
41. In this case, did your evaluation consider whether or not the GC/CM took any steps to ensure that they hired safe contractors?
42. In this case, did the GC/CM do anything to ensure that the contractors that they hired were safe contractors?
43. In the past, have you ever come across a GC/CM that had a safety manager or safety consultant assigned to a construction project?

44. In the past, have you ever come across a superintendent of a GC/CM who took any steps to ensure that the job site safety and health program was being implemented? If so, explain what steps.
45. Have you ever come across a representative of a GC/CM that monitored the construction site to see that the contractors were complying with OSHA?
46. Have you ever come across a representative of a GC/CM who performed safety inspections on their construction project?
47. In this case, did the defendant GC/CM have anyone assigned to oversee the project to ensure that contractors were complying with OSHA?
48. Did the GC/CM do anything to ensure that pre-planning took place with contractors to foresee hazards and decide upon hazard controls to be implemented before work began?
49. Did the GC/CM require weekly safety meetings?
50. Did the GC/CM perform daily safety monitoring to ensure that the work was being done safely?
51. Would it have been possible for this injury to have been prevented?
52. Would it have been possible for the GC/CM to have done anything that would have prevented this incident?
53. When you have performed evaluations in the past, have you ever relied upon any industry safety authority to support your opinions?
54. If so, list them.
55. In this case, list for me all of the industry safety authorities that you relied upon to perform your evaluation.

NOTES

1. 29CFR1926.32(f)—Competent person means one who is capable of identifying existing and predictable hazards in the surroundings or working conditions which are unsanitary, hazardous or dangerous to employees and who has authorization to take prompt corrective measures to eliminate them.

2. *Construction Safety Management and Engineering*, Darryl C. Hill, CSP, American Society of Safety Engineers, Des Plaines, IL, 2004, p. 179.

3. *Accident Prevention Manual*, Associated General Contractors of America, Chapter I-23, Washington, D.C., 1972.

4. 29CFR1926.32(f)—Competent person means one who is capable of identifying existing and predictable hazards in the surroundings or working conditions which are unsanitary, hazardous or dangerous to employees, and who has authorization to take prompt corrective measures to eliminate them.

Chapter Five

Evaluating the Conduct of the General Contractor/Construction Manager—Standard of Care

The method an attorney and safety professional should use to evaluate the conduct of the defendant GC/CM is to compare its conduct to the standard of care. The standard of care consists of compliance with OSHA standards and the customary safe practices established by industry safety authorities. They should consider the following:

- Principles and Practices of Safety Management—Industry Standard
- OSHA Compliance—Multi-Employer Citation Policy
- Contract Requirements of the GC/CM in its Contract with the Owner or Construction Project Owner (CPO)
- Whether or not the GC/CM violated its own Safety Program and Policy
- Compliance with relevant ANSI standards

For many decades, construction industry safety authorities have been consistent in their guidance to project managers, construction managers, general contractors and superintendents about the role they should take in preventing injuries on a construction site. Essentially all industry safety authorities and OSHA agree that general contractors, builders and construction managers should take reasonable steps to implement the job site occupational safety and health program, including:

- Holding pre-job safety conferences
- Weekly safety meetings
- Planning before work begins to identify hazards
- Performing the functions of hazard identification, evaluation and control
- Periodic monitoring of the site to ensure that the work is done safely
- Hiring safe contractors
- Safety training of the superintendent, project manager and foremen

All of the following construction industry safety authorities are in basic agreement with the principles and practices of construction safety management expressed in chapters 2 and 3.

AUTHORS OF THE STANDARD OF CARE IN CONSTRUCTION SAFETY

The following is a list of the highest and most authoritative construction industry safety authorities.

- The American National Standards Institute, 11 West 42nd Street, New York, NY 10036
- The Associated General Contractors of America, 1957 E Street, N.W. Washington, D.C. 20006
- The American Society of Safety Engineers, 1800 E. Oakton Street, Des Plaines, IL 60018
- The National Association of Home Builders, 15th and M Street N.W. Washington, D.C. 20005
- The Construction Industry Institute, 3925 W. Braker Lane (R4500), Austin, TX 78759-5316
- The National Safety Council, 1121 Spring Lake Drive, Itasca, IL 60143-3201
- The American Society of Civil Engineers, 101 Constitution Avenue, NW, Suite 375 East, Washington, D.C. 20001
- Construction Management Association of America, 7926 Jones Branch Drive, #800, McLean, Virginia 22102.

All of the above agree that general contractors and construction managers should plan, monitor and ensure that the work performed by construction workers is done safely and in compliance with OSHA standards. For example, the following is taken from the standards of the above construction industry safety authorities.

1. American National Standard for Construction and Demolition Operations—Safety and Health Program Requirements for Multi-Employer Projects ANSI A10.33-2011

This national consensus standard was promulgated in 2011. It sets forth the minimum elements and activities of a program that defines the duties and responsibilities of construction employers working on a construction project where multiple employers are or will be engaged in the common undertaking to complete a construction project. This standard is the basis for use as a minimum safety and health guideline for a program to provide a safe and healthful work environment and to accomplish cost effective construction. The following are some provisions from this standard:

> 2. Definition. **Project Constructor** (emphasis added). A person, firm, or corporation, **construction manager, general contractor**, prime contractor, or other entity, designated in the contract as being responsible for all construction work contained in the project documents.
>
> 3.2.3.1. Project Safety and Health Plan. The project constructor shall have a project safety and health plan specific for the scope of work to be performed.
>
> 3.4. Requirements of the Overall Project Safety and Health Plan. The following shall be specified in the project safety and health plan, and be assigned to the various levels of construction management and supervision with authority and capabilities to implement the plan.
>
> 3.4.1. Evaluation of contractor safety and health plans to determine their appropriateness to the specific job site and work to be performed.
>
> 3.4.2. Monitoring and documenting the implementation of the safety and health plans.
>
> 5. Senior Project Supervisor.
>
> 5.2. Responsibilities. In addition to other responsibilities required by this standard for all work to be performed on the project site, the senior project supervisor shall:
>
> 5.2.1. Ensure correction or abatement of hazardous conditions in compliance with this standard.
>
> 5.2.2. Verify that competent persons are designated by contractors and list the names along with the qualifications of the competent persons.
>
> 5.2.3. Monitor the project when work is being conducted, regularly (at least daily) for potential hazardous conditions.
>
> 5.2.4. Immediately notify the responsible contractor, and contractors whose employees may be exposed, of any conditions/acts that may cause injury or illness to employees.
>
> 6. Senior Contractor Supervisors:
>
> 6.1. Designation. Each contractor shall designate a senior contractor supervisor who shall have the final authority and responsibility for the contractor's safety and health program.

8. Pre-Work Planning:

8.1.1. Prior to the start of work, each contractor shall conduct a physical survey by walking through the job site, reviewing the drawings and contract documents and holding discussions as appropriate with the owner, engineer, general contractor and construction manager.

8.2. Hazard Analysis. At the initiation of the construction project, hazard analysis shall be conducted to provide a safe and healthful workplace.

2. American National Standard A10.1—Pre-Project and Pre-Task Safety and Health Planning:

5. **PROJECT CONSTRUCTORS**—PRE-PROJECT SAFETY AND HEALTH PLANNING:

5.1. **General Responsibilities in Project Safety and Health Planning**

5.1.1. The Project Constructor shall plan for overall safety and health on the project.

5.2.1. The Project Constructor shall perform project hazard identification using contract documents, project schedules, site assessments, drawings, plans, building information models, project specifications, etc. to identify the complex tasks that will be performed on the project.

5.3. **Project Specific Safety and Health Plan**

5.3.1. As part of the planning process, the Project Constructor shall develop a project specific safety and health plan which includes the impact of safety and health on the following critical topics where applicable.

6. PROJECT CONSTRUCTORS—PRE-TASK SAFETY AND HEALTH PLANNING

6.1.1. Project Constructor shall establish regular safety and health planning meetings with all contractors for the purpose of coordinating project activities.

6.1.3. The Project Constructor shall require all contractors to participate in the planning meeting.

6.1.4. The Project Constructor shall establish the agenda for each planning meeting.

Appendix C—**Project Hazard Identification Guidelines for Project Constructors and Contractors**

Purpose:

- To identify complex tasks and potentially hazardous tasks, and inform all contractors and other affected project personnel about them.

Procedure:

- Evaluate project schedules, site assessments, building information models, project specifications and/or any other documents that could help identify complex tasks and potentially hazardous tasks.
- Determine which tasks are likely to present a substantial probability of death, serious physical harm or significant impairment to health without appropriate safety and health protective measures.

Appendix D—**Task Hazard Analysis Guidelines**

Purpose:

- Identification of potential task specific safety and/or health hazards, and establishment of safety and/or healthful task procedures.

General:

- Perform the task hazard analysis as close to the task's start-up time as possible.
- Identify the potential hazards.
- Identify the construction methods and/or control measures to eliminate or control the risks.
- Identify the safety and health equipment and materials needed to perform the task safely.
- Establish safe task procedures.
- Provide task specific safety and health training for all affected craft labor.
- Ensure the availability of safety and health equipment needed for the task.
- Ensure a qualified safety professional or competent person participates when a complex task is involved.
- Perform a pre-task briefing immediately prior to the start of the task to remind affected craft labor about the hazards and the established safe task procedures.

3. Associated General Contractors of America

Manual of Accident Prevention in Construction

Since 1927, the Associated General Contractors of America have published their *Manual of Accident Prevention in Construction.* The following is taken from the 8th Edition of their Manual published in 2005. The Manual is intended to aid general contractors, specialty contractors, and subcontractors in the development of a safety and health program.

Chapter 1:

1-1 General
Planning and controlling are basic functions of management. Accident prevention is a part of both functions, assisting management to reach the goals of no accidents and lower operating costs.

1-2 Planning begins with management's written commitment to accident prevention objectives . . . It is imperative that management be dedicated to the accident prevention program . . . A management representative should be responsible for coordinating loss control activities. This assignment should be delegated to an individual with basic training in accident prevention . . . Areas of responsibility include pre-planning, employee supervisory training, establishment of minimum safety standards, . . . inspections . . .

1-4 Assignment of Responsibility. Line management should be responsible for achieving the objective of the accident prevention program. Safety staff should provide assistance to line management in delegating responsibilities for accident prevention.

1-7 Pre-Job Planning. Management and safety staff should meet to discuss accident prevention as soon as the bid documents have been obtained. Job layouts, plans, and schedules should be studied to determine the requirements of the project . . . Safety staff and the insurance company's loss control representative should be present at this meeting . . . A supplemental safety program for each specific job should be developed and disseminated to all supervisory personnel on the job.

A fundamental element in any safety program is monitoring to ensure that plans are being implemented.

Chapter 46. Project Safety Pre-Planning:

1- General. An effective method to ensure safety is to pre-plan safety activities into a project before construction starts. The management personnel responsible for the project should be the catalyst for any pre-planning meeting.

2- Pre-Job Site Planning. Project safety pre-planning should cover such topics as those listed below. (Note: This list may not be all inclusive . . .)

- Wind and lightning storms
- Work zone/traffic control
- Appoint safety responsibilities/competent person
- Locate underground utilities and overhead power lines
- Determine if job specific written plans will be needed for issues such as excavations, confined space, demolition, equipment inspection, fall protection, lockout/tagout, steel erection
- Site specific training requirements

3- Periodic audit during construction. Regular inspections of the project should be completed in order to assure your loss control program is being administered properly.

Supervisory Safety Training Program

In this training program, the Associated General Contractors of America sets forth the reasonable steps that a construction supervisor should take regarding implementation of a job site safety program and to provide a workplace free of recognized hazards in compliance with OSHA standards.

ACCIDENT PREVENTION AND LOSS CONTROL

Superintendent's Moral and Personal Obligations. As a supervisor, you have many obligations placed on you, not the least of which is the care of those working for you . . . Nowhere are the supervisor's obligation to workers more personal and obvious than in the area of accident prevention. During each hour they work, the lives and livelihood of all workers and their families are entrusted to your care. Decisions you make affect their future. You have a basic responsibility for their safety.

You start to fulfill your safety responsibilities by analyzing each specific task with safety and health considerations in mind . . . Falls have consistently caused between 30 and 40 percent of construction fatalities . . . You cannot watch each worker under your supervision all the time. You can, however, lay down the base for a safe site by clearly defining and enforcing all safety rules. You can make safety a priority by being an active advocate for safe and healthy construction.

Site Safety Management. The role and responsibility of the supervisor in safety planning cannot be overstated. Proper understanding of OSHA regulations, accompanied by good planning and site auditing processes, can ensure a safe worksite. Always review your site, identify major hazard areas, and take steps to address them before they become a potential danger.

- Plan for specific safety hazards.

Multi-Employer Jobsite Safety

- Supervise safety policy and procedures on multi-employer job sites.
- Coordinate safety compliance as the controlling site safety contractor.

SESSION 1—Introduction

Construction work is a hazardous occupation but it does not have to be dangerous. We have the technology and ability to plan and implement safety processes to achieve zero accidents.

SESSION 3—Planning for Site Safety

A world of safety problems can be avoided if you plan for site safety. By reviewing site plans and schedules, a supervisor can eliminate many hazards that would otherwise confront workers.

- Analyze and manage site hazards through planning.
- Develop and use a Job Hazard Analysis.

Safety planning requires a detailed review of the work tasks that are scheduled. Tasks cannot be undertaken before the work area or planned activities have been evaluated for safety issues and concerns . . . Scheduling a project must take safety into consideration. WORK SHOULD NOT BEGIN UNTIL A THOROUGH SAFETY REVIEW HAS BEEN COMPLETED.

Project Scheduling

Supervisor should review project schedules and look for safety issues that need to be addressed before work activities can begin . . . Task planning identifies the work process, materials, equipment, space, skills and information necessary for willing workers to complete an activity. Effective supervisors always plan tasks by reviewing these elements of work before assigning them to workers. A critical activity that should be completed during planning is the safety analysis that identifies all potential risks associated with the elements of the task. Make sure that all of your site activities and work tasks are properly planned and that each element has been evaluated for potential risk.

Planning and developing JHAs requires analyzing the task. A supervisor should question the work process and evaluate the potential for risk.

Session 6—Multi-Employer Job Site Safety

One approach reinforces the idea that safety is the responsibility of each contractor and everyone needs to take care of his or her own problems . . . This so-called "ostrich approach" amounts to sticking one's head in the sand. There are two distinct reasons why this approach is faulty.

The first is OSHA's policy that **the controlling contractor has responsibility for the actions of other contractors** . . . The second reason to keep your head out of the sand is **third party liability** . . . Preventing accidents is the best way to limit third party liability.

4. American Society of Safety Engineers—*Construction Safety Management and Engineering*

In this Manual published in 2004 the American Society of Safety Engineers gives guidance to business owners who hire contractors as well as general contractors and construction managers relative to reasonable steps that they can and should take to prevent contractor worker injury and death and to save money. In chapter 2, they set forth the essential elements of a construction safety program. The role and responsibilities of the project owner, general contractor, construction manager and contractor are essentially the same as those recognized by all the owner industry safety authorities indicated in this report. They point out the importance of planning, monitoring and taking reasonable steps to ensure that contract workers have a workplace free of recognized hazards, that is, in compliance with OSHA regulations.

The American Society of Safety Engineers also points out the importance of training. They state the following:

> Each new project should develop its own safety training program . . . Making sure the contractor employees are trained before they are allowed to work on the job site is the best way that the general contractor has of ensuring that all employees on the site have received at least the minimum training required. When developing a project specific training program, a job hazard analysis must be conducted to determine the needs of the training.

5. The National Association of Home Builders

The National Association of Home Builders gives guidance to literally tens of thousands of residential construction companies relative to ways to ensure that work is done in ways that contractors and subcontractors' workers are not needlessly injured and killed. They have provided several publications to guide this industry. The following are some examples:

- The Model Safety and Health Program for the Building Industry, Second Edition, 1995
- Construction Management—The Superintendent's Job, Second Edition, 1990
- How to Hire and Supervise Subcontractors, 1991
- Fall Protection Compliance Manual—An Employer's Compliance Manual for OSHA's Fall Protection Regulations, 1995
- An Ounce of Prevention—Job Site Safety and Ensurance for Builders and Remodelers, 1995
- An Occupational Safety and Health Program for Builders: Guidelines for Residential and Commercial Construction, 1990

In their publication, "An Ounce of Prevention," the National Association of Home Builders gives guidance to the builder to prevent injuries to subcontractors or their employees. They state:

> It's just not **your own employees** you have to worry about. You can also be held responsible for injuries of subcontractors or their employees . . . If you are doing business as a . . . builder, you have a legal obligation to provide your subcontractors and their employees with a safe place to work. If you do not, you are being negligent. The law requires you to supervise the project to ensure the safety of **all** the workers on the site, including the employees of subcontractors. Moreover, this is one of those **nondelegable** duties we mentioned in Chapter 2. The responsibility to supervise and inspect your job sites to ensure that safety practices meet the

> requirements for your industry is yours. If you assign that task to someone else, and they do not do it right, you are liable for the consequences of their mistakes.

Throughout these publications, the National Association of Home Builders guides general contractors and builders to implement a job site occupational safety and health program. That is, they exhort the builders in this industry to design and implement safety programs by requiring contractors and subcontractors to implement their own safety and health programs. They exhort the builder to manage safety, just as they manage all other aspects of construction such as scheduling, quality assurance, coordination, etc. The National Association of Home Builders recognizes the moral responsibility of the builder to take reasonable steps to manage safety to ensure that contractor and subcontractor employees are not needlessly exposed to hazards and risks which could cause catastrophic injury or death.

The National Association of Home Builders specifically addresses the relationship between general contractor and subcontractors when they state:

> More and more, builders are finding out that when an OSHA inspection takes place on their job site, they can be held responsible for the violations of their subs. Since March 1992, when OSHA increased their penalties by seven-fold, the effect of a subcontractor's violations can have an even greater impact on the builder's bottom line . . . One of the best ways a builder can avoid OSHA citations that result from a subcontractor's violations is to only utilize subs who have effective safety and health programs and policies that aggressively attempt to comply with OSHA standards. Builders should share information about developing a safer work site with the sub. Having a safe, OSHA-compliant job site is good business for everyone on the site. If there are no injuries, then workers' compensation rates go down and the concern for third party lawsuits is lessened . . . Remember, OSHA currently wants the builder or general contractor to ensure that all employers under contractual control comply with all requirements.

National Association of Home Builders—*Home Builder's Safety Program*

In 2007, the National Association of Home Builders published this safety program as a model that members should follow if they want to design and implement an effective safety program. In it, they state:

> Builders need to appreciate the value of good safety programs. A good safety program saves lives and protects your bottom line . . . There are three major motivator types for safety.
>
> - Humanitarianism
> - Economical
> - Legal

SAFETY STARTS AT THE TOP

If management does not make safety a priority, then neither will the rank and file. Simply telling people to practice job safety techniques is not enough . . . Your company mandate must be that everyone on the project is responsible for safety.

Site Superintendents

The superintendent should:

- Establish comprehensive project safety procedures that comply with OSHA.
- Monitor the project's safety status.
- Conduct project-safety and loss control training for employees.
- Ensure that each job site has the necessary safety equipment and materials.
- Monitor trade contractor performance to ensure compliance with the company's safety performance requirements.
- Enforce disciplinary action.

Establish Accountability Procedures

Develop and Deliver a Safety Program

The site superintendent is also responsible for:

- Conducting accident prevention and safety training.
- Ensuring that job site employees comply with applicable training provisions of OSHA.

Conduct Regular Job Site Inspections and Hazard Analysis

Jobsite inspections allow employers to gauge the effectiveness of their safety program and to determine employee training needs. As part of an effective job site inspection program, the site superintendent must:

- Set inspection responsibilities and schedules.
- Analyze inspection findings.
- Set program standards for observing employees' safety practices.
- Monitor employees' safety practice performance.

Job Site Hazard Analysis

It is important to include job site hazard analysis in your safety program. By performing a JHA, you can proactively address potential hazards and take corrective measures.

Successful safety program administrators will attest to the fact that good training is one of the most valuable investments a company can make.

6. Construction Industry Institute

The Construction Industry Institute is an association of major general contractors/construction managers and major corporations in the United States.

The Construction Industry Institute participates with leading universities in the United States. They funded research which resulted in the publication of a document entitled "Managing Subcontractor Safety," Publication 13-1, February 1991. The purpose of the CII Safety Task Force research was to identify the primary means by which general contractors influence the safety performance of their subcontractors . . . The goal was to add to the body of knowledge so that effective measures can be implemented to reduce the cost of accidents.

Conclusions of CII Explained in "Managing Subcontractor Safety"
Task Force research shows that, where subcontractor safety is concerned, the role of project managers is very important. On large and small projects alike, emphasizing safety and providing quality coordination have a favorable impact on the safety of subcontractors. On small projects, subcontractor safety performance also was influenced by the quality of the project management existent on the job and the degree to which workers were dealt with in a humanitarian or personal manner . . . **Since the general contractors have a significant influence on their subcontractors, owners too will have an influence on the safety performance of the general contractor and subcontractor. Thus, it can be inferred from the results of this study that owners also play a major role in construction safety** (emphasis added).

Guidelines for Managing Subcontractor Safety on Construction Projects
The following is a brief summary of the guidelines set forth by CII.

- They point out the importance of selecting subcontractors by evaluating their safety performance when evaluating bids.
- The contract should be detailed relative to how safety will be managed and reported. As a minimum, the scope of work should include requirements for a "Safety Plan," including such information as safety inspection, enforcement, safety staffing, permit required, preemployment testing, substance abuse testing, safety meetings, personal protective equipment required, . . . basic safety training . . .
- Pre-job safety conference to set forth safe procedures, training requirements and a schedule to discuss safety performance and training programs.
- Periodic safety progress reviews between managers and subcontractor safety representatives.
- Managers should conduct their own safety inspections of the subcontractor's work site, and a review of the inspection findings should take place at the periodic meetings.

Safety Rules—Enforcement Procedure

There must be a procedure for enforcing safety rules. This procedure should be written, and should be enforced equally among supervisors, managers, workers and other parties on the site. It should spell out what situations will result in immediate discharge and what actions will be taken on the first, second or third incidents involving violations of a less serious nature.

7. National Safety Council

The National Safety Council, chartered by Congress in 1953, is the nation's leading advocate for worker safety and health. It is comprised of approximately 37,000 members of major corporations and representatives of government, labor and the insurance industry. It has been giving guidance to business owners through many manuals and documents for close to 100 years. They have been giving guidance in their *Accident Prevention Manual* since 1946.

Accident Prevention Manual for Industrial Operations

The National Safety Council is considered by construction safety management professionals as a highly authoritative source for guidance in safety matters. In Chapter 2 of their ACCIDENT PREVENTION MANUAL FOR INDUSTRIAL OPERATIONS, it sets forth guidelines for controlling hazards in the construction industry. It has been available since at least 1969. In their Manual, they point out:

- The importance of insisting upon contractor compliance with all safety and health regulations.
- The need for advanced analyses and planning for safety.
- The need for a preconstruction safety conference.
- The need for periodic safety meetings during which plans are made for anticipating hazards associated with work so that controls can be put in place before the hazard evolves.

Essential to the principles established by the National Safety Council is the principle that all accidents are foreseeable, predictable, avoidable and preventable. Construction safety management should be proactive rather than reactive. That is, plans should be made to predict the hazards and to install the controls before the hazard evolves. This is a proactive approach. It is far more dependable than a reactive approach which would depend upon safety inspection to identify the hazard. Serious injury or death could result before the hazard is identified through safety inspection.

The National Safety Council further points out the importance of "assignment of responsibility" and "accountability" as key elements in a construction safety management program.

Core Safety Materials for the Construction Professional

A Manual entitled "Core Safety Materials for the Construction Professional" has been prepared by the National Safety Council's Construction Division. In it, it gives guidance regarding the elements of an effective construction site-specific safety plan:

> Introduction: An effective safety plan should get its start during the bid process. The owner should require the development of a pre-construction analysis by all successful bidders. The general contractor/project management team should take the lead in the developing process. All subcontractors—both first and second tier subs—should be invited to an initial meeting and encouraged to participate in the process.
>
> Construction Management Responsibility:
>
> a. Plan safety into the project.
>   1. Comply with owner's safety requirements and local, state and federal regulations.
>   2. Establish minimum safety history requirements (e.g., last five years, EMRs, OSHA inspection history, etc.) for all project contractors.
>   3. Investigate, and pre-qualify as acceptable bidders, contractors who meet the pre-determined safety history requirements.
>
> Establish and incorporate into contract documents the requirement for a Project Specific Safety and Health Plan to include:
>
> a. Construction process plan.
> b. Hazard analysis.
> c. Permit system.
> d. Designated project safety coordinator/administrator.

This document goes on to give guidance with regard to owners, general/prime contractors and subcontractors which is essentially the same as all of the other industry standards and authorities.

8. Construction Management Association of America

The Construction Management Association of America gives guidance to construction managers relative to safety management. They point out the following in their book entitled *Construction Management—Standards of Practice*, 2010:

> CMAA has long advocated a collaborative approach to safety management for construction projects and programs. In such a collaborative environment, some responsibility for safety is widely shared. All project participants, for example, have a duty to call attention to observed unsafe conditions as a key step in preventing injuries to themselves and others.
>
> Project safety should be considered a process that is elevated above other issues and resolved in a timely manner. The CM needs to make it clear to the owner that anyone on the CM staff observing a safety hazard will bring the issue to the contractor for corrective action.
>
> An early member of the project team should be the CM's safety coordinator. The safety coordinator begins to develop input from a safety perspective, for such items as the construction management plan, project procedure manuals, pre-construction drawings, constructability reviews, and the management information system.
>
> **Staffing Considerations.** In order to coordinate and monitor contractor safety efforts effectively, a separate safety staff is created within the Construction Management team. The safety staff is comprised of safety professionals with project-specific experience and knowledge of:
>
> - American National Standards
> - Occupational Safety and Health Administration Standards
> - Hazard Communication requirements
>
> **Contract Requirements.** Each prime contractor should be required to submit, as per the contract documents, the following for review by the CM:
>
> - Written safety program
> - Resume of safety representative
> - Hazard communication program
> - Safety training programs
> - Site-specific safety plan
> - Task-specific safety and health plans for high risk activities
>
> **Pre-Construction Conference.** The CM's safety representative addresses all prime contractors at the pre-construction conference. At this time, information should be reviewed with the contractors concerning submittal requirements, emergency response programs and procedures, safety meeting times and schedules, training requirements, site safety survey, accident investigations and reporting procedures. The contractor shall be reminded to transmit all safety related materials to all subcontractors of any tier.

> The CM monitors the contractor's daily construction activities and notifies the contractor in writing (with copies to the owner) of any deficiencies or imminent hazards or situations observed. The CM then follows up with the contractor to determine if corrective measures have been taken . . . Should the contractor fail to correct an unsafe condition, the CM immediately notifies the owner of the contractor's failure to correct the unsafe condition. The owner then notifies the contractor through the CM that the unsafe condition must be corrected or the work in question will be stopped until the condition is corrected to the satisfaction of the owner . . . A safety coordination meeting takes place between the CM, the contractor, and other affected contractors to discuss the job hazard analysis . . . The CM participates as a member of the job site safety committee . . .

There is general agreement among industry safety authorities with regard to steps that a GC/CM should take to implement the job site safety program. An analysis of causation considers the facts obtained from discovery and from the deposition of key defendant management representatives to determine if they took reasonable steps to identify, evaluate and ensure control of hazards by planning, monitoring and implementing the construction site safety program.

Chapter Six

Epidemiology of Fatal Falls from Elevation in the Construction Industry

The greatest number of construction worker third party cases involves falls from elevations. The following research gives some indication of the magnitude of the problem.

The National Institute of Occupational Safety and Health performed research from 1980 to 1989 and found that falls from elevation were the fourth leading cause of occupational injury/fatality in the United States.[1] The consensus of fatal occupational injuries of the Bureau of Labor Statistics found that falls from roofs, ladders and scaffolds were the most common fall location. Other studies have noted falls associated with steel erection,[2] falls from equipment or materials,[3] and falls through floor openings.[4]

Previous research identified falls as a leading cause of fatalities in the construction industry. Falls accounted for 25 percent of construction deaths identified by the National Traumatic Occupational Fatality Surveillance System for 1980 through 1989,[5] 32 percent reported by the 1996 Consensus of Fatal Occupational Injuries,[6] and 33 percent of construction fatalities investigated by the Occupational Safety and Health Administration between 1985 and 1989.[7] Falls comprised 29 percent of construction fatalities in Washington State between 1973 and 1983,[8] and 46 percent in New Jersey between 1983 and 1989.[9] Occupational groups identified with high frequencies of fatal falls include roofers, painters, ironworkers, carpenters, construction laborers, and tree trimmers.[10]

Fatal Falls by Location from Which Worker Fell, FACE, 1982–1997

Location	*N*	%
Stairs or steps	0	0.0
Ladder	8	8.8
Scaffolding	17	18.7
Scaffold collapse (n = 2)		
Building	40	44.0
Roof (n = 26)		
Floor (n = 10)		
Specified structures	7	7.7
Unspecified structure/building	11	12.0
Fall into hole or other opening	0	0
Other fall from one level to another	8	8.8
Tree (n = 1)		
Stationary vehicle/machine (n = 5)		
Fall, n.e.c./unspecified	0	0.0
Total	91	100.0

Circumstances of Fatal Roof-Related Falls, United States, 1980–1994

	N	%
Falls through roof		
Through roof opening	43	3.5
Through roof (non-supportive materials)	13	1.1
Through skylight	83	6.7
Through roof, n.e.c./unspecified	103	8.4
Falls from roof		
From roof structural member	19	1.5
From roof	961	78.1
Roof, n.e.c./unspecified	6	0.50
Total	1228	99.8

Source: National Traumatic Occupational Fatalities (NTOF) Surveillance System

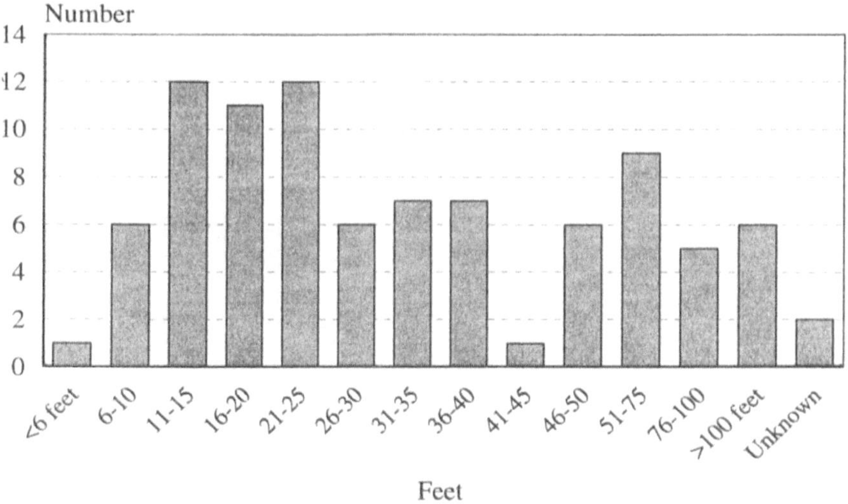

Figure 6.1. Distribution of Fatal Falls by Height of Fall, FACE Investigations, 1982–1997 (N = 91)

NOTES

1. Worker Fall by Death: A Summary of Surveillance Findings and Investigative Case Reports, National Institute for Occupational Safety and Health, U.S. Department of Health and Human Services, November 2000.

2. Injuries Resulting from Falls from Elevations, U.S. Department of Labor Bulletin 2195, U.S. Department of Labor, Bureau of Labor Statistics. Washington, D.C., U.S. Government Printing Office, 1984; Fatalities and Serious Injuries, McVittie D.J., Occupational Medicine: State of the Art Reviews. 1995, 10:285–293.

3. Injuries Resulting from Falls from Elevations, U.S. Department of Labor Bulletin 2195, U.S. Department of Labor, Bureau of Labor Statistics. Washington, D.C., U.S. Government Printing Office, 1984.

4. Fatalities and Serious Injuries, McVittie, D.J., Occupational Medicine: State of the Art Reviews. 1995, 10:285–293; Analysis of Construction Fatalities—The OSHA Database, 1985–1989, U.S. Department of Labor, Occupational Safety and Health Administration. Washington, D.C.: U.S. Government Printing Office, 1990.

5. Injury Hazards in Construction Industry, Kisner, S.M., Fosbroke, D.E., *J Occup Med.* 1994; 36:137–143.

6. Fatal Workplace Injuries in 1996: A Collection of Data and Analyses, U.S. Department of Labor Report 922, U.S. Department of Labor, Bureau of Labor Statistics. Washington, D.C.: U.S. Government Printing Office, 1998.

7. Analysis of Construction Fatalities—The OSHA Database, 1985–1989, U.S. Department of Labor, Occupational Safety and Health Administration. Washington, D.C.: U.S. Government Printing Office, 1990.

8. Fatal Injuries in the Construction Industry in Washington State. Buskin, S.E., Paulozzi, L.J. *Am J Indust Med.* 1987; 11:453–460.

9. Fatal Occupational Injuries in the New Jersey Construction Industry. Sorock, G.S., Smith, E.O., Poldoft, M. *J. Occup. Med.* 1993; 35:916–961

10. Ibid.; Fatal Work-Related Falls from Roofs. Suruda, A., Fosbroke, D., Braddee, R. *J Safety Res.* 1995; 26:1–8; NIOSH Alert: Request for Assistance in Preventing Falls and Electrocutions During Tree Trimming. National Institute of Occupational Safety and Health. Cincinnati, OH: DHHS (NIOSH) Publication No. 92-106.

Chapter Seven

Falls from Elevation—Residential Construction

Most falls from elevation in residential construction will likely have a viable theory of liability. If the worker had been provided fall protection, he/she would have been automatically prevented from falling by a guardrail, safety net or personal fall arrest system. From my experience, I can say that it is very rare to come across a residential builder who actually implements a fall protection plan and ensures that contract workers are trained as required by OSHA.

I remember being cross examined by a defense attorney who asked me: "Isn't it true, Mr. Gallagher, that in the real world workers commonly work in violation of OSHA standards?" She probably had a deposition of mine where I said that. I answered: "Yes, that is true because in the real world, Congress really wanted workers to be protected from falls that really cause serious injury and death to really precious people. Their hope was that workers would really be protected. Some GCs and builders just do not really care to comply with the law. That is why we are here today."

Roofers and framers are most vulnerable. They are often undocumented and paid under the table, sometimes just above minimum wage. They are easily intimidated and rarely complain. Often their employer has no workers compensation or liability insurance. Some suffer brain damage, paralysis, and end up in wheelchairs or nursing homes for the rest of their lives.

The plaintiff's employer is often hired by a framing or roofing contractor who actually does no work. The framer or contractor contracts with the builder and then hires a person who has a crew to do the work. It is common that no one at any level on the residential construction site sees to it that the workers doing the framing and roofing work are trained and certified in fall protection training as required by OSHA. They almost always permit the workers to work without fall protection. Usually they get away with it. OSHA has too few construction inspectors to give an adequate threat to builders.

The entity or person that hires the contractor who hires the crew is usually required by the builder to have liability insurance and to indemnify them in case of injury. The builder attempts to protect themselves from the economic risk that could result from lawsuits but does little or nothing to control the risks or hazards to which workers are exposed. They do not act unconsciously. They stack the deck against the safety of the workers.

OSHA requires standard fall protection for workers exposed to falls six feet or greater [29CFR1926.501(b)(13)]. This standard indicates that if the employer can demonstrate that it is infeasible or creates a greater hazard to use standard fall protection then the employer can implement a fall protection plan as indicated in paragraph 1926.502(k). This paragraph requires the fall protection plan to document why standard fall protection is infeasible or why it would create a greater hazard. However, I know of no fall hazard in residential construction that cannot be controlled through standard fall protection or other reasonable means such as the use of scissors lifts, scaffolds, telescoping and articulating boom lifts or other personnel lifts.

One day while training residential construction superintendents about OSHA requirements for fall protection, I sensed that they felt that actual OSHA compliance was not practical nor realistic. So I asked if anyone could tell me of a task performed by a worker at height in residential construction that could not be controlled by standard fall protection or other reasonable means. When no one answered, I said: Tell me of the fall hazard in residential construction that you would permit your son or daughter to be exposed to because you think OSHA compliance is a nuisance or impractical. Again, there was no answer—because there is no reasonable answer.

The following are some of the more common ways that residential workers have been injured. In all of these cases, the plaintiff's attorney pursued liability due to a breach in the standard of care. That is, the GC/CM violated principles and practices of safety management because they violated the standards of OSHA, American National Standards Institute (ANSI), National Association of Home Builders, Associated General Contractors of America, the National Safety Council, Construction Industry Institute, the American Society of Civil Engineers and the American Society of Safety Engineers.

~ ~ ~ ~

Description of Incident:	**Framer falls through stairway opening** from second floor to basement.
Failure:	Lack of guardrail or cover over the stairway opening. Failure to train worker in fall protection as required by OSHA.

~ ~ ~ ~

Description of Incident: **Framer applying plywood sheathing to roof slips** and falls to ground level.
Failure: No fall arrest system, slide guard or guardrail. Failure to train worker in fall protection as required by OSHA.

~ ~ ~ ~

Description of Incident: **Roofer applying roofing material falls** from sloped roof while applying roofing material.
Failure: No fall arrest system, slide guard or guardrail. Failure to train worker in fall protection as required by OSHA.

~ ~ ~ ~

Description of Incident: **Framer on roof building chimney slips** and falls to ground.
Failure: No fall arrest system, slide guard or guardrail. Failure to train worker in fall protection as required by OSHA.

~ ~ ~ ~

Description of Incident: **Roofing material slides down roof, strikes worker**, causing worker to fall.
Failure: Lack of slide guard, fall arrest system or guardrail. Failure to train worker in fall protection as required by OSHA.

~ ~ ~ ~

Description of Incident: **Framer installing** four by eight plywood **sheathing on side of house** from ladder falls.
Failure: Failure to train worker in fall protection as required by OSHA. Failure to prohibit the worker from climbing the ladder while carrying materials.

~ ~ ~ ~

Description of Incident: **Pump jack scaffold** used to install siding **collapses** and worker falls.
Failure: Failure to properly tie the pump jack scaffold into the building. Failure to train worker in scaffold safety as required by OSHA.

~ ~ ~ ~

Description of Incident: Worker **falls from scaffold** while performing masonry work on façade of building.
Failure: No guardrail on scaffold. Failure to train worker in fall protection as required by OSHA.

~ ~ ~ ~

Description of Incident: Bricklayer falls when **scaffold plank breaks** in half.
Failure: Use of non-scaffold grade planks. Failure to train worker in fall protection as required by OSHA.

~ ~ ~ ~

Description of Incident: Masonry **worker climbs up side of scaffold** without use of ladder.
Failure: Lack of standard ladder giving access to scaffold. Failure to train worker in fall protection as required by OSHA.

~ ~ ~ ~

Description of Incident: **Fall into trench** which was not shored or sloped to the angle of repose.
Failure: Lack of sloping, shoring or bracing of trench—lack of barrier at side of trench. Failure to train worker in fall protection as required by OSHA.

~ ~ ~ ~

Description of Incident: **Roofer slips and falls from sloped roof due to rain water**.
Failure: Permitting workers to work on wet, slippery, sloped roof. Failure to train worker in fall protection as required by OSHA.

~ ~ ~ ~

Description of Incident: **Roofer slips on morning frost on roof from dew**.
Failure: Permitting workers to work before the frost melted and was not slippery. Failure to train worker in fall protection as required by OSHA.

~ ~ ~ ~

Description of Incident: **Framer raised on plywood laid over forks of forklift truck falls** from elevation.
Failure: Permitting use of forklift truck to raise workers without using OSHA required platform with guardrails. Failure to train worker in fall protection as required by OSHA.

~ ~ ~ ~

Description of Incident: **Trusses collapse** causing framer installing trusses to fall.
Failure: Failure to follow Truss Manufacturers Institute's instructions for bracing. Failure to train worker in fall protection as required by OSHA.

~ ~ ~ ~

Description of Incident: **Installing drywall or sheetrock from stepladder—** worker falls.

Failure: Failure to use scissors lift or scaffold to prevent falls. Failure to train worker in fall protection as required by OSHA.

~ ~ ~ ~

Description of Incident: **Worker on stilts** installing drywall or sheetrock **falls over guardrail**.

Failure: Failure to extend guardrails the height of the stilts. Failure to train worker in fall protection as required by OSHA.

~ ~ ~ ~

Description of Incident: **Roofer falls from roof**. Roofing material delivered to wet roof during rainstorm while workers were on the roof.

Failure: Failure to prohibit work on roof when raining. Failure to train worker in fall protection as required by OSHA.

~ ~ ~ ~

Description of Incident: **Worker picks up a piece of plywood and then falls in hole that the plywood covered**.

Failure: Failure to secure cover and mark it with words COVER or HOLE. Failure to train worker in fall protection as required by OSHA.

There is almost always a viable theory of liability in residential fall cases because the GC/CM rarely requires employees who work at elevation to be properly trained. Rarely do they have a **Competent Person** on site. Rarely do they implement a job site safety program. Rarely do they have a **Fall Protection Plan**.

The OSHA residential fall protection standards require a fall protection plan when the employer can demonstrate that it is infeasible or creates a greater hazard to use conventional fall protection equipment [29CFR1926.501(b)(13)]. In order to implement a fall protection plan, the GC/CM has to know what is required of a fall protection plan. Questioning of the superintendent or project manager of the GC/CM will show whether or not they understood the requirements of a fall protection plan.

DEPOSITION OF GC/CM REGARDING FALL PROTECTION PLAN

1. Does your company have a written fall protection plan?
2. Does your company have a fall protection plan that is not in written form?
3. Have you ever seen a written fall protection plan?
4. Do you know the OSHA requirements for a fall protection plan?
5. List all of the OSHA requirements for a fall protection plan that you are aware of.
6. Does your company have any established procedures for framers to follow when installing trusses?
7. What are the safety requirements that framers or carpenters must follow when installing trusses?
8. Does your company have established procedures for fall protection while leading edge work is being done, that is, installing the plywood sheathing on floors?
9. What are the safety requirements for framers when doing the leading edge work of installing floor sheathing?
10. Does your company have established safety procedures to protect workers who perform work at the edge of a building?
11. What are those requirements?
12. Does your company have any established procedures as to when fall arrest systems are needed during roof sheathing installation?
13. What are those requirements?
14. On this job site, were sheathers and roofers protected by guardrails while working on roofs?
15. Were they protected by safety nets?
16. Were they protected by full body harnesses attached to lanyards and lifelines attached to a safe anchorage point, that is, did they use a fall arrest system?
17. Have you ever been trained by a qualified person in OSHA's fall protection requirements for work in the residential construction industry? Explain—when, where, who trained, how long did it last, what subjects were covered?
18. Were any certifications given to you?
19. Does your company's written safety program or your policy require roofers and framers to submit a fall protection plan to you for review?
20. Does your company policy require that roofers and framers submit documents of certifications to show that their workers have received the OSHA required safety training related to fall protection?

21. Did you require contractors at this site who employ workers who work at elevation to show you certifications which prove that those workers were trained as required by OSHA?
22. Did you ever require any roofer or framer contractor on any job site prior to this to submit a fall protection plan?
23. Did you ever require a roofer or framer on any job to show you documentation of certifications that their workers had received training related to fall protection?
24. In this case, did you determine if the roofers and framers had received safety training as required by OSHA?
25. Do you know if OSHA requires GC/CMs to have a **competent person** perform safety inspections?
26. Do you know what a competent person is according to OSHA's definition?
27. Have you ever been designated as a competent person with the responsibility to ensure that the roofer or framer implemented their fall protection plan?
28. Do you know if any of the contractors or subcontractors had OSHA competent persons working on this site?
29. Do you know the components of a fall arrest system?
30. Do you know the requirements of an anchorage point, according to OSHA standards?
31. Do you know the definition of a controlled access zone according to OSHA standards?
32. Do you know what OSHA's definition is of a warning line system?
33. Do you know OSHA's definition of a safety monitoring system?
34. Do you know when a safety monitoring system can be used?
35. Do you know when a controlled access zone can be used?
36. Do you know if the roofer and framing contractor or subcontractor on this job site had a fall protection plan prepared by a qualified person?
37. On this job site, who was the competent person charged with the responsibility to ensure implementation of fall protection plans of roofers?
38. Did you require the roofer and framing contractor or subcontractor at this site to have a fall protection plan?
39. Did they have one?
40. Did you review it?
41. Did the roofer or framer at this site have workers who received the OSHA required safety training?
42. Do you know what OSHA means by conventional fall protection? (Conventional fall protection consists of guardrails, nets or a fall arrest system.)

43. Can you identify all of the tasks performed at heights at this site where conventional fall protection was not feasible?
    Note: Conventional fall protection is a personal fall arrest system, guardrail, or safety net.
44. Have you identified any work at this job site that was required to be performed within a controlled access zone?
45. Have you identified any work on this site that was required to be done with a safety monitor?

DEPOSITION OF EXPERT REGARDING THE NEED FOR A FALL PROTECTION PLAN

1. Have you ever received any training regarding the requirements of an OSHA fall protection plan for residential construction?
2. Have you ever designed a fall protection plan?
3. Have you ever reviewed a fall protection plan?
4. Have you ever worked for a company that had a written fall protection plan?
5. Please list for me all of the OSHA requirements for a fall protection plan.
6. According to OSHA standards, should a residential builder, framing contractor and roofing contractor have a fall protection plan?
7. In this case, did any defendant have a fall protection plan developed for this site?
8. Do you know OSHA's definition of a qualified person as used in their standard regarding fall protection plans?
9. Do you know OSHA's definition of a competent person as used in their standard regarding a fall protection plan?
10. Do you know if there was a competent person with regard to fall protection at this site?
11. Do you know if there was a qualified person as defined by OSHA at this site with regard to fall protection?
12. When you performed your evaluation, were you aware that OSHA had a requirement that the fall protection plan be under the supervision of a competent person?
13. Do you know who, if anyone, supervised the fall protection plan at this site?
14. Should the fall protection plan establish ways to install trusses when standard fall protection is not feasible?
15. At this site, do you know what the fall protection plan said with regard to safe ways to install trusses?

16. Should a fall protection plan establish safe ways with regard to performing leading edge work for the installation of sheathing on floors?
17. At this site, do you know what the fall protection plan said with regard to safe ways for installing flooring?
18. Did the fall protection plan at this site say what safe procedures must be used to protect workers when performing leading edge work, that is, installing roof sheathing?
19. Did the defendant company do anything to ensure that the fall protection plan of the framer was under the supervision of a competent person?
20. Did the GC/CM or builder at this site do anything to ensure that the fall protection plan of any craft that worked at elevation is under the supervision of a competent person?
21. Do you know if any contractor or subcontractor had an OSHA competent person working for them at this job site?
22. Do you know if the roofer or framing contractor or subcontractor at this site had fall protection plans prepared by a competent person?
23. Who was the competent person?
24. What training qualified that person to be a competent person?

While many of these questions about OSHA regulations will seem irrelevant because they relate to fall hazard exposures different from the fall hazard in your case, they will nevertheless give your expert facts to show that the GC/CM representative was ignorant of OSHA's fall protection standards in general and permitted many exposures to fall hazards. It also shows the extent of the safety management failures of the GC/CM. The root cause of the plaintiff's injury is the defendant's failure to manage safety. All of the facts which show the extent of management's safety failures should be relevant.

OSHA TRAINING REQUIREMENTS

Properly trained workers should be instructed not to work when they are exposed to fall hazards in violation of OSHA standards. Below are the OSHA standards regarding training. I have yet to find a GC/CM in the residential construction industry that has required roofers and framers to show them certifications of the individual workers to verify that they have had the safety training required by OSHA. In fact, I have yet to come upon a bilingual safety trainer who was ever hired by a builder, roofer or framer to train Hispanic workers regarding OSHA fall protection requirements. However, OSHA requires employers to train workers in the language that they understand. The following are some OSHA standards which require fall protection training:

29CFR1926.503. Training requirements. The following training provisions supplement and clarify the requirements of 1926.21 regarding the hazards addressed in Subpart M of this part.

29CFR1926.503(a)(1). Training program. The employer shall provide a training program for each employee who might be exposed to fall hazards. The program shall enable each employee to recognize the hazard of falling and shall train each employee in the procedures to be followed in order to minimize these hazards.

29CFR1926.503(a)(2). The employer shall assure that each employee has been trained, as necessary, by a competent person qualified in the following areas:

(i) The nature of fall hazards in the work area;
(ii) The correct procedures for erecting, maintaining, disassembling, and inspecting the fall protection systems to be used;
(iii) The use and operation of guardrail systems, personal fall arrest systems, safety net systems, warning line systems, safety monitoring systems, controlled access zones, and other protection to be used;
(iv) The role of each employee in the safety monitoring system when this system is used;
(v) The limitations on the use of mechanical equipment during the performance of roofing work on low-sloped roofs;
(vi) The correct procedure for handling and storage of equipment and materials and the erection of overhead protection;
(vii) The role of employees in fall protection plans;
(viii) The standards contained in this Subpart.

29CFR1926.503(b)(1). Certification of Training.[1] The employer shall verify compliance with paragraph (a) of this section by preparing a written certification record. The written certification record shall contain the name or other identity of the employee trained, the dates of the training, and the signature of the person who conducted the training or signature of the employer.

29CFR1926.503(b)(2). The latest training certification shall be maintained.

INSTALLING PLYWOOD SHEATHING ON THE SIDES OF THE BUILDINGS

One way you can show a systematic abdication of safety management responsibilities relative to fall hazards is to question the GC/CM relative to the methods framers use to install plywood sheathing on the sides of the building. Almost always framers install plywood sheathing on the side of the houses using ladders. The framer carries the four by eight sheet of plywood up the ladder on his/her **head**. He/she uses one hand to hold the plywood while sliding the other hand up the side rail of the ladder. He/she then takes the plywood from his/her head and places it against the two by four studs at the side of the building. He/she then holds it there, gets the nail gun and secures the plywood sheet to the two by fours. This is extremely dangerous and violates 29CFR1926.1053(b)(22) which states that "an employee shall not carry any object or load while on a ladder that can cause the employee to lose balance and fall."

OSHA standard 29CFR1926.1060(a) requires workers who use ladders to be trained:

> 29CFR1926.1060(a). The employer shall provide a training program for each employee using ladders and stairways, as necessary. The program shall enable each employee to recognize hazards related to ladders and stairways, and shall train each employee in the procedures to be followed to minimize these hazards.
>
> (1) The employer shall ensure that each employee has been trained by a competent person in the following areas, as applicable:
>
> (i) The nature of fall hazards in the work area;
> (ii) The correct procedures for erecting, maintaining and disassembling the fall protection system to be used;
> (iii) The proper construction, use, placement, and care in handling all stairways and ladders;
> (iv) The maximum intended load-carrying capacities of ladders used; and
> (v) The standards contained in this subpart.

It is rare that framers are trained in ladder safety. If workers are trained in ladder safety, they would be instructed to never work in violation of the OSHA standards and to never carry plywood sheets up a ladder.

USE OF GUARDRAILS OR COVERS TO PROTECT STAIRWAY OPENINGS

Another common fall hazard exposure is to stairway openings. The stairway openings should be cut open just before installation of the stairs. This is the most reliable way to reduce the risk of a worker falling through a stairway opening, that is, by reducing exposure time. OSHA does not permit exposure to fall hazards even for short amounts of time. However, the stairway opening is usually cut when the plywood is placed to create the floor and is then left unprotected. The reason they do not protect the stairway opening immediately is because eventually it is going to be protected by walls, a banister or a permanent railing. So instead of installing a temporary guardrail right away and then having to take it down later, the framer is permitted by the GC/CM to leave the stairway open without a guardrail. It saves time and money. It also violates OSHA standards and can result in serious injury or death.

DEPOSITION OF GC/CM REPRESENTATIVE REGARDING FALL PROTECTION WHEN THERE ARE MANY SYSTEMATIC FAILURES

The following are questions for the GC/CM rep which can be used to show a **systematic failure to manage safety** and require fall protection in compliance with OSHA standards.

1. Is it your company's policy to determine if the subcontractors have a competent person as required by OSHA?
2. Do you know what OSHA's definition is of a competent person?
3. Are you required by your company's policy to determine if the subcontractors have a competent person on site as required by OSHA?
4. Do you know who the competent person was at this job site?
5. Do you know what OSHA's definition is of a qualified person?
6. Was there a person on this job site that was trained to be qualified with regard to OSHA's fall protection standards?
7. Do you know what training the qualified person had with regard to fall protection?
8. Do you know if that qualified person was required to decide when the roofing system could serve as an anchorage point so that a personal fall arrest system could be used?

   Note: It can be dangerous for a worker installing trusses to anchor to a truss because it is not yet strong enough to meet the OSHA requirement for strength of anchorage points. OSHA requires a qualified person to make the determination regarding when the trusses have been sufficiently braced to be able to serve as an anchorage point. It is rare that that is actually done.

9. Do you know if at any point during roof sheathing installation at this job site whether or not framers were at some point instructed to use the truss system as an anchorage point for a personal fall arrest system?
10. Have you ever worked as superintendent or project manager on any residential construction job where your company policy required a qualified person to make the decision when to begin to use personal fall arrest systems when installing trusses?
11. Are you qualified to make that determination?
12. Did your company policy require you to plan and communicate with contractors so that you knew how they planned to control fall hazards?

13. Did you have a pre-job safety meeting with contractors where you planned and communicated so that they knew your expectations with regard to specific ways to comply with OSHA standards at this site?
14. Approximately how many houses were constructed at this site?
15. Approximately how many developments have you worked on in your career?
16. Approximately how many houses altogether then have been built on jobs where you were superintendent or project manager?
17. Have you ever seen framers use ladders to install plywood sheathing on the sides of houses? (NOTE: It is a common practice for workers to install plywood sheathing by putting a four by eight sheet of plywood on their head and climb the ladder. They then take the sheet from their head and place it against the two by fours. They then get their nail gun and secure the plywood to the two by fours. That violates OSHA standards. However, it is a very common practice.)
18. Is it acceptable according to your company's policy to use ladders to install plywood sheathing?
19. Was it acceptable at any site where you worked as the GC/CM rep for sheathers to use ladders to install plywood sheathing on the sides of houses?
20. Were you ever trained with regard to OSHA's ladder safety standards?
21. According to your company's safety policy, is it acceptable for workers to climb ladders while carrying plywood?
22. Are you familiar with the OSHA standard that addresses the question of climbing while carrying material?
23. Have you ever seen workers climbing ladders while carrying material?
24. Is that acceptable according to your safety policy?
25. Is it your company's policy to require contractors and subcontractors' employees to be trained in OSHA's ladder safety standards?
26. Did you ever do anything at this site to verify if contractors or subcontractors' employees who use ladders were trained in OSHA's ladder safety training requirements?
27. Have you ever done anything on any site to verify if contractors or subcontractors' employees who use ladders have been trained in OSHA's ladder safety training requirements?
28. Approximately how high above the ground were the eaves of the roofs at this job site?
29. Did workers use ladders to install plywood sheathing on the entire sides of this building?
30. Did you see it being done?

31. Did you have any problem with the way they installed sheathing with regard to questions of safety?
32. Is it your company's policy to instruct framing contractors to not cut openings for stairways until it is time to install stairs? Note: It is rarely done.
33. Is it your company's policy to instruct framing contractors to install guardrails or covers over stairway openings immediately after cutting them open?
34. According to your company's safety policy, is there an acceptable period of time when stairways can be without fall protection?
35. If framers install guardrails or covers at stairway openings after they have installed all of the plywood flooring, is that acceptable according to your policy?
36. On this job, did you instruct the framing contractors to install guardrails or covers immediately after creating stairway openings?
37. Specifically who did you instruct? When?

NOTE

1. For residential construction, OSHA requires workers exposed to fall hazards six feet or more above a landing surface to receive the training as indicated in 1926.503(a)(1) and (2) but does not require certification in writing. For all other industries, 1926.503(b)(1) applies.

Chapter Eight

Falls from Scaffolds, Ladders, and Others

FALLS FROM SCAFFOLDS

The Bureau of Labor Statistics has found that each year, approximately 4,500 workers are injured while working on scaffolds. Workers suffer approximately 60 deaths per year from falls from scaffolds. Some of the common ways workers fall from scaffolds are:

- Over the side or off the end due to a lack of guardrail
- Between the scaffold and the face of the building when the gap exceeds 14 inches
- Scaffold plank breaks because it is not scaffold grade lumber
- From pump jack scaffold due to collapse because of failure to tie the scaffold to the building at top and bottom
- Fall while climbing the side of scaffold without the use of a ladder
- From tipover of rolling scaffold because elevated worker pulls the scaffold along by grabbing the ceiling or side of the building
- Worker steps into an opening between planks on platform of scaffold
- Worker steps on unsupported plank which tips down or see-saws
- Fall while building or disassembling scaffold
- From scaffold tipover because wheel of scaffold went into uncovered hole

Unfortunately, the current OSHA standard does not require fall protection until the scaffold is 10 feet above ground [1926.451(g)(1)]. Before this standard was revised in August of 1996, the OSHA standard required guardrails when the scaffold was four feet above ground. There is no reasonable explanation for making this change. Fortunately, many construction employers require fall protection on scaffolds at four feet or six feet. While there is no requirement for fall protection on a scaffold less than ten feet, there still may be a viable theory of liability.

As with ironworkers exposed to fall hazards where there is no violation of the OSHA standards (see Chapter 9), you may be able to prove that a violation of the contract was the cause of injury. Sometimes the contract between the owner and the GC/CM requires implementation of "reasonable precautions" for safety and to provide "reasonable protection" to prevent injury (AIA A-201 10.2.1) or to erect and maintain "reasonable safeguards" (AIA A-201 10.2.3.)[1] If the above language is in the contract, the GC/CM agreed to do what is reasonable. It is not reasonable to allow workers to be exposed to falls likely to lead to catastrophic injury or death when the hazard could be simply controlled by reasonable means, that is, even if OSHA allows it. Which argument would you like your expert to make to the jury? It is unreasonable to put workers at risk of paralysis, quadriplegia, brain damage and death when that risk could be controlled through methods which are reasonable? Or one who opines that while installation of guardrails is feasible, he or she finds it reasonable to permit workers to be exposed to falls from scaffolds at heights which make it likely to result in paralysis, quadriplegia, brain damage and death **because OSHA permits it**? Which expert do you think the jury will find to be most reasonable?

Another method to show the GC/CM's negligence is to show that it violated its own safety and health program. During deposition, the superintendent of the GC or CM will likely say that according to the company's safety policy and practices, if he/she had seen a worker at eight or nine feet above ground on a scaffold without any fall protection, they would have responded and required the worker to be protected. If that is the case, your expert could opine that the GC/CM permitted violations of its own safety policy and program. Your expert could then opine that the failure to comply with its own safety program and policy was the cause of the plaintiff's injury. Of course the facts would have to show that the GC/CM representative had knowledge, actual or constructive, of the fact that the plaintiff was exposed to the fall hazard.

The following are some safety standards that could be important in your evaluation in scaffold cases.

Standard 29CFR1926.451(a)(6) states: Scaffolds shall be designed by a **qualified person** and shall be constructed and loaded in accordance with that design according to 29CFR1926.450(b). A qualified person means one who by possession of a recognized degree, certificate, or professional training, or who by extensive knowledge, training, and experience, has successfully demonstrated his/her ability to solve or resolve problems related to the subject matter, the work, or the project.

Standard 29CFR1926.451(f)(3) states: Scaffolds and scaffold components shall be inspected for visible defects by a competent person before each work shift, and after any occurrence which could affect the scaffold's structural integrity. A competent person is one who knows OSHA standards and has the authority to make safety corrections.

Standard 29CFR1926.454(a) gives training requirements for workers who perform work on scaffolds. If you are not able to prove knowledge, actual or constructive, by the GC/CM of the fact that the worker was exposed to a fall hazard, you may be able to show that the failure of the GC/CM to verify that construction workers who used scaffolds were trained as required by 29CFR1926.454(a) was a cause of injury. The proximate cause then is that had the worker been trained by a qualified instructor, he/she would have been instructed never to work in violation of OSHA standards.

OSHA SCAFFOLD SAFETY TRAINING REQUIREMENTS

29CFR1926.454(a). Training requirements. This section supplements and clarifies the requirements of 1926.21(b)(2) as these relate to the hazards of work on scaffolds.

(a) The employer shall have each employee who performs work while on a scaffold trained by a person qualified in the subject matter to recognize the hazards associated with the type of scaffold being used and to understand the procedures to control or minimize those hazards. The training shall include the following areas, as applicable:

(1) The nature of any electrical hazards, fall hazards, and falling object hazards in the work area;
(2) The correct procedures for dealing with electrical hazards and for erecting, maintaining, and disassembling the fall protection systems and falling object protection systems being used;
(3) The proper use of the scaffold, and the proper handling of materials on the scaffold;
(4) The maximum intended load and the load-carrying capacities of the scaffolds; and
(5) Any other pertinent requirements of this subpart.

(b) The employer shall have each employee who is involved in erecting, disassembling, moving, operating, repairing, maintaining, or inspecting a scaffold trained by a competent person to recognize any hazards associated with the work in question. The training shall include the following topics, as applicable:

(1) The nature of scaffold hazards;
(2) The correct procedures for erecting, disassembling, moving, operating, repairing, inspecting, and maintaining the type of scaffold in question;

(3) The design criteria, maximum intended load-carrying capacity and intended use of the scaffolds;
(4) Any other pertinent requirements of this subpart.

(c) When the employer has reason to believe that an employee lacks the skill or understanding needed for safe work involving the erection, use or dismantling of scaffolds, the employer shall retrain each such employee so that the requisite proficiency is regained. Retraining is required in at least the following situations:

(1) Where changes at the worksite present a hazard about which an employee has not been previously trained;
(2) Where changes in the types of scaffolds, fall protection, falling object protection, or other equipment present a hazard about which an employee has not been previously trained; or
(3) Where inadequacies in an affected employee's work involving scaffolds indicate that the employee has not retained the requisite proficiency.

Another important standard is 29CFR1926.454(b) which requires the following:

The employer shall have each employee who is involved in erecting, disassembling, moving, operating, repairing, maintaining or inspecting a scaffold trained by a competent person to recognize any hazards associated with the work in question. The training shall include the following topics, as applicable:

(1) The nature of scaffold hazards;
(2) The correct procedures for erecting, dismantling, moving, operating, repairing, inspecting and maintaining the type of scaffold in question;
(3) The design criteria, maximum intended load-carrying capacity and the intended use of the scaffold;
(4) Any other pertinent requirements of this subpart.

Standard 29CFR1926.451(g)(2) states:

The employer shall have a **competent person** determine the feasibility and safety of providing fall protection for employees erecting or dismantling supported scaffolds. Employers are required to provide fall protection for employees erecting or dismantling supported scaffolds where the installation and use of such protection is feasible and does not create a greater hazard.

It is very common that the GC/CM did not require contractors using scaffolds to:

- Be built under the direction of a qualified person [1926.451(a)(6)].
- Be inspected by a competent person [1926.451(f)(3)].

- Verify that the workers using scaffolds were trained as required by 1926.454(a).
- Verify that workers who built and disassembled scaffolds were trained as required by 1926.454(b).

Violations of the above standards could be the proximate cause of the fall from elevation from the scaffold.

DEPOSITION OF GC/CM REGARDING SAFETY MANAGEMENT OF SCAFFOLDS

The following are some questions which can be used during the deposition of the GC/CM representatives to show systematic failures of the management system related to scaffold safety:

1. Have you ever worked on any construction project where scaffolds were used?
2. What are some of the types of scaffolds used on jobs that you have run?
    - Scissors lifts?
    - Pump jack scaffolds to install siding?
    - Masonry scaffolds to install block and brick?
    - Rolling scaffolds to install drywall in the interior?
    - Other types of scaffolds used?
3. What types of scaffolds were used on this job?
4. What contractors used scaffolds?
5. Have you been trained in OSHA standards regarding scaffold safety?
6. If so, who trained, when, where, how long did the training last? What was the purpose of the training?

    Note: The training could have been simply scaffold awareness training and not related to compliance with an OSHA training standard.
7. Did you receive any certification or documentation of that training?
8. Has anybody in your company who has worked at this site been trained in OSHA's safety requirements for scaffolds?
9. If so, did the training satisfy the requirements of any particular OSHA standard?
10. Do you know what OSHA's definition is of a qualified person?
11. Is it your company's policy to require scaffolds to be designed by qualified persons?

12. Who was the qualified person for the contractors who designed scaffolds at this site?
13. Do you know if any contractor employed a person who met the requirements of an OSHA qualified person relative to scaffolds at this site?
14. Do you know what OSHA's definition is of a competent person? (A competent person is one who is familiar with OSHA standards and has the authority to require compliance.)
15. Was there a competent person at this site who was qualified to perform inspections of scaffolds?
16. How do you know that he/she had been trained to be an OSHA competent person?
17. Is it your company's policy to require that scaffolds be inspected by a competent person?
18. Was there a competent person on this job site who had responsibility to inspect scaffolds?
19. Did a competent person inspect scaffolds at this site daily?
20. If so, who?
21. Did you perform safety inspections?
22. Did you perform safety inspections of scaffolds?
23. Have you been trained to know how to perform a safety inspection of scaffolds?
24. Is it your company's policy to ensure that contractor workers who use scaffolds have been trained as required by OSHA standard 1926.454(a) to safely use scaffolds?
25. In this case, did you or anyone from your company verify whether or not workers who used scaffolds were trained as required by OSHA?
26. Did you or anyone from your company do anything to ensure that the workers who built and disassembled scaffolds at this site were trained as required by OSHA standard 1926.454(b)?
27. In the past, have you ever done anything to verify whether or not workers who used scaffolds were trained as required by OSHA?
28. In the past, have you ever done anything to verify whether workers who built and disassembled scaffolds were trained as required by OSHA?
29. In the past, have you ever done anything to verify that scaffolds were built under the direction of a qualified person?
30. In the past, have you ever done anything to verify that scaffolds had been inspected by someone who meets OSHA's definition of a competent person?

DEPOSITION OF THE EXPERT IN SCAFFOLD FALL CASES

It is very common that the GC/CM does not require workers who build and use scaffolds to be trained as required by OSHA standards. The defense expert should agree that the GC/CM should take reasonable steps to verify that workers have received all of the OSHA required safety training. All of the industry safety authorities say that the GC/CM should take reasonable steps to make sure the work is done in compliance with OSHA standards.

1. Do you know if OSHA has a standard requiring training for workers exposed to falls greater than six feet? [29CFR1926.503]
2. Have you ever had responsibility to ensure that workers had received OSHA required training relative to fall protection?
3. If so, what did you do to verify training?
4. Does OSHA have a standard that requires workers in excavations and trenches to be trained?
5. Have you ever had the responsibility to ensure that workers received the OSHA required training when they worked in trenches?
6. If so, did you ever do anything to verify they had received that training?
7. If so, what?
8. Does OSHA have standards that require forklift operators to be trained? [29CFR1926.602(d)]
9. Have you ever had the responsibility to ensure that workers had received the OSHA required training for forklift truck operation?
10. If so, what did you do to verify that they had received the OSHA required training?
11. How did you verify the training? Answer: Email, fax or asking workers to show their certification card or documentation of training.
12. Does OSHA have standards that require workers exposed to chemicals to receive hazard communication training?
13. Have you ever had the responsibility to ensure that workers had received hazard communication training?
14. What did you do to verify that they had received that training?
15. Does OSHA have standards related to training workers who design, build and use scaffolds?
16. Did you ever have the responsibility to ensure that workers received the OSHA required training for designing, building or using scaffolds?
17. If so, what did you do to verify that they had received that training?
18. Have you ever worked in any position in construction safety management where you had jobs where scaffolds were used?
19. What types of scaffolds?

20. Are you familiar with OSHA's scaffold safety standards?
21. Have you ever been trained in OSHA's scaffold safety standards?
22. If so, who did the training, when, where, how long did it last, was it done so that you received training required by any specific OSHA scaffold standard?
23. Do you consider yourself to be expert in OSHA's scaffold safety standards?
24. Have you ever qualified as expert in OSHA's scaffold safety standards or scaffold safety in general?
25. Do you know what OSHA's definition is of a qualified person with regard to scaffold safety?
26. Are you an OSHA qualified person relative to scaffolds?
27. Do you know what OSHA's definition is with regard to a competent person relative to scaffold safety?
28. Are you a competent person regarding OSHA's scaffold standards?
29. Did you ever have safety responsibility to ensure that scaffolds were designed by a qualified person? Explain.
30. Did you ever have a job where you had the responsibility to ensure that scaffolds were installed by workers trained in scaffold safety? Explain.
31. Did you ever take any steps to ensure that workers who used scaffolds have received the OSHA required training?
32. Do you agree with the American Society of Safety Engineers where they say in *Construction Safety Management and Engineering* published by the American Society of Safety Engineers: "Making sure that subcontractor employees are trained before they are allowed to work on the job site is the best way that the general contractor has of ensuring that all employees on the site have received at least the minimum training required?"[2]
33. In your opinion, should the GC/CM take reasonable steps to ensure that contractors and subcontractor workers have received the OSHA required training?
34. In this case, was there any evidence that the incident scaffold was built under the direction of a qualified person as required by OSHA standard 1926.451(a)(6)?
35. At this site, was the incident scaffold inspected by a competent person before the shift began on the day of the incident, that is, as required by 1926.451(f)(3)?
36. In your review of documents provided in this case, did you find any written evidence of certification or training of workers who used scaffolds, that is, to show that they were trained in compliance with 1926.454(a) to safely use a scaffold?

37. In this case, did you see any evidence that the workers who built and disassembled scaffolds were trained as required by 1926.454(b)?
38. Was it possible for the superintendent of the GC/CM to have verified that there was a qualified person overseeing while scaffolds were built?
39. Was it possible for the GC/CM to have ensured that scaffolds were inspected by a competent person before each shift?
40. In this case, did you see any evidence that the GC/CM ensured that scaffolds were inspected by a competent person before each shift?
41. Prior to coming here today, did you give any thought as to whether or not the defendant could have done anything at all prior to this incident that would have prevented this incident?
42. As we sit here today, can you imagine anything that the defendant could have done before this incident that would have prevented this incident?

LADDERS

Some common ways that workers on ladders are injured are:

- Ladder placed on slippery surface, not secured—ladder slips out.
- Worker uses only one part of extension ladder which does not have slip-resistant base—ladder slips out.
- Ladder placed on top of scaffold—scaffold tips over.
- Ladder side rails do not extend at least three feet above the upper landing surface—worker getting onto or off of ladder slips and falls.
- Ladder with defect not inspected by a competent person (defects include broken or missing rungs, cleats or steps, broken or split rails, corroded parts).
- Worker works from ladders while using two hands to work—weight shifts and worker falls. A scissors lift, scaffold or personnel lift should be used instead of ladders.
- Worker falls while carrying material while climbing ladder.

Workers who use ladders are required by OSHA to be trained according to 29CFR1926.1060(a) which states:

> The employer shall provide a training program for each employee using ladders and stairways, as necessary. The program shall enable each employee to recognize hazards related to ladders and stairways, and shall train each employee in the procedures to be followed to minimize these hazards.
>
> (1) The employer shall ensure that each employee has been trained by a competent person in the following areas, as applicable:

(i) The nature of fall hazards in the work area;
(ii) The correct procedures for erecting, maintaining, and disassembling the fall protection systems to be used;
(iii) The proper construction, use, placement, and care in handling of all stairways and ladders;
(iv) The maximum intended load-carrying capacities of ladders used; and
(v) The standards contained in this subpart.

(2) Retraining shall be provided for each employee as necessary so that the employee maintains the understanding and knowledge acquired through compliance with this section.

DEPOSITION OF GC/CM REPRESENTATIVE REGARDING LADDER SAFETY

It is not unusual for a worker to have received some training about ladder safety, if only during a Tool Box meeting. However, it is rare for workers to have been trained by a competent person about all of the OSHA ladder safety standards as required by 29CFR1926.1060(a)(1)(v). The following are questions which may be of use in your deposition of the GC/CM:

1. Does OSHA require workers who use ladders to have special training?
2. If the answer is yes—when did you first become aware of that?
3. Have you ever required a contractor or subcontractor to show evidence that their workers have received ladder safety training? How did you verify training?
4. Tell me all of the people who had the responsibility to inspect ladders at this site.
5. Have you been trained in ladder safety as required by OSHA? If so, by whom? When? How long did it last?
6. Is it your company's policy to require contractors and subcontractors to comply with OSHA standards regarding safe use of ladders?
7. Is it your company's policy to require contractors and subcontractors whose employees who use ladders to ensure that the workers are trained by a competent person about the hazards associated with the use of ladders, that is, as required by OSHA standard 1926.1060(a)?
8. Is it your company's policy to verify that workers who use ladders have been trained by a competent person as required by OSHA? If so, how?
9. On this job, do you know if anyone verified whether or not contractors and subcontractors' workers who used ladders had been trained by a competent person in ladder safety as required by OSHA?

10. Is it your company's policy to verify who the competent person was that performed the training?
11. On this job, do you know who the competent person was who trained the workers who used ladders at this site?

DEPOSITION QUESTIONS FOR EXPERT IN LADDER FALL CASES

1. According to OSHA's ladder safety standards, should all workers who use ladders receive training?
2. Should all workers at this site who used ladders have received the OSHA required ladder safety training?
3. Have you ever worked on a ladder safety case before?
4. Have you ever criticized any defendant for failing to take reasonable steps to ensure that workers who used ladders had received the OSHA required safety training?
5. In your opinion as an expert, should ladder safety training including instructing workers to not work in violation of OSHA standards when to do so could result in serious injury or death?
6. In this case, did you find any evidence that the defendant took reasonable steps to verify that ladders were used by workers who were trained in OSHA ladder safety standards?
7. In your expert opinion, should workers who use ladders be trained regarding how to inspect ladders?
8. On this job, did any representative of the GC/CM verify that workers were trained by a competent person in ladder safety as required by OSHA standards?
9. Have you been trained in OSHA ladder safety standards? If so, who, when, where, how long did the training last?
10. Have you been trained in how to use ladders safely?
11. Have you been trained on how to inspect ladders?
12. Have you ever worked for a company whose workers used ladders?
13. Did that company require their workers to be trained according to the OSHA standard?
14. Did that company require any contractor or subcontractor workers to be trained in ladder safety as required by OSHA standards?
15. Did you ever perform safety inspections on a construction site where ladders were used?
16. Did you ever have the responsibility to determine if OSHA ladder standards were violated?

17. Did you ever do anything to verify that workers who used ladders were trained as required by OSHA standards?
18. If workers are trained by a competent person related to the requirements of OSHA standard 1910.1060(a), would you expect the workers to be told not to work in violation of the safety requirements of OSHA if that exposure could result in serious injury or death?
19. Was the plaintiff trained and instructed not to use the ladder in the way it was used at the time of this incident?

NOTES

1. American Institute of Architects A201—General Conditions of the Contract for Construction 2007, and A232-2009—General Conditions of the Contract for Construction—Construction Management.
2. CONSTRUCTION SAFETY MANAGEMENT AND ENGINEERING, Darryl C. Hill, CSP, American Society of Safety Engineers, Des Plaines, IL, 2004, p. 179.

Chapter Nine

Falls During Steel Erection

Ironworkers by far suffer more fatal injuries from falls than any other construction craft.

In all of the following incidents, the theory of liability was that the GC/CM failed to comply with the principles and practices of safety management of industry authorities such as the Associated General Contractors of America, the American Society of Safety Engineers, the National Safety Council, and the Construction Industry Institute, and they failed to comply with OSHA and/or ANSI standards.

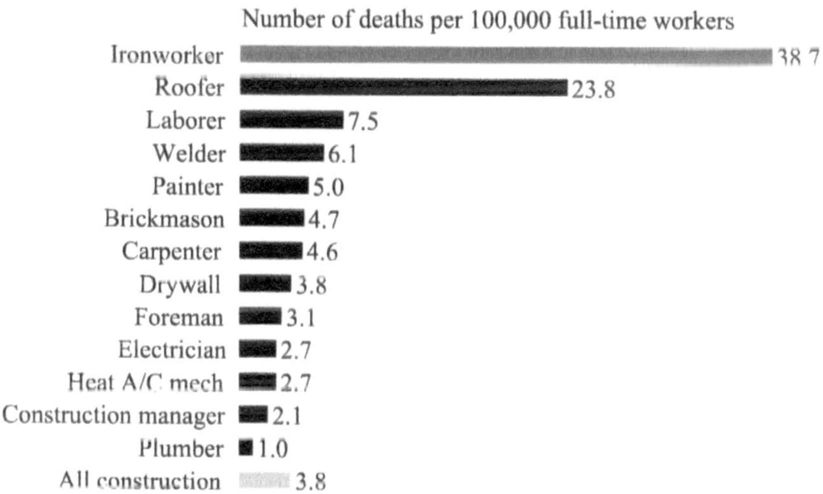

Figure 9.1. Rate of Deaths from Falls (Selected construction occupations, 2003–2005 average)

Source: The Construction Chart Book, fourth edition, Chart 37b. Published by CPWR—The Center for Construction Research and Training, 2008, p. 4.

~ ~ ~ ~

Description of Incident: **Walking horizontal steel beam**—slips and falls.
Failure: Failure to have available lifeline or safety net installed on horizontal beam.

~ ~ ~ ~

Description of Incident: **Connecting structural steel**—slips and falls.
Failure: Failure to install lifeline or to provide a scissors lift or anchorage point for fall arrest system.

~ ~ ~ ~

Description of Incident: Crane offloads decking onto **joists which were not secured causing collapse.**
Failure: Failure to require fastening and bridging of joists before loading decking onto joists.

~ ~ ~ ~

Description of Incident: **Spreading joists while standing on beam, slips and falls.**
Failure: Failure to use scissors lift or other personnel lift.

~ ~ ~ ~

Description of Incident: **Crane operator moves load which causes worker to fall.**
Failure: Failure to move load only upon direction of a signalman.

~ ~ ~ ~

Description of Incident: **Fall through hole in decking—skylight opening.**
Failure: Failure to install guardrail or cover over hole as soon as opening was created.

~ ~ ~ ~

Description of Incident: **Fall through stairway opening.**
Failure: Failure to install guardrail or cover.

EVALUATING STEEL ERECTION FALL INJURY CASES

Perhaps the easiest fall hazard for a superintendent of a GC/CM to identify is the ironworker without fall protection. It is not unusual for ironworkers to be without standard fall protection. One of the reasons is that OSHA does not require fall protection for all ironworker exposures. However, there may be a viable theory of liability despite the fact that the ironworker was working in compliance with OSHA standards when the fall occurred.

The current OSHA standard requires standard fall protection for ironworkers beginning at 15 feet.[1] Standard fall protection consists of guardrails, safety nets or a fall arrest system. OSHA does not require fall protection for ironworkers who work below 15 feet. Serious injury and death can result from falls less than 15 feet.[2] OSHA also does not require standard fall protection for workers performing **connecting work** and while **installing decks** at elevations between 15 and 30 feet.[3] As you will see, it is economically and technologically feasible to provide ironworkers with 100 percent fall protection for **all** exposures beginning at six feet above ground level. If an ironworker falls while exposed to a hazard but was not working in violation of OSHA standards, it is nevertheless still **likely** that you will be able to successfully pursue liability on the part of the GC/CM.

CONNECTORS

Connecting work involves ironworkers placing and connecting elevated structural members and/or components.[4] The ironworker stands or sits on the structural steel to guide the beam in place and then connect it with only several bolts and nuts. Afterwards another crew of ironworkers comes back to "bolt up." That is, the bolting crew will install more than a dozen bolts and nuts while staying in one place. OSHA requires workers who bolt up at 15 feet or higher to be protected by standard fall protection.[5] However, for connectors working between 15 feet and 30 feet, they must be **provided** with a personal fall arrest system, positioning device system or fall restraint system and wear the equipment necessary "to be able to be tied off" **or** be provided with other fall protection.[6] They do not have to be actually connected to a fall arrest system nor use other fall protection.[7] That is, to comply with OSHA standards, the ironworker does not need to be protected from falling. He/she can simply wear a full body harness but not connected to a fall arrest system. However, he/she must have the opportunity to choose to connect to an available anchorage point. More often than not, when a connector falls, there was no available anchorage point. But there could have been.

OSHA gives this exemption because ironworkers have testified that they feel that there could be a greater danger of being connected and anchored with a fall arrest system during a time when they receive an uncontrolled incoming load of structural steel from a crane.[8] If the crane operator overshoots or moves the load unexpectedly, ironworkers say that they want the ability to be able to move away quickly from the load which otherwise could push him or her off of the steel. However, the ironworker could have mobility by using a beamer or by connecting their lanyard to a horizontal lifeline installed on the horizontal I-beam before it is raised. The beamer allows the ironworker to walk and work while anchored to it. See figures 9.2 and 9.3.

Stanchions and a lifeline could be installed on the horizontal beam before it is raised. This will give the connector a place to attach the lanyard to the lifeline and have mobility.

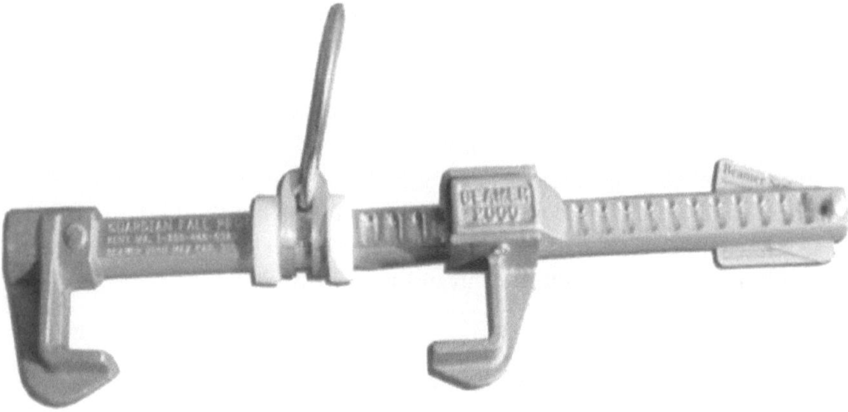

Figure 9.2. **The beamer adjusts to the width of the beam. The worker attaches his or her lanyard to it and it slides as the worker walks. It gives the ironworker the ability to move.**

Courtesy of Guardian Fall Protection.

Figure 9.3.

National Safety Council, Safety and Health, December 2004, p. 33.

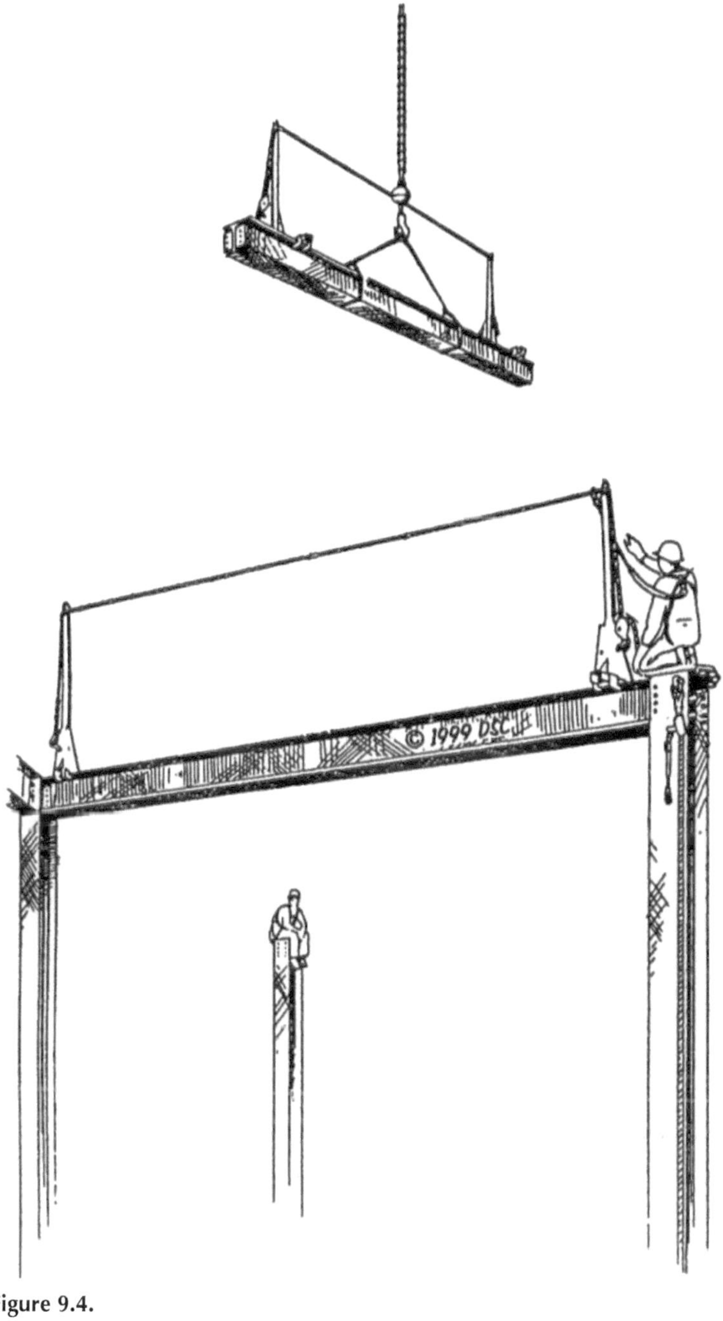

Figure 9.4.

American Society of Safety Engineers, Introduction to Fall Protection, Third Edition, 2001, J. Nigel Ellis, p. 73.

Also, an articulating and telescoping boom lift or scissors lift could be used by the ironworker to connect beams. It is entirely feasible to provide reliable 100 percent fall protection for connectors for all exposures yet OSHA does not require standard fall protection until the ironworker is working 30 feet above the lower surface.

DECK INSTALLATION

As with connectors, OSHA recognizes the feasibility of reliable standard fall protection for deck installation at 30 feet and above.[9] OSHA requires standard fall protection for deck installation for all exposures 30 feet and higher, but not for exposures 15 to 30 feet.[10] If it is feasible to provide 100 percent fall protection at 30 feet and above, it is also feasible to provide fall protection below 30 feet. Decking consists of corrugated sheets of metal approximately three feet wide and 12 to 20 feet long which are laid over joists to form the floor or roof of the building.

It does not make sense for OSHA to require connectors and workers installing deck at 30 feet and above to have standard fall protection and not those working below 30 feet. A personal fall arrest system could be designed and used for both heights.

Figure 9.5. Ironworkers installing decking using personal fall arrest systems

The Center for Construction Research and Training, Leading the Way to Safety with the Leading Edge Fall Protection System—A Manual for Installation and Use, 2010, p. 1.

THEORY OF LIABILITY WHEN OSHA DOES NOT REQUIRE FALL PROTECTION

It is likely that there is a contract between the CPO and the GC/CM. Sometimes the safety language regarding responsibility of the GC/CM requires the GC/CM to implement "reasonable precautions" for safety and to provide "reasonable protection" to prevent injury (AIA A-201—10.2.1) or to erect and maintain "reasonable" safeguards (AIA A-201—10.2.3).[11] If the above language is in the contract, the GC/CM agreed to do what is **reasonable**. It is not reasonable to allow ironworkers or anyone to be exposed to risks of injury likely to lead to catastrophic injury or death, even if OSHA allows it. Which argument would you like your expert to make to the jury? It is unreasonable to put ironworkers at risk of paralysis, quadriplegia, brain damage or death when that risk can be controlled by methods which are reasonable, that is, technologically and economically feasible. Or one who opines that while it is possible and not cost prohibitive to provide fall protection to prevent ironworkers from falling, he or she finds it **reasonably acceptable** to permit ironworkers to be exposed to risks likely to lead to paralysis, quadriplegia, brain damage or death because OSHA allows it. Which expert do you think the jury will find to be the most reasonable?

Another method to show the GC/CM's negligence is to show that it violated its own safety program and policy. Sometimes the safety program of the GC/CM requires fall protection for all exposures beginning at six feet. In those cases, the facts will show that the defendant GC/CM permitted violations of its own safety program. Your expert could then opine that that failure was a cause of the plaintiff's injury.

While OSHA does not say that the connector or decker have to have 100 percent fall protection, they do not say that the erector can do nothing with regard to fall protection. For example, regarding connectors, OSHA says that they must be provided with an anchorage point to connect his or her lanyard but has the choice to not connect to an anchorage point. Most of the time, the facts will show that the connector had no anchorage point available. Your expert could then opine that the GC/CM, as controlling employer, violated OSHA standards and that violation was a cause of injury because it is more likely than not that the plaintiff would have used the available anchorage point to prevent the fall. The best argument the defense would have is that, while the defendant violated OSHA standards, had there been an anchorage point, the worker may have chosen not to use it. You could also argue that the ironworker was denied the possibility of being protected.

With regard to deck installation, OSHA does not require ironworkers to have fall protection between 15 and 30 feet. However, they do require the installation of a controlled decking zone. A controlled decking zone is an area in which initial installation and placement of metal decking can take place without the use of standard fall protection and where access to the zone is controlled. OSHA requires that the controlled decking zone be established so that only employees engaged in leading edge work have access to that area. There is really not much likelihood of any other craft wanting to be anywhere near a controlled decking zone because there is no possibility of any other craft having any other work in an area where they are in the process of building the floor. However, in many cases, the ironworkers do not establish a controlled decking zone. Therefore, at the time of a fall, the workers were working in violation of OSHA standards. The plaintiff's safety expert could argue that there was a violation of the OSHA standard at the time of the incident. However, he or she could not convincingly argue that a controlled decking zone would have prevented injury. His/her argument would be that the customary safe practice is for a conscientious GC/CM to require a personal fall arrest system rather than a controlled decking zone because a controlled decking zone is really no fall protection at all for the ironworker. The defense argument would be that the defendant violated OSHA but had the defendant decided to comply with OSHA by establishing a controlled decking zone, this incident would not have been prevented. That expert could be challenged:

- Do you agree that it is entirely feasible to provide deckers with a personal fall arrest system for exposures 30 feet and more above the ground?
- Do you know if OSHA requires standard fall protection for workers installing decks 30 feet and above? (Answer: It does.) [1926.760(c)]
- If it is feasible to provide personal fall arrest systems for deckers working above 30 feet, is it also possible to provide the same personal fall arrest system for work between 15 and 30 feet? Answer: Of course it is.
- Is a personal fall arrest system more reliable fall protection than a controlled decking zone? Answer: A controlled decking zone is really no fall protection at all.
- Does a controlled decking zone actually provide any fall protection for the ironworker working at the leading edge? Answer: It does not.
- In your opinion, what would be more reliable fall protection—an ironworker between 15 and 30 feet with a personal fall arrest system or the same ironworker working in a controlled decking zone?
- In your opinion, what would be more reasonable fall protection—an ironworker between 15 and 30 feet with a personal fall arrest system or a controlled decking zone?

- Can you point to any place in OSHA where it prohibits a general contractor or construction manager from requiring a personal fall arrest system for deck installation between 15 and 30 feet?
- If you were working at the leading edge of a deck, would you rather your fall protection be a personal fall arrest system or a controlled decking zone?
- Could a fall of 15 feet result in brain damage, quadriplegia or death?
- Have you ever worked on a job where 100 percent fall protection was required for ironworkers?
- Are you aware that the Associated General Contractors of America has advocated for 100 percent fall protection for all ironworker exposures greater than six feet to which ironworkers could be exposed?
- If you had construction safety management responsibilities on a job and saw a connector or decker working between 15 and 30 feet above ground and not protected from falls by a personal fall arrest system or restraint, would you say anything?
- Have you ever seen an ironworker working between 15 and 30 feet doing connecting or decking work without a personal fall arrest system? What did you do?

RECOGNITION OF THE DANGER OF OSHA'S STEEL ERECTION STANDARDS

Respected safety authorities have recognized the danger of OSHA's steel erection standard. For example, in 1986, OSHA published a Proposed Rule to change the fall protection standard for construction. OSHA hired a consultant to study the economic impact of the proposed "six-foot fall protection rule" in Subpart M. The study concluded that the implementation of the six-foot fall protection rule would have no adverse economic impact on the steel erection industry, if adopted.[12] The six foot fall protection rule requires the use of standard fall protection devices.

The Associated General Contractors of America likewise recognizes the danger of OSHA's steel erection standard. They are an advocate for the six foot fall protection rule for all construction workers' exposures including steel erectors. The AGC is keenly aware of the feasibility of 100 percent fall hazard control for all workers in the construction industry. On August 27, 2001, Stephen Sandherr, the CEO of the AGC, wrote to John Henderson, the Assistant Secretary of Labor for OSHA. He stated:

> AGC has long been the industry leader in this critical field. Improving working conditions for the industry was one of the first commitments that its founding

> fathers made back in 1918. General contractors have worked long and hard over many years to improve their work sites and they have made significant progress. Reinforcing the commitment, AGC signed a Partnering Charter with OSHA in March of 1998. AGC and OSHA have also signed an agreement to implement the Construction Health and Safety Excellence (CHASE) Partnering Program which requires, among other things, **all workers be protected from falls at six feet** (emphasis added) . . . AGC believes that OSHA has not met its obligation to protect all employees from fall hazards. This final rule puts connectors' lives in serious jeopardy. A fall from 15–30 feet is likely to cause a greater injury than a fall from 6 feet. If a connector falls to his or her death, or is seriously injured, who will be responsible? AGC believes that all workers should be tied off or otherwise protected at 6 feet, regardless of the type of work being performed. OSHA has already recognized that it is feasible for steel erectors to ensure 100 percent fall protection. In 1998, OSHA even gave special recognition to the Steel Erection Safety Association of Colorado, in part, because this group of steel erectors was using 100 percent fall protection on its projects . . . AGC believes that OSHA should fulfill its responsibility to protect all workers.[13]

Other respected safety voices in the United States testified during OSHA hearings that 100 percent standard fall protection is entirely feasible for all steel erection work as evidenced by the fact that they have been requiring it for years. For example, OSHA published comments of the following industry authorities in the Federal Register on January 18, 2001, where it provided background for promulgation of the current OSHA steel erection standard.[14] Kellogg, Brown and Root testified during OSHA hearings that they have had a six foot fall protection policy for several years. U.S. Bellows Construction Corporation testified to OSHA that their six foot fall protection policy for steel erection increased productivity, decreased insurance costs and saved lives. CENTEX Construction Company's policy also includes hiring only subcontractors who use a six foot fall protection policy. Turner Construction Company argued to OSHA that they would prefer OSHA to adopt the six foot rule for steel erection. Others who argued to OSHA that technology exists to protect all ironworkers above six feet were Nigel Ellis (author of *Introduction to Fall Protection* published by the American Society of Safety Engineers), Beacon Skanska Construction Company, Clark Construction Company and Joseph Fitzgerald. The American Society of Safety Engineers in their book entitled *Construction Safety Management and Engineering* also recognizes the feasibility of standard fall protection for connectors and deck installers.

OSHA's "Reasoning" for the Compromise

OSHA cited three reasons for not requiring fall protection beginning at six feet.[15] First OSHA said that the injury data is "not clear" regarding how much of a need there is to provide fall protection below fifteen feet. Essentially OSHA justified permitting ironworkers' exposures below fifteen feet because of lack of injury data. However, on August 9, 1994, OSHA published in the Federal Register the following with regard to fall protection:

> Based on the Bureau of Labor Statistics' Injury and Fatality Data, discussed above, OSHA believes that employees performing construction work on walking and working surfaces six feet or more above lower levels are exposed to a significant risk of injury and death.

The second reason that OSHA permits ironworkers to be exposed to falls is because "many situations" do not permit the use of a fall arrest system (full body harness with lanyard attached to a lifeline or anchorage point) below fifteen feet.[16] It is true that while using a fall arrest system for some falls below fifteen feet, the fall would not be arrested before a worker strikes a lower surface. But a fall arrest system is not the only means of fall protection that could be used. Ironworkers could use restraint devices, work from scaffolds, scissors lifts or other personnel lifts. In fact, scissors lifts are very commonly used by conscientious steel erectors and required by conscientious general contractors/construction managers. OSHA could have required fall protection beginning at six feet and could have said that they will accept scissors lifts, personnel lifts, restraints and scaffolds as fall protection.

OSHA further indicates the reason to permit ironworkers exposed to falls up to fifteen feet is because steel erectors often use scaffolds and work platforms at heights between six and fifteen feet.[17] In essence, OSHA is saying that they will not require the use of fall protection below fifteen feet because scaffolds or work platforms are often used.[18] However, that is not a reasonable explanation to justify not requiring scaffolds, work platforms, or other means of fall protection to be used between six and fifteen feet.

OSHA also says that ladders are "often used" as a justification for not requiring fall protection.[19] However, the use of ladders for ironworkers is often a dangerous practice. Ironworkers sometimes use heavy impact wrenches and crowbars while working from ladders. In those instances, the entire work platform consists of a twelve inch long rung which is one inch in diameter. With both hands off of the ladder, the ironworker pushes and pulls and exerts forces to the ladder. A slip is likely to result in serious injury or death. A ladder should not be used by ironworkers for many types of work they commonly perform. OSHA should have said that the use of ladders as a work platform for tasks requiring the use of tools and/or two hands is prohibited.

The American Society of Safety Engineers, in their book entitled *Introduction to Fall Protection*, points out the following about the dangers of working from ladders: "Portable ladders have rungs with very little structure to stand on, and so require a worker to use at least one hand at all times for securely maintaining balance. This means that ladders can be dangerous when used for work involving hands, either for lifting, carrying, holding, manipulating, or other purposes, particularly while moving."[20]

The National Safety Council also recognizes the danger of working from ladders. In their *Accident Prevention Manual*, they state: "The use of ladders at any time when applied for work and not solely access to another level calls for serious consideration of appropriate fall protection. The higher the ladder is used, the more fall protection consideration must be given."[21] However, OSHA does not prohibit workers from working from portable ladders even at heights of 50 feet or more above ground level.

Despite unsafe OSHA standards, many conscientious owners, general contractors and construction managers require steel erectors to provide 100 percent fall protection for all exposures of ironworkers above six feet. When the current OSHA steel erection standard was debated, there was a significant amount of testimony by major general contractors who urged OSHA to require 100 percent fall protection for all ironworkers above six feet. They found it was technologically feasible, morally responsible and it saved money.[22]

100 PERCENT FALL PROTECTION VS. OSHA COMPLIANCE

Recently an incident occurred where an ironworker without fall protection fell while performing decking work at 22 feet above the ground.[23] The injured worker had worked on many other jobs where this same general contractor did require 100 percent fall protection for all ironworkers. The steel erector's superintendent was deposed as a result of litigation and was asked why he did not require fall protection. He said it was because OSHA standards did not require it. When asked why he required it on some jobs and not others, he explained that this job was run with an Owner Controlled Insurance Policy. That is, with an owner-controlled insurance policy, the construction project owner's insurance company wrote one policy for all of the workers comp and liability insurance for all the contractors on the project. Owner-controlled insurance policies require 100 percent fall protection for **all** elevated work, including ironworkers.

The insurance industry is aware that money can be saved by preventing injury by requiring 100 percent fall protection for ironworkers. The superintendent went on to explain the reasons he provides fall protection on some jobs and not on others is because many times the CPO simply selects the lowest bid without regard to safety performance or safety plans. If the steel erector were to include the costs of 100 percent fall protection, his/her bid would likely be higher than his/her competitors who did not include the extra costs for 100 percent fall protection. He/she would likely not get the work. His/her bid would be too high to be competitive because of the added costs of the use of scissors lifts, articulating boom lifts, nets, and the costs of installing and using fall arrest systems.

THEORY OF LIABILITY—CONSTRUCTION PROJECT OWNER

The facts will probably show that the GC/CM had worked on many other projects where ironworkers installed structural steel. The facts will probably also show sometimes 100 percent fall protection was implemented and sometimes simple OSHA compliance was implemented. While one might appreciate the dilemma of the GC/CM in cases where the CPO does not require the steel erectors' work to be done with 100 percent fall protection, from the point of view of the ironworker and his/her family members, it is nevertheless unfair for both the GC/CM and CPO to agree to a deal which puts their lives at risk.

What should a GC/CM do when the CPO is silent about the question of 100 percent fall protection for ironworkers or is clear that it does not want to spend the money for it? If the GC/CM includes all of the costs for 100 percent fall protection, he/she may be less likely to be hired by the CPO.

If the GC/CM makes the added costs of 100 percent fall protection clear in bid documents, the CPO would then be on notice of the issue. The GC/CM could let the CPO know in as diplomatic a way as possible that its policy is to not participate in deals that unnecessarily risk workers' lives because it is not only morally and ethically responsible to not risk workers' lives needlessly, it is in the long run good business. Maybe the GC/CM will lose business because of this policy. Alternatively, the GC/CM might have to answer the following questions in deposition.

DEPOSITION QUESTIONS FOR GC/CM

1. Have you ever worked on a job where ironworkers were required to have 100 percent fall protection for all exposures six feet or more above ground level? NOTE: If this representative has experience in the construction industry, it is highly likely that they have worked on both 100 percent fall protection ironworker jobs and OSHA compliance jobs.

2. Have you ever worked on jobs where ironworkers performing decking operations beginning at 15 feet above ground were required to use standard fall protection?
3. Have you ever worked on jobs where ironworkers performing connecting work 15 to 30 feet above ground were required to be actually connected or protected from falling by standard fall protection?
4. Approximately how many jobs have you worked on where ironworkers were required to have 100 percent fall protection?
5. Approximately what percentage of the jobs that you have worked on where there was steel erection where ironworkers were required to have 100 percent fall protection versus OSHA compliance?
6. Does your company policy recognize that falls from 15 feet or more could result in quadriplegia, brain damage or death?
7. Is it your company's policy to require 100 percent fall protection for ironworkers all the time?
8. Do you agree that there are costs associated with providing 100 percent fall protection?
9. Do you agree that it takes more time to require 100 percent fall protection than to let workers work without being connected to a personal fall arrest system?
10. Aside from costs and time, do you know of any reason for not requiring ironworkers to have 100 percent fall protection?
11. At this job, did you require all ironworkers to have 100 percent fall protection for all exposures above six feet?
12. Why not?
13. Can you think of anything you or anyone in your organization could have done that would have prevented this fall?
14. Could you have implemented 100 percent fall protection at this job site?
15. Why didn't you?

NOTES

1. U.S. Department of Labor, Occupational Safety and Health Administration Standard 29CFR1926.760(a)(1).

2. "Worker Deaths by Falls: A Summary of Surveillance Findings and Investigative Case Reports," Center for Disease Control and Prevention, National Institute of Occupational Safety and Health, November 2000, p. 17. NIOSH found that of 91 fatal fall injuries, 19 were suffered by workers who fell 15 feet or less.

3. U.S. Department of Labor, OSHA Standard 29CFR1926.760(b) and (c).

4. U.S. Department of Labor, OSHA Standard 29CFR1926.751.

5. U.S. Department of Labor, OSHA Standard 29CFR1926.760(a)(1).

6. U.S. Department of Labor, OSHA Standard 29CFR1926.760(b)(3).
7. Ibid.
8. Federal Register, Vol. 66, No. 12, January 18, 2011, pp. 5246 and 5247.
9. U.S. Department of Labor, OSHA Standard 29CFR1926.760(c).
10. U.S. Department of Labor, Occupational Safety and Health Administration Standard 29CFR1926.760(b).
11. American Institute of Architects A201—General Conditions of the Contract for Construction 2007, and A232-2009—General Conditions of the Contract for Construction—Construction Management.
12. American Society of Safety Engineers (ASSE). (2004). *Construction Safety Management and Engineering.* Des Plaines, IL: Darryl C. Hill, CSP, p. 270.
13. August 27, 2001, letter from Stephen Sandherr, CEO of AGC, to the Honorable John L. Henshaw, Assistant Secretary of Labor for OSHA.
14. Federal Register, January 18, 2001, Safety Standard for Steel Erection—66:5317–5325, p. 98.
15. Ibid, p. 99.
16. Ibid.
17. Ibid.
18. Ibid.
19. Ibid.
20. American Society of Safety Engineers (ASSE). (1993). *Introduction to Fall Protection,* Second Edition. Des Plaines, IL, Author: Nigel Ellis, p. 154.
21. National Safety Council, *Accident Prevention Manual*, 11th Edition, Itasca, IL, p. 63.
22. Federal Register, Vol. 66, No. 12, January 18, 2001, pp. 2244 and 2245.
23. Personal experience of author.

Chapter Ten

Trenching and Excavation Hazards[1]

One of the most common ways that construction workers are injured and killed is when trenches and excavations collapse and bury them. NIOSH reports that the trenching fatality rate is 112 percent greater than all construction accidents. They have also found that cave-ins result in an estimated 1,000–1,500 annual work-related injuries of which 50–140 are identified as permanent disability cases.[2]

Excavation cave-ins should not be called accidents. In the construction safety business, trench cave-ins are notorious for killing workers by burying them alive. The OSHA standards are well known to all excavation contractors and GCs/CMs who have any experience with trenching and excavation work. Cave-ins are by far the most serious hazard associated with trenching and excavation. It is costly to comply with OSHA standards and to protect trenches.

Before work begins, decisions should be made and are made about whether or not the trench or excavation is going to be made safe. When a worker is buried in a collapse, it is no accident. Safe trenches in compliance with OSHA standards do not collapse. The GC/CM and excavation contractor should know before the excavation is opened how the excavation is going to be protected from collapsing.

TRENCHING SAFETY STANDARDS ARE "WRITTEN IN BLOOD"

The trenching and excavation standards of OSHA have resulted from serious thought given to prevent recurrences of workers being buried when excavations collapse. GC/CMs and excavation and trenching contractors are very often keenly aware that death and disabling injury can occur in unsafe trenches and excavations. They are also aware of the costs associated with OSHA compliance. If the GC/CM does not make it clear that the excavation contractor must make the trench or excavation safe, the excavation contractor is more likely to try to save time and money by cutting corners. When they prepare their bids, they may exclude the cost of safety.

There are three ways to make trenches safe. Each method takes time and has its costs:

SLOPING AND BENCHING

To slope or pull the sides of the bank back "collapses" the bank so it cannot cave in. There are different angles or slopes required depending upon the type of soil.

Type A Soil: Cohesive soils made of clay, silty clay, sandy clay, clay loam and, in some cases, silty clay loam and sandy clay loam.
Type B Soil: Granular cohesionless soil including: angular gravel, silt, silt loam, sandy loam and, in some cases, silty clay loam and sandy clay loam.
Type C Soil: Granular soil including gravel, sand and loamy sand or submerged soil or soil from which water is freely seeping. It also includes submerged rock that is not stable.

The maximum allowable slopes and benching requirements are shown in Appendix B of standard 1926.652.

Maximum Allowable Slopes

SOIL OR ROCK TYPE	*MAXIMUM ALLOWABLE SLOPES (H:V)[1] FOR EXCAVATIONS LESS THAN 20 FEET DEEP[3]*
STABLE ROCK	VERTICAL (90°)
TYPE A[2]	3/4: 1 (53°)
TYPE B	1:1 (45°)
TYPE C	1½:1 (34°)

1. Numbers shown in parentheses next to maximum allowable slopes are angles expressed in degrees from the horizontal. Angles have been rounded off.
2. A shore-term maximum allowable slope of 1/2 H : IV (63°) is allowed in excavations in Type A soil that are 12 feet (3.67 m) or less in depth. Short-term maximum allowable slopes for excavations greater than 12 feet (3.67 m) in depth shall be 3/4 H : IV (53°).
3. Sloping or benching for excavations greater than 20 feet deep shall be designed by a registered professional engineer.

In some places, sloping and benching may not be the most practical method to use because it may require demolition of paved surfaces to achieve the required slope. Or there may be a building near the trench that would prevent a safe slope. There may be no place to temporarily store the spill so dump trucks may be required to remove and return the spill. There are also costs related to removing the soil and refilling the trench or excavation and costs associated with compaction.

SHORING OF BANKS

Shoring involves leaving the banks vertical and using timber or metal braces to hold the banks in place. If a shoring system is used, it must conform to OSHA specifications and must be approved by a registered engineer. See Appendix C of standard 1926.652 for OSHA specifications for shoring systems. This data must be in writing and must include enough explanatory information, including the criteria for making the selection and the limits on the use of the data, for the user to make a selection. At least one copy of the data, including the identity of the registered professional engineer who approved it, must be kept at the work site during construction of the protective system. After the system is completed, the data may be stored away from the job site, but a copy must be provided upon request to the Assistant Secretary of Labor for OSHA.

The costs associated with shoring systems involve the purchase and transportation of the shoring system, the costs associated with design by a registered professional engineer, the costs related to training of workers to install the system and the costs related to the time to install and remove the shoring system.

SHIELDING SYSTEMS OR TRENCH BOXES

Shielding systems or trench boxes consist of two steel walls parallel to the trench and connected by supports. See Appendix B and D of standard 1926.652. Workers are required to stay within the confines of the walls of the box. A trench box must be designed and approved by a registered professional engineer or must be based on tabulated data prepared or approved by a registered professional engineer. Timber, aluminum, or other suitable materials may also be used. OSHA standards permit the use of a trench shield if it provides the same level of protection or more than the appropriate shoring system.

The costs associated are purchase or rental of the trench box, transportation to the job site and perhaps cost of the crane to install and remove the trench box if the excavator is not capable of safely lifting the trench box. There are also all of the costs associated with the time it takes to move the trench box as work progresses.

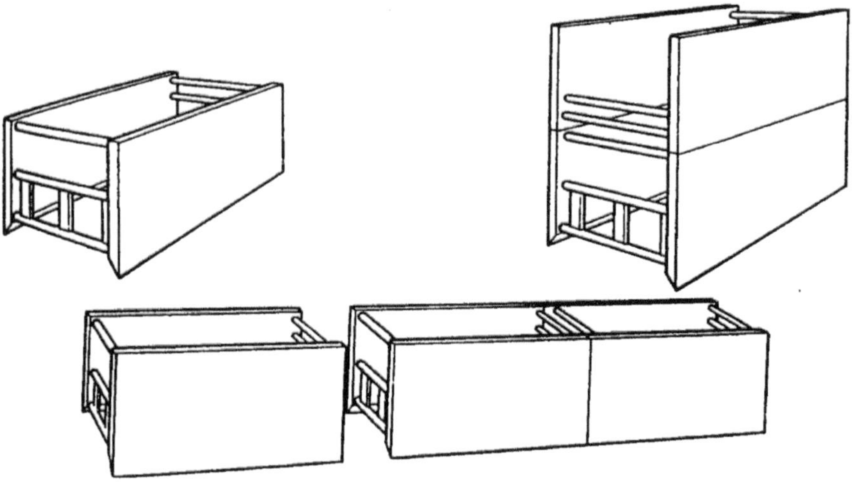

The GC/CM knows before bid documents are sent out what the characteristics of the soil are and the depth of the excavation/trench. Soil samples are taken and analyzed. Drawings are made giving the depth of the installation. The GC/CM should require all bidders to indicate the type of trench and excavation protection they plan to use. They should require the costs to be included and made visible in the bid. That way, the evaluator can be sure that the bidder is not excluding the costs of safety in order to present a low bid.

The GC/CM should hold a pre-job safety conference with the excavator and reaffirm the need to use the selected method of protecting workers in the trench. Periodic safety inspections should be performed to verify that the protection is being used.

It usually takes relatively little time to install and connect a pipe. It is very tempting to ignore safety to save money. Because a significant amount of money can be saved by not protecting the trench or excavation, unscrupulous contractors will too frequently risk workers' lives.

In the industry, they say that the "safe trenches" are the ones that kill. That is, if the trench is obviously unsafe, the excavator will do something to protect workers because the danger is clear. It is the trench that violates the OSHA standard but "appears" safe that kills. You cannot be sure by just looking. You must determine the type of soil and then comply with the OSHA standards.

The risk factors that increase the probability of collapse are:

- Type of soil
- Depth
- Moisture content of soil

- Surface or underground water
- Rocks or boulders in the bank
- Excavated material stored above the bank
- Equipment stored above the bank
- Vibrations from traffic on a road near the trench or excavation

The GC/CM will probably be aware of many, if not all of the risk factors.

OSHA standard 1926.652(a)(1)(ii) indicates that excavations less than five feet in depth need not be protected but only if a competent person performs an evaluation and finds no indication of a potential cave-in. Trenches less than five feet deep have seriously injured and killed workers.

DEPOSITION OR CROSS EXAMINATION OF REP OF GC/CM

1. Tell me all of the safety training that you have ever received in your career. Who trained you? Where? When? How long did it last? What subjects were covered?
2. How long have you worked for the defendant company?
3. Approximately how many jobs have you run for the defendant?
4. Approximately how many jobs have you run for the defendant that involved trenches or excavations five feet deep or more?
5. Before working for the defendant company, how many jobs did you work on where you had trenches and excavations five feet or deeper?
6. Other than the defendant company, have you ever worked for a company that had an occupational safety and health program in written form?
7. Other than the defendant company, have you ever worked for a company that had a policy of taking reasonable steps to ensure that trenches and excavations were safe?
8. Which companies? What was the policy? What were you required to do?
9. With regard to trenching and excavation, does your company's safety program and policy require you to plan to foresee hazards and communicate with contractors and subcontractors about controls that should be in place before work begins?
10. At this job site, did your company policy require you to have a pre-job safety conference with the trenching and excavation contractor?
11. Did you have one?
12. Were minutes kept of that meeting?
13. Did you and the trenching contractor foresee any hazards associated with trenching and excavations before work began at this site? If so, list them.

14. Did you make any plans with regard to the ways those hazards would be controlled before work began?
15. Did you expect the trenching contractor to protect this trench?
16. How did you expect the trenching contractor to protect this trench?
17. Did you receive a copy of the drawings or specs that showed the depth of equipment to be installed in the trench/excavation before work began?
18. When did you receive them?
19. Are you able to read the drawings or specs with regard to elevations?
20. Did you review them to determine the depths of trenches and excavations at this site?
21. What was the depth of the incident trench or excavation?
22. Before work began, did you have any information available to you concerning the type of soil in this area?
23. Before work began, did you do anything to determine the type of soil which would be excavated?
24. Did the trench and excavation contractor tell you beforehand what they determined the type of soil to be?
25. Did you know the type of soil of this trench?
26. When did you find out?
27. How did you find out the type of soil in this trench?
28. Do you know what OSHA's definition is of a competent person with regard to trenching and excavation?
29. Is it your company's policy to require that the job have an OSHA competent person during trenching/excavation work?
30. Are you a competent person?
31. Did the trenching and excavation contractor have a competent person at this job site? Who was it?
32. Prior to this incident, were you aware that the risk of trench collapse was more likely when the soil is looser?
33. Prior to this incident, were you aware that the risk of trench collapse was more likely as the trench gets deeper?
34. Prior to this incident, were you aware that the risk of trench collapse was more likely when there is greater moisture content in the soil?
35. Prior to this incident, were you aware that the risk of trench collapse was more likely when there is surface or underground water?
36. Prior to this incident, were you aware that the risk of trench collapse was more likely when there are rocks or boulders in the material?
37. Prior to this incident, were you aware that the risk of trench collapse was more likely when the excavated material is stored at the edge of the bank?

38. Prior to this incident, were you aware that the risk of trench collapse was more likely when equipment is stored above the bank?
39. Prior to this incident, were you aware that the risk of trench collapse was more likely when there is traffic on a road near the trench or excavation?
40. Does your company's occupational safety and health program and policy require you to do anything specifically to ensure that workers in trenches and excavations are not exposed to cave-in hazards?
41. List for me all of the steps that you are required to take to prevent people from being buried in trenches and excavations.

    NOTE: You should find out how long the work was done in this trench or excavation prior to the injury. Was it also opened and in violation of OSHA standards on days prior? You want to show that daily monitoring by the GC/CM rep should have identified the dangers associated with trenches and excavations on the day of the incident and days prior.

42. When did trenching and excavation work begin at this job site? (Job records should show when the trenching and excavation contractor arrived, worked and left.)
43. Did you make frequent and periodic inspections of the trenches and excavations?
44. Do you have any records?
45. Did you ever see the trenching and excavation work while it was being performed?
46. Did you ever see the trenching and excavation at other times when workers were not in it?
47. Did you see a trench box?
48. Did you see a shoring system?
49. Did you see adequate sloping?
50. What did you see?
51. When did you see the trench and excavation?
52. Did you ever point out any hazards at all to the trenching and excavation contractor prior to this incident?
53. Prior to this deposition, did you give any thought as to what could have been done to have prevented this incident?
54. Prior to this deposition, did you give any thought as to what your company could have done to prevent this incident?
55. Prior to this deposition, did you give any thought to what you could have done that would have prevented this incident?

DEPOSITION OR CROSS EXAMINATION OF TRENCH/EXCAVATION EXPERT

You will likely have uncovered many facts related to management system failures of the defendant before questioning the defense expert. In preparation for the deposition or cross examination, you could identify and list the key factual testimony of various witnesses that is most beneficial to your case. Often the defense expert focuses on the failure of the employer and plaintiff and ignores facts related to the failure of the defendants. You could begin by asking the expert if before performing his/her evaluation, he/she was aware of each of those facts and whether or not they were relevant in any way for his/her evaluation.

1. Do you know of any industry safety authorities that give guidance to GC/CMs regarding the need for the GC/CM to foresee hazards and to make plans as to particular hazard controls **before work begins**?
2. Do you agree that **before work begins** at a construction site involving trenching and excavation (T/E) work, evaluations are typically made which indicate the type of soil on the construction site where T/E work is to be performed?
3. Do you agree that information regarding the type of soil is customarily available to the GC/CM before work begins?
4. Do you know of any reason why a GC/CM could not find out the type of soil to be excavated at this site before work began?
5. In your experience, before work begins, do GC/CMs have copies of drawings and specs?
6. Do drawings and specs typically indicate elevations or depths of T/Es where pipes or other equipment are to be installed?
7. Can you read drawings and specs with elevations?
8. In your experience, are representatives of GC/CMs usually able to read drawings, plans and specs with regard to elevations or depth of the T/E?
9. In your opinion, should the GC/CM representative know the depth that the T/E will be before work begins?
10. In your opinion, should the GC/CM representative know the type of soil that will be excavated before work begins?
11. Is knowledge of the type of soil and the depth of the trench important information needed to understand potential hazards associated with work in T/Es?
12. Do you agree that the GC/CM should have that information about the depth of the T/E available before work begins in order to foresee hazards associated with T/Es?

13. In this case, did the GC/CM know the depth and type of soil regarding this trench?
14. In your opinion, should there be a pre-job safety conference held by the GC/CM with the T/E contractor to discuss the soil type, depth and plans to protect workers therein?
15. Have you ever heard of the saying "safety pays"? Do you know what that means?
16. Do you agree that there are various costs associated with the different methods which can be used to make a T/E safe?
17. In your experience, does the T/E contractor need to know the depth of the T/E and the type of soil in order to prepare cost estimates for the bid?
18. In your experience, is information about depth and type of soil typically made available to the T/E contractor? (Answer: It is.)
19. Is that information typically made available to the GC/CM?
20. Do you agree that one of the reasons OSHA was passed is because sometimes some contractors would cut corners regarding safety and risk workers' lives because they can save money?
21. Do you know of any safety authorities that say the GC/CM has the responsibility to take reasonable steps to monitor and verify that the work is done safely and in compliance with OSHA? Which?
22. Do you know of any safety authorities that say the GC/CM should have a pre-job safety conference?
23. Was a pre-job safety conference regarding trenching and excavation held at this site?
24. Do you know of any safety authorities that say the GC/CM should monitor the work on a construction site to see that it is done safely as planned?
25. In your opinion, should that include monitoring T/Es?
26. Was periodic monitoring regarding trenching and excavation done by the GC/CM rep at this site?
27. Do you know of any safety literature prepared by OSHA related to T/E hazards which gives guidance regarding the importance of planning before work begins to evaluate and decide upon controls so T/Es do not collapse on workers?
28. Are you familiar with OSHA's requirement for a "competent person" to be available to perform certain tasks during T/E work?
29. Should a GC/CM determine who the competent person of the T/E contractor is?
30. Was there a competent person at this site regarding T/E hazards?
31. Have you ever heard the expression that the safety standards are "written in blood"?
32. Do you know what that expression means?

33. Would you agree with me that regarding T/E work there is no hazard more important than the cave-in hazard?
34. Would you agree with me that the more moisture there is in soil, the looser it is and the greater the danger of collapse?
35. Would you agree with me that the risk of T/E collapse is greater as the T/E gets deeper?
36. Do you agree that the T/E is more likely to collapse when excavated material is stored at its edge?
37. Would you agree with me that vibrations from construction vehicles can make it more likely that a T/E will collapse?

With regard to the risk factors associated with the collapse of the T/E in your case, you should ask if those risk factors were important for his/her evaluation.

38. Would you agree with me that when a trench or excavation collapses, there was a violation of an OSHA standard?
39. That is, do you agree that safe trenches which are protected as required by OSHA cannot collapse?
40. In your opinion, before work begins, should the person performing the excavation know what the plans are for protecting the T/E from collapsing?
41. In this case, was there any communication by the GC/CM rep to the excavator regarding safe ways to dig this trench?
42. In your opinion, should the GC/CM rep take reasonable steps to ensure that the person digging the excavation knows what the plans are regarding how the T/E will be protected?
43. In your opinion, should an excavator be instructed to not dig trenches or excavations that would be in violation of OSHA standards if workers have to enter the T/E?
44. Before this deposition, did you give any thought as to what the defendant could have done which would have reduced the risk of this incident?
45. Can you now think of anything that the defendant could have done before this incident occurred that would have prevented this injury?
46. Did the GC/CM plan and know how this T/E was going to be protected before it was dug?
47. Did the GC/CM evaluate bids to ensure that all costs associated with protecting the trench were included?
48. Do you agree it takes time and costs money to shore trenches and excavations?
49. Do you agree it takes time and costs money to slope trenches and excavations to the angle of repose?

50. Do you agree that it takes time and costs money to use a trench box or shield?
51. Did the GC/CM communicate to bidders that all of the costs associated with safety must be included in the bids?
52. Should a GC/CM communicate with bidders to ensure that they include all costs related to safety in their bids?
53. If so, why?
54. Would it be important for a GC/CM to know if a contractor did not plan to spend the money to safely protect a trench?
55. Is it possible for a bidder to make a bid lower because they did not include the cost for making a trench or excavation safe?
56. If a GC/CM does not require the contractor to include the costs related to making a trench safe, is it possible for them to submit a bid lower than others who do plan to include those costs?

NOTES

1. OSHA defines an excavation as a man-made cut, cavity, trench, or depression in the earth's surface formed by earth removal. This can include excavations from anything from cellars to highways. A trench is defined as a narrow underground excavation that is deeper than it is wide, and no wider than 15 feet. When the word excavation is used in this chapter, it is meant to include trenches.

2. "An Exploratory Analysis of Excavation Cave-In Fatalities" by Ron L. Stanevich and Dannie C. Middleton, *Professional Safety*, February 1988.

Chapter Eleven

Demolition Hazards

The primary hazards associated with demolition are: "falls from elevation" and being "struck by" falling material. The safety authorities who give guidance regarding demolition are:

- American National Standard A10.6-1990—"Safety Requirements for Demolition Operations"
- National Association of Demolition Contractors
- American Society of Safety Engineers—Construction Safety Management and Engineering
- National Safety Council
- U.S. Department of Labor, Occupational Safety and Health Administration

All of these authorities say that planning and hazard analysis should take place before work begins.

AMERICAN NATIONAL STANDARDS INSTITUTE A10.6-1990

This standard requires an engineering survey of the structure to be performed by qualified or competent persons to determine whether steps need to be taken to prevent premature collapse of any portion of the structure. It requires shutting off all utility lines or otherwise controlling them before demolition work begins. It requires consideration for public safety. It includes a document to be used to survey the job site. It is essentially a check list of all the hazards that must be considered before demolition work begins.

NATIONAL ASSOCIATION OF DEMOLITION CONTRACTORS

In their "Demolition Safety Manual," the National Association of Demolition Contractors indicates:

> 2.3. Pre-Job Safety Briefing. One of the best ways to integrate safety into each job is the pre-job safety briefing . . . Supervisors will be able to explain, in detail, the safe ways of doing each of the tasks assigned.
>
> 3.0. Preparatory Operations. Before the start of every demolition job, the demolition contractor should take a number of steps to safeguard the health and safety of workers at the job site. These preparatory operations involve the overall planning of the demolition job, including the methods to be used to bring the structure down, the equipment necessary to do the job, and the measures to be taken to perform the work safely. Planning for a demolition job is as important as actually doing the work . . .
>
> 3.1. Engineering Survey. Prior to starting all demolition operations, an engineering survey of the structure must be conducted by a properly qualified person. The purpose of the survey is to determine the condition of the framing, floors, and walls so that measures can be taken, if necessary, to prevent the premature collapse of any portion of the structure . . . The demolition contractor must maintain a written copy of the survey . . . The engineering survey provides the demolition contractor with the opportunity to evaluate the job in its entirety. The contractor should plan for the wrecking of the structure, the equipment to do the work, manpower required and the protection to the public.

The National Association of Demolition Contractors supplies a "Suggested Form for Engineering Survey." (See page 119.)

AMERICAN SOCIETY OF SAFETY ENGINEERS

In their publication entitled CONSTRUCTION SAFETY MANAGEMENT AND ENGINEERING, the American Society of Safety Engineers gives guidance regarding demolition safety. The following is taken from Chapter 23 entitled "Demolition."

> Preparatory Operations. Before the start of any demolition project, steps should be taken to safeguard the safety and health of each and every worker at the job site. The overall demolition plan should include all elements to successfully complete the project, including the methods used to bring down the structure or to remove various components of the building structures. The sequence of demolition work to be followed, the equipment necessary to perform the project, and the measures to be used to perform the work safely should be included in the plan.

SUGGESTED FORM FOR ENGINEERING SURVEY

____ DATE __________

TYPE OF STRUCTURE

LOCATION ____________________ BASEMENT ______________

STORIES OR HEIGHT ______________ SIZE OF STRUCTURE __________

LOCATE PARTY WALLS ____________________

ARE WALL TIES REQUIRED? ______ HOW MANY? ______ TYPE ______

STRUCTURAL HAZARDS ____________________________________

____

IS SHORING OF WALLS OR FLOORS REQUIRED?

____

TYPE OF SHORING AND LOCATION ____________________________

____

PROTECTION FOR ADJACENT PROPERTIES ______________________

____

EXISTING DAMAGE IN ADJACENT STUCTURES ___________________

____

PROTECTION FOR PUBLIC ___________________________________

____

METHODS OP DEMOLITION __________________________________

____

UTILITIES ____

LOCATION OF POWER LINES _______________________________

LOCATION OF TANKS ____________________________________

TANKS' PREVIOUS USE ___________________________________

HAVE TANKS BEEN PURGED AND TESTED? _________ BY WHOM? ________

MATERIAL SAFETY DATA SHEETS PROVIDED BY CUSTOMER/OWNER

____

PCB'S ____

ASBESTOS ____

LOCATE PITS OR OPEN HOLES ______________________________

____

SPECIAL HAZARDS AND REMEDIES ___________________________

____

OTHER COMMENTS ____

____

SIGNED ________________________________

> Engineering Survey. Planning for a demolition job is as important as performing the work. A competent person with the necessary experience and/or training in demolition operations should therefore plan all demolition work . . . Prior to the start of every demolition project, a competent person must conduct an engineering survey of the structure. The purpose of the survey is to determine the condition of the framing, floors and walls so that measures can be taken to prevent the premature collapse of any portion of the structure.

THE NATIONAL SAFETY COUNCIL

The National Safety Council in their ACCIDENT PREVENTION MANUAL, 12th Edition gives some guidance related to demolition safety. They state the following in Chapter 3.

> The following are some fundamental safety procedures and suggestions for minor demolition work:
>
> - Make provisions to keep the public and unauthorized facility employees at least 15 feet away from the structure.
> - Have a competent person make an engineering survey of the structure. Determine the condition of the framing, floors, and walls, and check for any unanticipated conditions. Check for hazardous chemicals, gases, explosives, flammable materials, asbestos, hazardous wastes, electrical circuits that may be damaged, etc.
> - Have a competent person or qualified engineer detail the demolition sequence.

OCCUPATIONAL SAFETY AND HEALTH ADMINISTRATION

29CFR1926.850(a). Preparatory Operations. Prior to permitting employees to start demolition operations, an engineering survey shall be made, by a competent person, of the structure to determine the condition of the framing, floors, and walls, and possibility of unplanned collapse of any portion of the structure. Any adjacent structure where employees may be exposed shall also be similarly checked. The employer shall have in writing evidence that such a survey has been performed.

The GC/CM cannot be expected to be expert in the safe techniques of demolition. However, they should hire a safe demolition contractor and require a copy of the survey and safe plans that should be developed. They should take reasonable steps to monitor and ensure that the safe plan is being followed.

It is very common that the demolition contractor has not been required to perform an engineering survey and to develop a specific safe plan. Sometimes the GC/CM simply accepts a low bid and does nothing to ensure that contract workers are protected. The following are some suggested questions for the representative of the GC/CM:

DEPOSITION OF THE GC/CM REP IN DEMOLITION

1. Prior to working for the defendant, did you ever work for a GC/CM who hired a demolition contractor to perform demolition work?
2. Did any of your prior employers require any of the demolition contractors to have written occupational safety and health programs?
3. Did any of your prior employers have a requirement for the GC/CM to hold a pre-job safety conference with contractors?
4. On any of those jobs, did you ever hold a pre-job safety conference with the demolition contractor?
5. On any of those jobs, did you ever meet with the demolition contractor and determine what hazard controls or work procedures would be in place to control foreseeable demolition hazards?
6. Do you recognize that collapse of the structure is possible if demolition work is not properly planned?
7. Do you recognize that fall hazards can result from work involving the demolition of floors and the support for the floors?
8. From your experience, do you recognize that planning regarding hazard control is important for all construction activity but is especially important for demolition work?
9. Does your company have a written safety and health program?
10. Does your company have a requirement for a pre-job safety conference?
11. Did you hold a pre-job safety conference with the demolition contractor?
12. Were minutes kept?
13. Was a written demolition plan developed?
14. Does your company policy require demolition contractors to prepare an engineering survey to foresee unexpected collapses?
15. In this case, was an engineering survey prepared?
16. Did you have the responsibility to oversee the work to see that it was done according to the contract?
17. Did you have the responsibility to oversee the work to ensure that it was done safely?
18. Did you have the responsibility to oversee the work to see that it was done in compliance with OSHA standards?

19. Did you have any responsibility at this job site to monitor construction activity?
20. According to your company's safety policy, how frequently are you or other representatives required to monitor the work to identify hazards?
21. How frequently was this demolition contractor's activity monitored by someone from your company?
22. Have you ever been trained in OSHA demolition standards?
23. Before this work began, were you familiar with an OSHA requirement with regard to an engineering survey being performed to identify the possibility of unexpected collapse?
24. In your career, have you ever required an engineering survey be given to you by a demolition contractor before work began?
25. On this job, did you require the demolition contractor to show you that an engineering survey had been done?
26. Before this job began, were you aware that a safety practice regarding demolition would be for a competent person or qualified engineer to detail demolition sequence?
27. On demolition jobs prior to this one, did you ever see a plan prepared by a competent person or qualified engineer which detailed demolition sequences?
28. At this job, did a competent person or qualified engineer develop a plan which detailed demolition sequence?
29. Have you ever worked on a job prior to this one where a worker was injured as a result of demolition work? Explain.
30. Before this deposition, did you give any thought regarding what anyone from your company, including you, could have done to prevent this incident?
31. As you sit here now, can you think of anything anyone from your company, including you, could have done to prevent this incident?

DEPOSITION OF EXPERT IN DEMOLITION

1. Have you ever developed a demolition safety plan?
2. Have you ever performed an engineering survey to identify unforeseen ways of collapse during demolition?
3. Have you ever had the responsibility to oversee demolition work?
4. Have you ever been trained in demolition safety?
5. Have you ever taught regarding demolition safety?
6. List all of the reasons why you should be considered a demolition safety expert.

7. Are you familiar with the ANSI standard A10.6 related to Safety Requirements for Demolition Operations?
8. Did you review ANSI A10.6 before forming your opinion in this case?
9. Are you familiar with the National Association of Demolition Contractors' Manual for Safety?
10. Did you review the Manual of the National Association of Demolition Contractors before forming your opinions in this case?
11. Are you familiar with the National Safety Council's ACCIDENT PREVENTION MANUAL with regard to their requirements for safe demolition?
12. Did you read the National Safety Council's ACCIDENT PREVENTION MANUAL before forming your opinion in this case?
13. Do you disagree with anything in the ANSI standard A10.6 related to demolition safety?
14. Do you have any disagreement with the National Association of Demolition Contractors with regard to steps that they say should be taken to prevent injury during demolition?
15. Do you disagree with what the National Safety Council says with regard to demolition safety?
16. Did you perform your evaluation of the conduct of the defendant based on what these three demolition authorities say should be done regarding demolition safety?
17. Have you ever been involved in demolition activity in any capacity where you found that the demolition contractor violated a provision of ANSI? Explain. When? Where? What standard? What did you do?
18. Have you ever been involved in demolition activity in any capacity where you found a demolition contractor violated any of the standards set forth in the Safety Manual of the National Association of Demolition Contractors? Explain. When? Where? What standard? What did you do?
19. Have you ever been involved in any construction activity in any capacity where you found that the demolition contractor had not performed an engineering survey as required by OSHA?
20. What is a demolition safety plan?
21. Do you know of any safety authorities that give guidance in the demolition industry to say that a safety plan should be developed before work begins?
22. Have you ever seen a demolition safety plan? When? Where? Who did it? What was on it?
23. Did you see a demolition safety plan for this job?
24. Do you agree that planning before work begins is an essential task to perform in order to prevent injury related to demolition?

25. According to the industry standard as you understand it, what are all the things that the demolition contractor should do before work begins with regard to safety?
26. Did the GC/CM hire the demolition contractor in this case?
27. Did you perform an evaluation to see whether or not the GC/CM took reasonable steps to hire a safe demolition contractor?
28. Would you agree that the GC/CM who hires a demolition contractor should take reasonable steps to make sure that demolition workers are not killed or injured during the demolition work?
29. Tell me all of the steps that you as an expert believe should be taken by a GC/CM to manage safety and to prevent injury and death to demolition workers?
30. Have you ever worked on a job site involving demolition work?
31. Have you ever worked on a job site involving demolition work where there was a demolition plan prepared which detailed demolition sequence?
32. Have you ever worked on a job involving demolition work where a competent person or qualified engineer prepared a survey of the structure to determine the condition of the framing, floors, walls and the possibility of unforeseen collapse?
33. In this case, should there have been a survey of the structure to determine the condition of the framing, floors, walls and possibility of an unforeseen collapse?
34. In this case, was there a demolition survey performed by a competent person or qualified engineer to determine the condition of the structure?
35. In this case, was there a plan which detailed the demolition sequence?
36. I would list all of the important facts which support your arguments and ask the expert whether or not these facts were important when he/she performed their evaluation. For example:

    - Did you read the GC/CM representative's deposition where he said that there was no written survey performed to determine the possibility of unforeseen collapse?
    - Was that fact important to you in your evaluation?
    - Did you read where he said there was no safety plan detailing the sequence of demolition work? Was that relevant for your evaluation?
    - Did you read where he said that his company had no written safety program? Was that relevant for your evaluation?
    - Did you read where he said he had no training with regard to demolition safety? Was that relevant for your evaluation?
    - Did you read where he said his safety performance was never evaluated by his supervisors? Was that relevant for your evaluation?

- Did you read where he said there were no weekly safety meetings at this job site? Was that relevant for your evaluation?
- Did you read where he said there were no written reports of safety inspections? Was that relevant for your evaluation?
- Did you read where he said he did not know what OSHA standards were related to demolition? Was that relevant for your evaluation?

Chapter Twelve

Injuries Involving Forklift Trucks

OSHA estimates that there are more than 68,400 injuries each year caused from the operation of forklift trucks. Approximately 100 are fatal injuries.

Classification of Forklift Fatalities, 1991–1992

Tip over	25.3%
Struck by powered industrial truck	18.8%
Struck by falling load	14.4%
Elevated employee on truck	12.2%
Ran off dock or other surface	7.0%
Improper maintenance procedures	6.1%
Lost control of truck	4.4%
Truck struck material	4.4%
Employees overcome by CO or propane fuel	4.4%
Faulty powered industrial truck	3.1%
Unloading unchocked trailer	3.1%
Employee fell from vehicle	3.1%
Improper use of vehicle	2.6%
Electrocutions	1.0%

Source: OSHA Study, "First Report of Serious Accidents 1985–1990," as published in *Forklift Safety* by George Swartz. Rockville, MD: Government Institutes, p. 1.

The Bureau of Labor Statistics studied forklift truck fatal accidents. The following information was provided from 170 fatal incidents involving forklift trucks.

Percentages of Forklift Accident Causes

OSHA has identified key factors which have contributed to employee accidents from lift trucks. Tip overs are responsible for over 25 percent of all accidents.

How Accident Occurred	*Number*	*Percentage*
Forklift overturned	41	24
Worker struck by material	29	17
Worker struck by forklift	24	14
Worker fell from forklift	24	14
Worker pinned between objects	19	11
Forklift struck something or ran off the dock	13	8
Worker died during forklift repair	10	6
Other accident	10	6

Source: OSHA Study, "First Report of Serious Accidents 1985–1990," as published in *Forklift Safety* by George Swartz. Rockville, MD: Government Institutes, p. 2.

OSHA has projected what compliance with their operator training standard would accomplish. OSHA found that each year there are approximately 85 fatal injuries which occur from improper operation of forklift trucks. There are approximately 34,902 serious injuries from improper operation and 61,800 non-serious injuries.

OSHA found that if employers were to comply with the training requirements of their standard, the risks would fall to:

- 68–63 fatalities—25% reduction
- 10,898 to 14,118 serious injuries
- 15,450 non-serious injuries

	Current OSHA Data	*After New Program Compliance*
Fatalities	85	68–63
Serious injuries	34,902	10,898–14,118
Non-serious injuries	61,800	15.450

These numbers are significant. Effective training programs are estimated to reduce injuries by as much as 70 percent.

Source: OSHA Study, "First Report of Serious Accidents 1985–1990," as published in *Forklift Safety* by George Swartz. Rockville, MD: Government Institutes, p. 3.

CAUSES OF ACCIDENTS—OSHA INVESTIGATION SUMMARIES

OSHA researched some 4,268 accident reports on lift truck accidents and was able to identify specific accident causes.

	Cause	Number of Reports
1st	Operator inattention	59
2nd	Overturn	53
3rd	Unstable load	45
4th	Operator struck by load	37
5th	Elevated employee	26
6th	No training	19
7th	Overload, improper use	15
8th	Accident during maintenance	14
9th	Obstructed view	10
9th	Improper equipment	10
11th	Falling from platform or curb	9
11th	Not powered industrial truck accident	9
13th	Other employee struck by load	8
13th	Carrying excess passenger	8
15th	Vehicle left in gear	6
15th	Falling from trailer	6
17th	Speeding	5
Total		339

Source: OSHA Study, "First Report of Serious Accidents 1985–1990," as published in *Forklift Safety* by George Swartz. Rockville, MD: Government Institutes, p. 4.

The following are the common ways that forklift truck operators cause injury to themselves or others:

- Carrying unsafe loads that fall onto workers
- Turning sharply causing tail swing which results in pedestrian runover
- Lifting workers on forks or on pallets without fall protection
- Backing up over workers
- Operate on dangerous slopes which cause tipovers
- Overloading the forklift truck which causes tipover
- Failure to wear seatbelt and forklift truck tips over
- Driving forward with an obstructed view striking pedestrian. With obstructed view, the operator should "trail" the load or travel in reverse.

It is not unusual that forklift operators in the construction industry have received the OSHA required training. Training is a fundamental element in an occupational safety and health program. According to the American Society of Safety Engineers, the GC/CM has a responsibility to verify if workers have received OSHA training. They state:

> Making sure that subcontractors' employees are trained before they are allowed to work on the job site is the best way that the general contractor has of ensuring that all employees on the site have received at least the minimum training required.[1]

According to all industry safety authorities, the GC/CM should take reasonable steps to ensure that contractors work in compliance with OSHA standards. That includes all OSHA standards including those which require training of forklift truck operators.

In many cases involving injury caused by a forklift truck you will find that if the operator had been properly trained and instructed, the injury would not have occurred. Proper safety training should instruct the forklift operator to refuse to work in dangerous ways which violate the OSHA standards.

It is very common that forklift truck operators learn on the job. A foreman, co-worker or a representative from a rental company may explain to the operator how the controls work. Often, the workers watch others and then learn by trial and error. Perhaps they have operated a forklift truck for several years without injuring or being injured. That does not mean that they operated safely for those years. A person can operate a vehicle unsafely and without injury for many years. For example, a person suffering alcoholism may drink and drive for years without harming someone or him or herself. It is surely unsafe to drive a car while intoxicated. Likewise, it is unsafe to operate a forklift truck without any safety training.

The OSHA construction standard related to forklift trucks is 29CFR1926.602(d). It refers to the General Industry Standard for forklift operator training, 29CFR1910.178(l).

1910.178(l) Operator training:

(1) Safe operation.
   (i) The employer shall ensure that each powered industrial truck operator is competent to operate a powered industrial truck safely, as demonstrated by the successful completion of the training and evaluation specified in this paragraph (1).
   (ii) Prior to permitting an employee to operate a powered industrial truck (except for training purposes), the employer shall ensure that each operator has successfully completed the training required by this paragraph (l), except as permitted by paragraph (l)(5).
(2) Training program implementation.
   (i) Trainees may operate a powered industrial truck only:
      (A) Under the direct supervision of persons who have the knowledge, training, and experience to train operators and evaluate their competence; and
      (B) Where such operation does not endanger the trainee or other employees.
   (ii) Training shall consist of a combination of formal instruction (e.g., lecture, discussion, interactive computer learning, video tape, written material), practical training (demonstrations performed by the trainer and practical exercises performed by the trainee), and evaluation of the operator's performance in the workplace.

(iii) All operator training and evaluation shall be conducted by persons who have the knowledge, training, and experience to train powered industrial truck operators and evaluate their competence.

(3) Training program content. Powered industrial truck operators shall receive initial training in the following topics, except in topics which the employer can demonstrate are not applicable to safe operation of the truck in the employer's workplace.

(i) Truck-related topics:

(A) Operating instructions, warnings, and precautions for the types of truck the operator will be authorized to operate;
(B) Differences between the truck and the automobile;
(C) Truck controls and instrumentation: where they are located, what they do, and how they work;
(D) Engine or motor operation;
(E) Steering and maneuvering;
(F) Visibility (including restrictions due to loading);
(G) Fork and attachment adaptation, operation, and use limitations;
(H) Vehicle capacity;
(I) Vehicle stability;
(J) Any vehicle inspection and maintenance that the operator will be required to perform;
(K) Refueling and/or charging and recharging of batteries;
(L) Operating limitations;
(M) Any other operating instructions, warnings, or precautions listed in the operator's manual for the types of vehicle that the employee is being trained to operate.

(ii) Workplace-related topics:

(A) Surface conditions where the vehicle will be operated;
(B) Composition of loads to be carried and load stability;
(C) Load manipulation, stacking, and unstacking;
(D) Pedestrian traffic in areas where the vehicle will be operated;
(E) Narrow aisles and other restricted places where the vehicle will be operated;
(F) Hazardous (classified) locations where the vehicle will be operated;
(G) Ramps and other sloped surfaces that could affect the vehicle's stability;
(H) Closed environments and other areas where insufficient ventilation or poor vehicle maintenance could cause a buildup of carbon monoxide or diesel exhaust;
(I) Other unique or potentially hazardous environmental conditions in the workplace that could affect safe operation.

(iii) The requirements of this section.

(4) Refresher training and evaluation.
  (i) Refresher training, including an evaluation of the effectiveness of that training, shall be conducted as required by paragraph (l)(4)(ii) to ensure that the operator has the knowledge and skills needed to operate the powered industrial truck safely.
  (ii) Refresher training in relevant topics shall be provided to the operator when:
    (A) The operator has been observed to operate the vehicle in an unsafe manner;
    (B) The operator has been involved in an accident or near-miss incident;
    (C) The operator has received an evaluation that reveals that the operator is not operating the truck safely;
    (D) The operator is assigned to drive a different type of truck; or
    (E) A condition in the workplace changes in a manner that could affect safe operation of the truck.
  (iii) An evaluation of each powered industrial truck operator's performance shall be conducted at least once every three years.

(5) Avoidance of duplicative training. If an operator has previously received training in a topic specified in paragraph (l)(3) of this section, and such training is appropriate to the truck and working conditions encountered, additional training in that topic is not required if the operator has been evaluated and found competent to operate the truck safely.

(6) Certification. The employer shall certify that each operator has been trained and evaluated as required by this paragraph (l). The certification shall include the name of the operator, the date of the training, the date of the evaluation, and the identity of the person(s) performing the training or evaluation.

(7) Dates. The employer shall ensure that operators of powered industrial trucks are trained, as appropriate, by the dates shown in the following table:

If the employee was hired:	*The initial training and evaluation of that employee must be completed:*
Before December 1, 1999	By December 1, 1999
After December 1, 1999	Before the employee is assigned to operate a powered industrial truck

DEPOSITION OF GC/CM REP

1. Before working for defendant company, did you ever work in a management capacity on a construction project where forklift trucks were used? Explain. How many projects, how many forklift trucks?

2. Who were you employed by?
3. When did you work for those companies?
4. Prior to working for the defendant company, did you ever determine if a forklift truck operator had been evaluated by a competent person to determine whether or not the forklift truck operator was competent to safely operate a forklift truck?
5. Prior to working for the defendant company, did you ever verify in any way that forklift operators had been trained as required by OSHA? If so, how?
6. Does your company have a written occupational safety and health program?
7. Does it require a pre-job safety conference?
8. Did you hold a pre-job safety conference with the employer of the forklift operator at this site?
9. Before this work began, did you know that OSHA requires forklift operators to be formally trained with certification proving that they had been trained?
10. At this project, did you verify that forklift operators had certifications or documents proving that they had been trained by a competent trainer?
11. Did you ever require any contractor whose workers use forklift trucks to show certification proving that they had been trained as required by OSHA?
12. Since this incident, has your company policy changed in any way with regard to verification of training of forklift operators?
13. Did you know that the OSHA standard requires workers who work at heights of six feet or more above ground level to have training in fall protection with certifications?
14. Have you ever verified that workers who work at heights had certifications as required by OSHA?
15. Did you ever do anything to verify that any worker received the OSHA required safety training regarding installation and use of scaffolds?
16. Did you ever do anything to verify that any workers received OSHA required training related to ladder safety?
17. Have you received any OSHA training?
18. Did any OSHA trainer ever inform you that forklift operators had to be trained and had to have training certification?
19. Today does your company do anything to verify that forklift truck operators of contractors and subcontractors have been trained as required by OSHA?
20. Prior to this deposition, did you ever give any thought as to how this incident may have been prevented?
21. Was there anything preventing you from verifying that forklift operators had been trained as required by OSHA?

CROSS EXAMINATION OF DEFENSE EXPERT

1. Do you know what the American Society of Safety Engineers is?
2. Are you a member?
3. Do you recognize that the American Society of Safety Engineers is a leading industry safety authority?
4. Do you know the name of the *Journal of the American Society of Safety Engineers*? (Answer: *Professional Safety)*
5. Have you ever attended any of the professional conferences of the ASSE?
6. Have you ever published in their journal?
7. Tell me whether you agree or disagree with this statement: "Making sure that subcontractor employees are trained before they are allowed to work on the job site is the best way that the general contractor has of ensuring that all employees on the site have received at least the minimum training required."[2]
8. In this case, did the GC/CM verify that forklift truck operators were trained and certified?
9. Would you agree that it is quite easy to verify forklift operator training by asking the employer of the forklift operator to fax or email a copy of the certification document which shows forklift operator training?
10. Are you familiar with the OSHA standard related to forklift operator training?
11. Do you have any disagreement with OSHA or that standard as it is written?
12. Are you familiar with OSHA's requirement for training of workers who work six feet or more above a lower surface?
13. Does OSHA require training and certification for workers who work six feet or more above a lower surface?
14. In your expert opinion, should a general contractor do anything to verify that people who work at heights have received the required OSHA training?
15. Do you agree that falls from elevation can cause catastrophic injury and death?
16. Do you agree that operating a forklift truck without safety training can be very dangerous?
17. Would you agree that operating a forklift truck without training is dangerous not only for the operator, but for all workers on the job site who may be run over or hit by falling material?
18. Do you know of any industry safety authorities that say the GC/CM has overall responsibility for safety management at a construction site?
19. And you agree that it is much safer to have forklift operators trained related to safety than not?

20. Tell me all of the things that a GC/CM should do to make sure that contractor workers have received the OSHA required safety training regarding forklift truck operation.
21. Tell me all of the things that a GC/CM could do to make sure that contractor workers have received the OSHA required safety training regarding forklift truck operation.
22. Was there anything preventing the GC/CM from verifying that forklift operators had been trained?

NOTES

1. CONSTRUCTION SAFETY MANAGEMENT AND ENGINEERING, Darryl C. Hill, CSP, American Society of Safety Engineers, Des Plaines, IL, 2004, p. 179.
2. CONSTRUCTION SAFETY MANAGEMENT AND ENGINEERING, Darryl C. Hill, CSP, American Society of Safety Engineers, Des Plaines, IL, 2004, p. 179.

Chapter Thirteen

Public Safety in Construction

On most construction sites there is some potential exposure to the public to construction hazards. Some common injury incidents are:

- Struck by falling object
- Tripping over construction debris
- Struck by object which is blown off of a building by wind
- Struck by construction vehicle
- Struck by automobile during highway maintenance or road construction
- Children playing on construction site
- Sales representative or prospective buyer on residential construction site falls from elevation

OSHA has no jurisdiction over hazards to which the public is exposed. However, if the public is exposed to a hazard, there is probably at least potential exposure to workers as well. You can show that the GC/CM should have taken reasonable steps to ensure that the work site was safe for both workers and people who could reasonably be expected to be on or near the construction site.

Construction industry safety authorities recognize the need for the GC/CM to include public safety in their occupational safety and health program.

ASSOCIATED GENERAL CONTRACTORS OF AMERICA

The Associated General Contractors of America in their MANUAL OF ACCIDENT PREVENTION IN CONSTRUCTION give guidance to the general contractor with regard to public safety. They recognize that the general public is often impacted by construction operations. They give guidance with regard to steps that the general contractor should take to protect the public. Some examples are contacting area residents to advise them of the work to be done, providing adequate fencing and barricades, and performing surveys to determine the condition of properties prior to the start of construction. They also suggest control measures including advertising in local publications and posting signs and posters.

AMERICAN NATIONAL STANDARD—PROTECTION OF THE PUBLIC ON OR ADJACENT TO CONSTRUCTION SITES

In standard ANSI/ASSE A10.34-2001, ANSI gives guidance regarding public safety. ANSI requires the creation of a Public Hazard Control Plan. It requires the general contractor to ensure that the plan is enforced. The Public Hazard Control Plan must consider all of the hazards to which the public may be exposed. Some of the hazards that the general contractor is required to consider in the plan are noise, dust, traffic hazards, pedestrian hazards, vehicle hazards, falling object hazards and others. It gives a checklist that the general contractor can use to identify hazards.

DEPOSITION OF GC/CM REP REGARDING PUBLIC SAFETY

The following are questions which could be used for the deposition of the GC/CM representative.

1. On approximately how many job sites have you acted as representative of the GC/CM in your career?
2. What are some of the types of construction projects that you ran as a superintendent of a GC/CM?
3. Before working for this defendant, did you ever work for a company that had a policy for you to take reasonable steps to protect the public from exposures to construction hazards? Explain all of the hazards that you were required to consider.
4. Prior to this project, did you ever consider how the public could be exposed to falling and flying objects?
5. Prior to this project, did you consider how the public may be exposed to being struck by construction vehicles?
6. Prior to this project, did you ever install barriers or blockades to keep the public away from construction activity?

7. Prior to this project, did you ever establish fences or warning lines?
8. Prior to this project, did you ever do anything to keep children away from the construction site?
9. At this site, did you consider how the public could be exposed to falling and flying objects?
10. At this site, did you do anything to protect the public from construction hazards?
11. At this site, did you consider how the public may be exposed to being struck by construction vehicles?
12. At this site, did you ever install barriers or blockades to keep the public away from construction activity?
13. At this site, did you ever establish fences or warning lines?
14. At this site, did you ever do anything to keep children away from the construction site?
15. Does your company have a written safety and health program?
16. Does it include policies and procedures regarding protection of the public?
17. Are you familiar with what the Associated General Contractors of America says regarding the responsibility of the general contractor for public safety?
18. If so, what does it say?
19. Are you familiar with the American National Standard which gives guidance to general contractors with regard to public safety?
20. If so, what does ANSI say?
21. Is it your company's policy to plan before work begins to identify potential hazards to which the public may be exposed?
22. Is it your company's policy to write a Public Safety Plan?
23. Have you ever seen anything in writing which relates to your company's policy with regard to preventing injuries to the public?
24. With regard to the hazard that led to injury in this case, did your company plan to foresee the possibility of exposure to that hazard before work began?
25. Was it possible for anything to have been done by anyone in your company which would have prevented this injury?
26. How could it have been avoided?
27. Could plans have been made beforehand to avoid this injury?
28. Did you monitor this job site to ensure that the public was not exposed to hazards related to this work?
29. Were written reports made?
30. How frequently did you monitor the site?
31. If you had seen this hazard prior to this incident, according to your company policy, were you required to do anything?

32. After this incident, were any steps taken to prevent a recurrence of this type of injury?
33. Prior to this deposition, had you given any thought to anything you could have done that would have prevented this incident?

DEPOSITION OF EXPERT IN PUBLIC SAFETY

1. Have you ever had the responsibility to oversee a construction project where there was a potential of exposure of the public to construction hazards?
2. List all of the steps that were taken when you worked for that company to prevent injury to the public.
3. Have you ever worked for a company that had a written safety program that included steps to take to prevent the public from being injured by construction activity?
4. Should a company such as the defendant have a written safety program that includes steps to be taken to prevent the public from being injured by construction activity?
5. Have you ever taught on the subject of public safety related to construction projects?
6. Have you ever written on the subject of public safety related to construction projects?
7. List all of the reasons why you should be considered expert in the area of public safety regarding construction sites.
8. Have you ever been on a construction site where there was a potential for exposure to the public to hazards from the construction work?
9. Explain all instances of potential exposure to the public.
10. Have you ever seen safety precautions taken by general contractors to prevent injury to the public?
11. Tell me all of the hazard controls that you are aware of that have been installed to protect the public from injury due to construction work.
12. Did you ever see any controls related to the hazard that caused this plaintiff's injury?
13. What types of controls have you seen?
14. In your opinion, should a general contractor take reasonable steps to make sure that the public is not injured by the construction activity?
15. In your opinion, should the general contractor plan before work begins to identify ways that the public may be injured?
16. In your opinion, should the general contractor then decide upon acceptable controls to prevent injury to the public, that is, before exposure to a hazard takes place?

17. In this case, is there any evidence of any planning done by the general contractor to foresee the injury that had resulted to the plaintiff?
18. Have you ever been involved in any cases prior to this case where a member of the public was injured because of construction activity?
19. Have you ever worked for a plaintiff's attorney in a public safety case related to construction?
20. Explain.
21. Have you ever worked for a defendant's attorney in a public safety case related to construction?
22. Explain.
23. Can you provide me with reports you have prepared for plaintiff attorneys and defense attorneys that involve public safety at construction sites?
24. Do you agree that all general contractors should take reasonable steps to make sure the work is done in ways that there are no hazards to which the public is exposed?
25. What was the hazard that led to injury in this case?
26. Was that hazard foreseeable before work began?
27. Was it possible to have controlled that hazard to prevent this injury?
28. Do you know what the Associated General Contractors of America is?
29. Are you familiar with their safety manual?
30. Do you consider the Associated General Contractors of America as an organization which speaks with authority with regard to what general contractors should do to prevent injury on construction sites?
31. Have you ever based an opinion on any of the guidance given by the Associated General Contractors of America to contractors?
32. Do you know what the Associated General Contractors of America says with regard to a general contractor's role in preventing injury to the public?
33. Tell me everything that the Associated General Contractors of America says a general contractor should do.
34. When you performed your evaluation in this case, did you do so based on what the Associated General Contractors of America says a general contractor should do with regard to preventing injury to the public?
35. Are you familiar with the ANSI standard A10.34 related to public safety?
36. Do you consider ANSI as an industry standard setter that is a respected authority in the field of injury prevention?
37. Have you ever based an opinion on any guidance given by any ANSI?
38. Can you tell me all of the steps that a general contractor should take to prevent injury to the public?
39. Did you perform your evaluation in this case based on the ANSI standard regarding public safety?

40. Can you tell me what the ANSI standard says a general contractor should do with regard to controlling the hazard that led to the plaintiff's injury?
41. Was it possible for the defendant to have done anything prior to this incident which could have prevented this incident?
42. Could the hazard that led to injury in this case have been controlled prior to this incident?
43. How?

Part III

CONSTRUCTION OWNER/PREMISE CASES—STANDARD OF CARE

Chapter Fourteen

Construction Project Owner

A construction project owner (CPO) is a corporation that hires a GC/CM or contractor to perform new construction work. An example is Wal-Mart, Target or any corporation that contracts with a company to perform construction work. A CPO could also be a Public Owner. A public owner could be the federal government, state government, or local government that contracts to have construction work done. The standard of care for a CPO regarding reasonable steps to take to prevent contractor worker injury has been established by the following industry safety authorities:

- The Business Roundtable
- The Construction Users Roundtable
- American National Standards Institute
- The National Safety Council
- The American Society of Safety Engineers
- The American Society of Civil Engineers

The following is taken from the standards of the above industry safety authorities:

1. The Business Roundtable

The Business Roundtable is an association of the largest 200 corporations in the United States. They have had research performed to identify the best practices to ensure safe performance by contractors when a corporation/business owner contracts for new construction and for construction work to be done on their premise.[1] The following is taken from *Improving Construction Safety Performance*:

Owners[2] have long recognized and honored a moral obligation to provide a safe work environment to minimize injuries. The primary purpose of this study report is to demonstrate that owners have, in addition to their moral commitment, an economic incentive to help reduce the number of accidents that occur on their construction projects. The high cost of accidents gives owners as construction users good reason to concern themselves with the safety efforts of the contractors they hire. Past research has shown that accidents are, to some extent, controllable by all levels of construction management. Reasonable reductions in the frequency and severity of accident would lower the $8.9 billion cost of accidents by as much as $2.75 billion, or 8 percent of direct construction labor payroll, a year. So there is ample economic incentive, in addition to humanitarian concerns, for owners to play an important role in construction safety.

Owners cannot maintain a completely hands-off policy towards construction activity on the owner's property . . . Owners should recognize that the principles of management control commonly applied to costs, schedules, quality and productivity are equally applicable to safety and that, if used, will improve safety performance. By showing more concern for construction safety, owners can help reduce injuries and loss of life and the billions of dollars needlessly wasted by construction accidents.

RECOMMENDATIONS. It is fully recognized by the Business Roundtable that contractors have the primary responsibility for execution of onsite safety . . . The Owners should:

- Become familiar with the high cost of construction accidents to reinforce their moral commitments to provide a safe work environment.
- Be prepared to financially support contractors' efforts to ensure an effective safety program.
- Realize that merely adopting a safety program will not yield the desired results without a serious and persistent management commitment.
- Recognize that the principles of management control commonly applied to cost, schedule, quality and productivity are equally applicable to safety and that, when used, they will improve safety performance.
- Make safety an important consideration in the selection of contractors for bidding on their construction projects, including evaluation of contractors' past safety performance, safety attitude, and present programs and practices.
- Become more directly involved in the safety activities of their construction projects and take proper measures to achieve better safety performance, such as:
    - Provide safety and health guidelines that the contractor must follow.
    - Require a formal site safety program.
    - Require the use of permit systems for potentially hazardous activities.
    - Require the contractor to designate the responsible supervisor to coordinate safety on the site.
    - Discuss safety at owner-contractor meetings.

  - **Conduct safety audits during construction** (emphasis added).
  - Require prompt reporting and full investigation of accidents.
- Establish with the contractor lines of communication at all levels so that safe work practices are understood by both parties.

The Business Roundtable published their conclusions in a document entitled **Improving Construction Safety Performance: A Construction Industry Cost Effectiveness Project Report.** They published this report to disseminate it to members and to owners and industry throughout the United States. Over 100,000 copies of their summary report has been distributed to owners and contractors throughout the United States.

2. The Construction Users Roundtable

The Construction Users Roundtable is an association of construction owners (corporations), contractors and contractor associations (see Appendix D).

The Construction Users Roundtable has also commented on the owner's role regarding construction safety in their Publication UP-802, July 2004. This publication is the result of their research regarding best practices to prevent construction worker injury. The following are excerpts from this publication entitled *Construction Safety: The Owner's Role.*

> Owners have a clear vested interest in contractor safety performance . . . Unsafe contractor work practices can endanger the owner's employees, property and plant operations.
>
> Owners must develop a construction safety program to be implemented aggressively and consistently at all owner sites and projects. Owners must recognize and actively support construction safety as a high priority, with corporate objectives and project goals focused on the elimination of incidents . . . The owner's role in safety does not end in the planning stages. Continued owner involvement during project execution is critical for safety performance. Safety plans must be executed. Contract provisions must be enforced. **The owner must monitor contractor behavior to ensure effective implementation** (emphasis added). Effective involvement includes:
>
> - Monitoring contractor safety performance.
>   The owner's representative monitors contractor safety compliance through auditing. Auditors check for implementation of the contractor safety program, compliance with local site requirements, and conformance with contractual obligations . . . The owner's representative should periodically tour the construction site and observe contractor employees, making note of both safe and unsafe behaviors . . . Owners can reduce injuries at their project sites through aggressive, proactive involvement and site operations. Owners must

make safety an important criterion when making critical decisions. Owners continue to be involved in promoting safe operations by measuring and monitoring contractor safety performance, participating in Behavior Observation Surveys and incident investigations, funding safety initiatives, networking contractor safety personnel, and participating in contractor safety training and employee orientation.

In their publication UP-804 entitled *Construction Safety: Contract Terms and Conditions*, they state the following:

The owner is responsible for:

- Defining the project context.
- Providing project oversight.
- Auditing staff behavior.
- Documenting performance.

These owner safety responsibilities are further shown in the following table:

Owner Safety Responsibilities

Defining the project context	Δ Setting goals, expectations, and requirements Δ Allocating project risk through the contract Δ Selecting the Project Team
Providing project oversight	Δ Training field staff to monitor adherence Δ Detecting non-conformance and compelling correction Δ Invoking remedies for failure to cure non-conformance
Auditing staff behavior	Δ Ensuring adherence to policy and procedure Δ Ensuring use of appropriate methods and process
Documenting performance	Δ Completing and maintaining documentation including: • Safety plans • Inspections and audits • Performance metrics • Incident reports • Investigations • Orientations, meetings, and training • Project completions

Once the contract is established and construction work begins, the owner must provide proactive project oversight by:

- Training their own (the owner's) field staff.
- Monitoring contractor adherence to contract provisions.
- Detecting deviations from the contract.
- Compelling corrections of nonconformance.

- Implementing consistent policy.
- Documenting owner and contractor action, behavior and results.

The owner must proactively support the contractor's safety operation without assuming control of the work . . . The owner should periodically audit the project and/or the site to ensure effective performance of their staff and areas of policy, procedure, methods and processes.

Owners who establish contract terms and conditions that reflect their safety objectives and who aggressively manage contractors to meet those objectives experience better safety results on their projects and are shielded from unnecessary liability for contractor accidents and injuries.

3. American National Standard for Construction and Demolition Operations—Safety and Health Program Requirements for Multi-Employer Projects ANSI A10.33-2011

This industry national consensus standard sets forth reasonable steps that a construction project owner should take to ensure the safety of contract workers on their construction site.

2.11. Owner. The legal entity entering into a contract with the project constructor for completing all work contained in the project documents, not to include a homeowner who has no involvement or expertise in the construction industry.

2.13. Project Constructor. A person, firm or corporation, construction manager, general contractor, prime contractor, or other entity designated in the contract as being responsible for all construction work contained in project documents.

3.2.1. Owner Responsibilities. It is the responsibility of the project constructor, through the owner's designated safety representative, to hold parties accountable including the owner, that work on the project will be implemented following this standard.

3.2.2. Evaluation of Contractor Qualifications. The owner or project constructor, through their designated safety representative, shall develop and implement a system to evaluate bidder's past safety and health performance.

3.2.2.1. The evaluation shall include a copy of the proposed safety and health plan and pre-task planning.

3.2.2.2. The evaluation shall include a written review of the bidder's past safety and health performance.

3.2.2.3. In instances where an owner chooses to contract with a bidder who fails to meet the owner's criteria, the owner shall require special plans to ensure improved project safety and health performance. Such action may include requirements for a qualified safety and health professional, enhanced training and/or more frequent inspections.

3.2.3. Project Safety and Health Plan

3.2.3.4. The owner's designated safety representative shall review the plan and certify in writing to the owner that the plan is adequate for the work to be performed, and meets company and other regulatory requirements.

3.2.3.5. The plan shall be accepted by the owner and constructor when it is adequate for the work to be performed.

3.2.4. The plan shall be made readily accessible to all construction workers on the project.

3.4. Requirements of the Overall Project Safety and Health Plan. The following shall be specified in the project safety and health plan and be assigned to the various levels of construction management and supervision with authority and capabilities to implement the plan.

3.4.1. Evaluation of contractor safety and health plans to determine their appropriateness to the specific job site and work to be performed.

3.4.2. Monitoring and documenting the implementation of the safety and health plans.

8. Pre-Work Planning

8.1.1. Prior to the start of the work, each contractor shall conduct a physical survey by walking through the job site, reviewing the drawings and contract documents, and holding discussions as appropriate with the owner, engineer, general contractor and construction manager.

8.2. Hazard Analysis. At the initiation of the construction project, a hazard analysis shall be conducted to provide a safe and healthful workplace.

14. Owner's Representative.

14.1. The owner's designated safety representative shall review with the owner the project's organizational hierarchy to ensure continuity and consistency and accountability for safety, including the implementation and effectiveness of the contractor's safety and health efforts.

14.2. The owner's designated safety representative shall conduct frequent and regular reviews of the project to evaluate the effectiveness and the implementation of the project safety and health plan.

14.3. Non-compliance with safety programs and plans that create or could create hazardous conditions shall be corrected.

AMERICAN NATIONAL STANDARD A10.33-2011

PRE-WORK PLANNING

1. Project Survey:

1.1 Project Site Visit ____________ Initial & Date

1.2 Review Drawings ____________ Initial & Date

1.3 Meet with Project Team ____________ Initial & Date

2. Hazard Analysis:

Potential Hazard	Preventative Action	Responsible Supervisor
2.1		
2.2		
2.3		
2.4		
2.5		
2.6		
2.7		
2.8		
2.9		
2.10		

3. Pre-Phase Planning Meeting: Supervisor Attendance List

3.1 ____________

3.2 ____________

3.3 ____________

3.4 ____________

3.5 ____________

3.6 ____________

3.7 ____________

3.8 ____________

3.9 ____________

3.10 ____________

AMERICAN NATIONAL STANDARD A10.33-2011

APPENDIX B: (This Appendix is not a part of American National Standard A10.33, but is included for informational purposes only.)

JOB HAZARD ANALYSIS (ACTIVITY HAZARD ANALYSIS)

1. Scope.
This suggested procedure will outline the purpose for job hazard analysis for safe work operations and the method of pre-phase planning.

2. Purpose.
Accident prevention preplanning identifies hazards that are likely to occur during construction and makes sure that each contractor performing an operation will have the necessary material and equipment on hand when needed. Due to the speed at which construction jobs proceed, time does not allow a single operation to continue long enough to become safe through trial and error. Pre-phase planning will enable the contractor to anticipate the hazards and develop an appropriate plan to prevent accidents.

3. Responsibility.
It will be the responsibility of an individual designated by the project constructor to ensure that pre-phase job hazard analyses are conducted for work operations and activities performed by the contractors.

a) Pre-phase job hazard analysis should be developed by the contractor field supervisory personnel who will actually be running the job that is being preplanned. The attached job hazard analysis form can be used for this analysis.
b) The project constructor should consult and coordinate with project contractors in the preparation of pre-phase plans to ensure their acceptability. In addition, the plans should be reviewed and updated at reasonable periods of time to reflect changes in hazards and job conditions.

4. Pre-Phase Meeting.
After the contractors have completed their necessary preparations and have a pre-phase job hazard analysis written out on the attached form or another acceptable form, the contractors should call a pre-phase meeting. This meeting should be attended by the contractors submitting the plans, the project constructor and the senior contractor supervisors responsible for that particular phase of work.

Copies of the written plan should be distributed to all persons present, and the originator of the plan should explain each item and allow time for comments from all present. When appropriate, employees involved with these operations should be consulted. After the final decision to accept the plan as written or revise the submitted plan, it should be discussed with the employees who will perform the work. Under no circumstances should work be allowed to begin without first going through this procedure and having the job hazard analysis approved by the project constructor.

4. American National Standard for Construction and Demolition Operations—Pre-Project and Pre-Task Safety and Health Planning, ANSI A10.1

3.3. **Construction Owner.** The entity or entities who contract with a project constructor to perform construction or demolition work.

4. **Construction Owner's—Pre-Project Safety and Health Planning:**

4.1. **General Responsibilities in Safety and Health Planning**

4.1.1. The construction owner shall ensure that project specific expectations, goals and policies for safety and health are established for the project.

4.1.2. The construction owner shall ensure that the project specific safety and health policies are implemented by the project constructor and evaluated for necessary changes throughout project construction.

4.1.2. Throughout the design phase of the project, the construction owner shall provide leadership and maintain a decision making policy to enhance worker safety and health on the project.

4.2.2. The construction owner shall ensure safety and health design specifications are established and incorporated into the appropriate contract documents.

4.2.3. The construction owner shall ensure all safety and health design specifications and information on any remaining identified risks are provided to the project constructor in a pre-project meeting.

4.2.4. The construction owner shall require the project constructor to become familiar with the project safety and health design specifications, and convey the specification requirements to all contractors and other project personnel.

4.2.6. The construction owner shall ensure that sufficient time and resources are made available for pre-project safety and health planning.

4.3.1. The construction owner shall establish and implement an evaluation process that measures the safety and health performance of project constructor candidates.

4.3.3. The construction owner shall require project constructor candidates to submit an operational plan and their company safety and health program.

4.3.3.1. The plans and programs shall be evaluated as part of the project constructor selection process.

5. National Safety Council

The National Safety Council, chartered by Congress in 1953, is the nation's leading advocate for worker safety and health. It is comprised of approximately

37,000 members of major corporations and representatives of government, labor and the insurance industry. It has been giving guidance to business owners through many manuals and documents for close to 100 years. They have been giving guidance in their *Accident Prevention Manual* since 1946.

Accident Prevention Manual for Industrial Operations:

The National Safety Council is considered by construction safety management professionals as a highly authoritative source for guidance in safety matters. In Chapter 2 of their ACCIDENT PREVENTION MANUAL FOR INDUSTRIAL OPERATIONS, it sets forth guidelines for controlling hazards in the construction industry. It gives guidance to industrial owners of construction projects relative to reasonable steps that they can take to prevent contractor worker injury. In their Manual, they point out:

- The importance of insisting upon contractor compliance with all safety and health regulations.
- The need for advanced analyses and planning for safety.
- The need for a preconstruction safety conference.
- The need for periodic safety meetings during which plans are made for anticipating hazards associated with work so that controls can be put in place before the hazard evolves.

Essential to the principles established by the National Safety Council is the principle that all accidents are foreseeable, predictable, avoidable and preventable. Construction safety management should be proactive rather than reactive. That is, plans should be made to predict the hazards and to install the controls before the hazard evolves. This is a proactive approach. It is far more dependable than a reactive approach which would depend upon safety inspection to identify the hazard. Serious injury or death could result before the hazard is identified through safety inspection.

The National Safety Council further points out the importance of "assignment of responsibility" and "accountability" as key elements in a construction safety management program.

Core Safety Materials for the Construction Professional

A Manual entitled "Core Safety Materials for the Construction Professional" has been prepared by the National Safety Council's Construction Division. In it, it gives guidance regarding the elements of an effective construction site-specific safety plan:

> Introduction: An effective safety plan should get its start during the bid process. The owner should require the development of a pre-construction analysis by

all successful bidders. The general contractor/project management team should take the lead in the developing process. All subcontractors—both first and second tier subs—should be invited to an initial meeting and encouraged to participate in the process.

Construction Management Responsibility:

a. Plan safety into the project.
    1. Comply with owner's safety requirements and local, state and federal regulations.
    2. Establish minimum safety history requirements (e.g. last five years, EMRs, OSHA inspection history, etc.) for all project contractors.
    3. Investigate, and pre-qualify as acceptable bidders, contractors who meet the pre-determined safety history requirements.
    4. Establish and incorporate into contract documents the requirement for a Project Specific Safety and Health Plan to include:
        a. Construction process plan.
        b. Hazard analysis.
        c. Permit system.
        d. Designated project safety coordinator/administrator.

This document goes on to give guidance with regard to owners, general contractors, construction managers and contractors which is essentially the same as all of the other industry standards and authorities.

6. American Society of Safety Engineers—Construction Safety Management and Engineering

In this Manual published in 2004 the American Society of Safety Engineers gives guidance to business owners, general contractors, construction managers and contractors relative to reasonable steps that they can and should take to prevent contractor worker injury and death and to save money. In Chapter 2, they set forth the essential elements of a construction safety program. The role and responsibilities of the project owner, general contractor, construction manager and contractor are essentially the same as those recognized by all the owner industry safety authorities indicated in this report. They point out the importance of planning, monitoring and taking reasonable steps to ensure that contract workers have a workplace free of recognized hazards, that is, in compliance with OSHA regulations.

With regard to the owner's responsibility, they indicate the following:

> Owners can, and do, successfully influence construction job safety. The degree to which owners should involve themselves in the process should be based on the cost, benefits, and risks involved . . . Owners must ensure that contractors recognize and conform to their contractual responsibilities to perform safely

> . . . Owners must recognize and honor the moral and legal obligations to provide a safe work environment to minimize injuries. Owners have, in addition to their moral and legal obligations, an economic incentive to help reduce the number of accidents that occur on their construction projects . . . Owners cannot maintain a completely hands off policy toward construction activity . . . Owners must recognize the principles of management control commonly apply to costs, schedules, quality and productivity are equally applicable to safety and that if properly used, will improve safety performance.

The American Society of Safety Engineers also points out the importance of training. They state the following:

> Each new project should develop its own safety training program . . . Making sure the contractor employees are trained before they are allowed to work on the job site is the best way that the general contractor has of ensuring that all employees on the site have received at least the minimum training required. When developing a project specific training program, a job hazard analysis must be conducted to determine the needs of the training.

7. American Society of Civil Engineers

a. **Policy Statement 350 on Construction Site Safety** (adopted by the Board of Directors on July 25, 1998):

The American Society of Civil Engineers (ASCE) believes improving construction site safety requires attention and commitments from all parties involved. It is the ASCE's policy that:

Safety issues be addressed for each project on a project-specific basis.

Role of Owner:

- Assigning overall project safety responsibility and authority to a specific organization or individual.
- Including prior safety performance as a criterion for contractor selection.
- Designating an individual or organization to monitor safety performance during construction and have the responsibility for developing a coordinated project safety plan.
- Designating in contract documents responsibility for final approval of shop drawings and details.

ASCE believes that site safety responsibilities should be assigned to the general contractor, construction manager, or other organization with the required expertise and resources, who is in control of the project site.

Effective improvements in construction site safety can be achieved through a committed, cooperative relationship between owners, contractors, subcontractors, construction managers, . . .

b. **Quality in the Constructed Project—A Guide for Owners, Designers and Constructors** (ASCE Manuals and Reports on Engineering Practice No. 73)

The American Society of Civil Engineers published this document in response to a catastrophic construction accident at the Kansas City Regency in 1981 which killed 114 people and injured 185 people. The ASCE agreed to develop and publish a comprehensive guide for quality in design and construction to prevent injury. The following is taken from that document.

The owner takes an active role in promoting site safety by assigning overall project safety responsibility and authority to a specific organization or individual (often the constructor) that is qualified in construction safety principles, rules and practices appropriate for the particular project (see ASCE Policy Statement 350 "Construction Site Safety").

Typical requirements for the owner—addressing of environmental, health, permitting, **safety** (emphasis added), user impact, and sustainable development considerations.

- Owner is responsible for compliance with applicable laws, regulations, codes, standards, and practices.

Owner should support the constructor by following the plan themselves . . . Construction safety plans may include the following:

- Clearly posted safety rules, inspection procedures, and enforcement action.
- Safety training sessions.
- Safety certification of equipment, operators, and personnel entering the construction site.
- Personal safety equipment.

Safety on the construction site is a critical responsibility of the owner.

Risk Liability and Handling Conflicts: Responsibility of Owner

- Evaluate project risks
- Address risks in contractual agreements
- Reduce risks by ensuring contract performance

Chapter 23: Risk, Liability, and Handling Conflict: Typical Responsibilities

Responsibility ↓	*Owner*	*Design Professional**	*Constructor**	*Design-Builder*
Evaluate project risks	•	•	•	•
Evaluate other team members	•	•	•	•
Address risk in contractual agreements	•	•	•	•
Reduce risk by ensuring contract performance	•	•	•	•
Assess insurance requirements	•	•	•	•
Use bonds and warranties when appropriate to ensure performance	•	•	•	
Evaluate liability	•	•	•	•
Establish conflict resolution procedures (contracts, partnering agreements, ADR)	•	○	○	○

*For design-bid-build situation. In a design-build situation, the Design Professional and Constructor are part of the Design-Builder team.
• = Primary Responsibility ○ = Assist or Advise

DEPOSITION OF CPO MOST KNOWLEDGEABLE ABOUT SAFETY POLICY

There is essential agreement by industry authorities relative to the role of the CPO to take reasonable steps to hire safe contractors and to ensure implementation of the project safety program by the GC/CM or contractor.

The following are proposed questions for the person most knowledgeable about the CPO's safety policy.

1. Before working for the defendant company, had you ever worked for a company that had established procedures to oversee a construction project to ensure that the GC/CM or contractors implemented a safety program?
2. If so, what companies had you worked for?
3. For each company, ask him or her to list the specific safety management tasks that he/she was required to perform.
4. Is it your company's policy to hire safe contractors?
5. What does your company do to ensure that they hire safe contractors?
6. Regarding this project, did your company have a policy to ensure that the GC/CMs or contractors complied with the contract?

7. Regarding this project, did your company have a policy to ensure that the GC/CMs or contractors complied with the contract regarding safety responsibility?
8. What is that policy?
9. What specific steps are your company representatives required to take in order to ensure that the contractors work safely and in compliance with the contract?
10. Did your company policy require the GC/CMs and contractors at this site to implement safety programs?
11. Tell me all of the steps that your company representatives are responsible to take to ensure implementation of the job site safety program by the GC/CM.
12. Did your company policy require GC/CMs and contractors to submit safety programs to anyone in your company for review?
13. Did your company policy require any representative of your company to attend a pre-job safety conference to identify hazards and controls before work began?
14. Is it your company policy to monitor the work site to ensure that GC/CMs and contractors are implementing their safety programs?
15. Is it your company policy to perform periodic safety inspections?
16. If so, how frequently?
17. Is it your company's policy to require contractors to hold safety meetings?
18. Is it your company policy to attend safety meetings?
19. Prior to this project, has your company ever hired other GC/CMs or contractors?
20. Approximately how many times?
21. What are some of the types of construction work that has been performed for your company?
22. Did your company have the same policy then as for this project?
23. Were you assigned any safety management tasks for this project?
24. What tasks?
25. Is it your company's policy for representatives with safety management tasks to have their safety performance evaluated?
26. Do you know if there are any written evaluation reports related to the safety performance of any representatives of your company?
27. Has your safety performance ever been evaluated?
28. Have you ever evaluated anyone's safety performance?
29. Has your company ever been sued before because of contractor worker injury? Explain.
30. Before this deposition, did you give any thought as to what anybody in your company could have done before this incident occurred that would have prevented this injury?

31. Sitting here today, do you know if there was any possible way that somebody from your company could have done something that would have prevented this injury?
32. Have you ever been deposed before?
33. If so, explain.
34. According to your company policy, if you had seen the plaintiff in the moments before this incident exposed to this hazard, would you have been required to do anything?
35. Before this deposition, did you give any thought as to whether or not this exposure to a hazard was foreseeable?
36. Would it have been possible for exposure to this hazard to have been identified in a pre-job safety conference?
37. Was a pre-job safety conference held before the work involved in this incident was performed?
38. Do you know of anyone who anticipated worker exposure to this hazard before this incident occurred?
39. Is it your company's policy to investigate incidents of worker injury to learn how to prevent recurrences?
40. In this case, did your company investigate this incident?
41. If so, were any lessons learned?
42. Would it have been possible for you to have done anything that would have prevented this incident?

EVALUATION OF EXPERT'S METHODOLOGY OF EVALUATION IN NEW CONSTRUCTION CASES: DEFENDANT CONSTRUCTION PROJECT OWNER

The following are questions for the expert in cases where a corporation hires a GC/CM or contractor to perform **new construction**. These are not for cases of construction work done on the corporation's **premise**.

1. Do you know what I mean by the standard of care relative to construction worker injury prevention by a construction project owner (CPO), that is, a corporation or business owner, that hires a GC/CM or contractor to perform new construction work for them? If so, explain.
2. Do you know of any construction industry authorities that give guidance to CPOs who hire GC/CMs or contractors to perform new construction for them relative to safety management oversight that should be performed by the CPO?
3. Do you know what the National Safety Council is?

4. Do you know what the National Safety Council says with regard to a CPO who hires a GC/CM or contractor to perform new construction work for them?
5. Do you know what the Business Roundtable is? Note: The Business Roundtable is an association of the 200 largest corporations in America.
6. Do you know what the Business Roundtable says that a business owner such as the defendant should do with regard to safety management and injury prevention of contractor workers when they hire a GC/CM or contractor to perform new construction work for them?
7. Do you know what the American Society of Safety Engineers is?
8. Do you know what the American Society of Safety Engineers says that a business owner such as the defendant should do with regard to safety management and injury prevention of contractor workers when they hire a GC/CM or contractor to perform new construction work for them?
9. Do you know what the Construction Industry Institute is?
10. Do you know what the Construction Industry Institute says that a business owner such as the defendant should do with regard to safety management and injury prevention of contractor workers when they hire a GC/CM or contractor to perform new construction work for them?
11. Do you know what the American Society of Civil Engineers is?
12. Do you know what the American Society of Civil Engineers says that a business owner such as the defendant should do with regard to safety management and injury prevention of contractor workers when they hire a GC/CM or contractor to perform new construction work for them?
13. Do you know what the American National Standards Institute is?
14. Do you know of any American National Standards Institute standard that says what a business owner such as the defendant should do with regard to safety management and injury prevention of contractor workers when they hire a GC/CM or contractor to perform new construction work for them?
15. Did you ever perform an evaluation of a CPO by evaluating whether or not the CPO complied with the steps that the National Safety Council says a CPO should take to prevent contractor worker injury?
16. Did you ever perform an evaluation of a CPO by evaluating whether or not the CPO complied with the steps that the Business Roundtable says a CPO should take to prevent contractor worker injury?
17. Did you ever perform an evaluation of a CPO by evaluating whether or not the CPO complied with the steps that the American Society of Safety Engineers says a CPO should take to prevent contractor worker injury?
18. Did you ever perform an evaluation of a CPO by evaluating whether or not the CPO complied with the steps that the Construction Industry Institute says a CPO should take to prevent contractor worker injury?

19. Did you ever perform an evaluation of a CPO by evaluating whether or not the CPO complied with the steps that the American Society of Civil Engineers says a CPO should take to prevent contractor worker injury?
20. Did you ever perform an evaluation of a CPO by evaluating whether or not the CPO complied with the steps that the American National Standards Institute says a CPO should take to prevent contractor worker injury?
21. In this case, did you perform your evaluation by considering what the National Safety Council says that a CPO should do regarding injury prevention of contractor workers when they hire GC/CMs or contractors to perform work for them?
22. If so, what did you find? If not, why not?
23. In this case, did you perform your evaluation by considering what the Business Roundtable says that a CPO should do regarding injury prevention of contractor workers when they hire GC/CMs or contractors to perform work for them?
24. In this case, did you perform your evaluation by considering what the American Society of Safety Engineers says that a CPO should do regarding injury prevention of contractor workers when they hire GC/CMs or contractors to perform work for them?
25. In this case, did you perform your evaluation by considering what the Construction Industry Institute says that a CPO should do regarding injury prevention of contractor workers when they hire GC/CMs or contractors to perform work for them?
26. In this case, did you perform your evaluation by considering what the American Society of Civil Engineers says that a CPO should do regarding injury prevention of contractor workers when they hire GC/CMs or contractors to perform work for them?
27. In this case, did you perform your evaluation by considering what the American National Standards Institute says that a CPO should do regarding injury prevention of contractor workers when they hire GC/CMs or contractors to perform work for them?
28. Have you ever heard of any "principles of construction safety management"?
29. Do you know what principles are?

    Answer: Principles are fundamental beliefs within a particular society. The following are some construction safety management principles. The industry safety literature is permeated with fundamental agreement with these principles.

    - *Safety begins at the top.*
    - *A proactive rather than a reactive approach is best.*

- *Assigning specific responsibility and holding people accountable are key to successful management.*
- *Planning is of the essence.*
- *Accidents are foreseeable and predictable.*
- *Safety pays.*

30. You could ask the expert to explain each principle and ask if he/she agrees with those principles and practices.
31. Did you apply any principles of safety management in your evaluation of the defendant's conduct in this case? If so, explain each.
32. In your opinion, should a CPO such as the defendant company have written policies regarding the role of the CPO relative to safety management oversight of the GC/CMs or contractor that they hire?
33. In your experience, have you ever come across a CPO, that is, a corporation or business owner, that had a policy to require the GC/CM or contractor to implement construction safety programs?
34. If so, what steps did the CPO take relative to safety management?
35. In your experience, do CPOs normally require the GC/CM or contractor to implement construction safety programs?
36. Do CPOs normally require GC/CMs to implement safety programs by putting that requirement in the contract?
37. In your experience, do CPOs customarily take steps to see that the contract is complied with?
38. In this case, can you list for me all of the steps that the CPO took to ensure that the GC/CM or contractor performed their work safely in compliance with the contract?
39. In your opinion, should a CPO take reasonable steps to hire safe contractors?
40. Are you familiar with any industry authorities that give guidance relative to steps to take to ensure that a CPO hires safe contractors?
41. In this case, did the CPO do anything to ensure that the GC/CM that they hired were safe contractors?
42. In the past, have you ever come across a CPO that had a project manager or contract liaison assigned to a construction project?
43. In the past, have you ever known of a project manager or contract liaison of a CPO who took any steps to ensure that a job site safety and health program was being implemented by a GC/CM?
44. Have you ever come across a CPO who employed or hired a safety manager to oversee their construction project?
45. Have you ever come across a CPO that monitored the construction site to see that the GC/CM or contractor was implementing the job site safety program?

46. Have you ever come across a CPO who performed safety inspections on their construction project?
47. In this case, did the defendant have anyone assigned to oversee the project to ensure that the GC/CM or contractor was implementing the job site safety program?
48. Did a CPO representative do anything to ensure that pre-planning took place?
49. Did a CPO representative attend safety meetings?
50. Did a CPO representative monitor to ensure that the work was being done safely?
51. Would it have been possible for this injury to have been prevented?
52. Would it have been possible for a representative of the CPO to have done anything that would have prevented this incident?

DISCOVERY REQUESTS

1. Copy of the written safety and health policy and program.
2. Copy of the contractor safety program.
3. Copy of the pre-job safety conference meeting minutes.
4. Copy of all safety inspections reports.
5. Copy of minutes from all safety meetings.
6. Copy of job description of contract liaison representative of CPO.
7. Copy of incident investigation report.
8. Copy of all documents related to this project.

NOTES

1. *Improving Construction Safety Performance—A Construction Industry Cost Effectiveness Project Report* A-3, January 1982, Business Roundtable.

2. In this context, the Business Roundtable is referring to the Business Owner/Corporation who contracts to have construction work performed for them. Their research was related to the Business Owner/Corporation. They make no distinction relative to landlord or landowner.

Chapter Fifteen

Premise Owner/Host Employer—Standard of Care

There is an accepted Standard of Care relative to the reasonable steps that a corporation should take to prevent injury to Contract Workers and other Non-Employees who perform work on its premise. This chapter is related to the role of the corporation that does business in the building where the incident occurred. It is not related to the role of the corporation that hires a GC/CM to build a new building. It is not related to the responsibility of the landlord or land owner (LL/LO). The LL/LO may have the responsibility to ensure that the building itself is maintained in a reasonably safe manner, depending upon its contract with the lessor. However, there is no industry safety standard that applies to the entity that simply holds the title of the building or the land regarding the safety of construction workers and other invitees who perform work within that building. However, there is a standard of care related to the corporation that hires contractors or other non-employees to perform work on its premise.

The corporation that hires the contractor or other non-employee to perform work on its premise could be called a premise owner or host employer (PO/HE). Under OSHA's Multi-Employer Citation Policy, the PO/HE would likely be a controlling employer. Contractors and other non-employees who could perform work on a corporation's premise include all construction contractors as well as truck drivers, security workers, maintenance workers, landscapers, janitors, temporary workers and all business invitees. The safe practices or standards for contractors and non-employees who work on the PO/HE premise have been established by the highest industry safety authorities in the United States. The responsibility for **construction workers** will be considered first. Then the corporation's responsibility for other **non-employees** will be considered.

STANDARD OF CARE FOR INJURY PREVENTION OF CONTRACTOR WORKERS

For decades, business owners and executives (corporations) have recognized their responsibility to take reasonable steps to prevent injury, disease and death to people invited to be on their premise to work. Those industry safety authorities that demonstrate that business owners and executives (corporations) **care** about injury prevention of contractor workers have standardized methods to manage safety and prevent injury to others on their premise are:

- The Business Roundtable
- The National Safety Council
- The American Society of Safety Engineers
- American Society of Civil Engineers
- American National Standards Institute
- Others

1. The Business Roundtable

The Business Roundtable is an association of the largest 200 corporations in the United States. In 1980, it contracted with Stanford University, Department of Civil Engineering, to perform research to identify the best methods to ensure safe performance by contractors on an owner's premise and during new construction. Study Team Members and Owners interviewed were drawn from a wide variety of industries. They published their conclusions in a document entitled **Improving Construction Safety Performance: A Construction Industry Cost Effectiveness Project Report.** They published this report to disseminate it to members and to owners and industry throughout the United States. Over 100,000 copies of their summary report has been distributed to owners and contractors throughout the United States. As a result of this research, Stanford University researchers also wrote a book entitled *Construction Safety Mangement* published in 1987 by McGraw-Hill, Inc. They published this book to further advise business owners and corporate representatives of the benefits of controlling construction costs by managing safety to prevent contractor worker injury.

Some relevant quotes from their summary report are:

> Owners have long recognized and honored the moral obligation to provide a safe work environment to minimize injuries. The primary purpose of this study report is to demonstrate that owners have, in addition to their moral commitment, an economic incentive to help reduce the number of accidents that occur on their construction projects . . . Owners should recognize that the principles

of management control commonly applied to costs, schedules, quality and productivity are equally applicable to safety in that, if used, will improve safety performance. By showing more concern for construction safety, owners can help reduce injuries and loss of life and the billions of dollars needlessly wasted by construction accidents . . . This study calls upon owners to be concerned and involved in construction-contractor safety performance. In addition to the humanitarian reasons for preventing personal injury and loss of life, increased attention to safety and health is essential to the long-term economic health of the construction industry. An effective construction-safety program will result in lower job costs . . . This study was conducted by a team of nine men who have responsibility in the area of safety and health and who represent industrial owners, construction contractors, and the insurance industry. The recommendations of this report are intended to establish the supportive role required of owners in the effort to improve construction safety performance.

Owners should:

- Be prepared to financially support contractors' efforts to ensure an effective safety program.
- Realize that merely adopting a safety program will not yield the desired results without a serious and persistent management commitment.
- Recognize that the principles of management control commonly applied to costs, schedules, quality and productivity are equally applicable to safety in that, when used, they will improve safety performance.
- Explain to the contractor prior to the bidding process what is expected regarding safety performance.
- Become more directly involved in the safety activities of their construction project and take proper measures to achieve better safety performance such as:
    - Provide safety and health guidelines that the contractor must follow.
    - Require a formal site safety program.
    - Discuss safety at owner-contractor meetings.
    - Conduct safety audits during construction.
- Function with the contractor as a cohesive safety team during the planning and execution of the construction project.
- Establish the contractor lines of communication at all levels so that safe work practices are understood by both parties.

2. The National Safety Council

The National Safety Council is considered by industrial safety management professionals as a highly authoritative source for guidance in safety matters. In Chapter 2 of their ACCIDENT PREVENTION MANUAL FOR INDUSTRIAL OPERATIONS, they set forth guidelines for controlling hazards in the construction industry. In their Manual, they point out:

- The importance of insisting upon contractor compliance with all safety and health regulations.
- The need for advanced analyses and planning for safety.
- The need for a preconstruction safety conference.
- The need for periodic safety meetings during which plans are made for anticipating hazards associated with work so that controls can be put in place before the hazard evolves.

Essential to the principles established by the National Safety Council is the principle that all accidents are foreseeable, predictable, avoidable and preventable. Industrial safety management should be proactive rather than reactive. That is, plans should be made to predict the hazards and to install the controls before the hazard evolves. This is a proactive approach. It is far more dependable than a reactive approach which would depend upon safety inspection to identify the hazard. Serious injury or death could result before the hazard is identified through safety inspection.

The National Safety Council further points out the importance of "assignment of responsibility" and "accountability" as key elements in a construction safety management program.

3. American Society of Safety Engineers

Construction Safety Management and Engineering

In this Manual published in 2004 the American Society of Safety Engineers gives guidance to business owners, general contractors, construction managers and contractors relative to reasonable steps that they can and should take to prevent contractor worker injury and death and to save money. In Chapter 2, they set forth the essential elements of a construction safety program. The role and responsibilities of the project owner, general contractor, construction manager and contractor are essentially the same as those recognized by all the owner industry safety authorities indicated in this report. They point out the importance of planning, monitoring and taking reasonable steps to ensure that contract workers have a workplace free of recognized hazards, that is, in compliance with OSHA regulations.

With regard to the owner's responsibility, they indicate the following:

> Owners can, and do, successfully influence construction job safety. The degree to which owners should involve themselves in the process should be based on the cost, benefits, and risks involved . . . Owners must ensure that contractors recognize and conform to their contractual responsibilities to perform safely . . . Owners must recognize and honor the moral and legal obligations to pro-

vide a safe work environment to minimize injuries. Owners have, in addition to their moral and legal obligations, an economic incentive to help reduce the number of accidents that occur on their construction projects . . . Owners cannot maintain a completely hands off policy toward construction activity . . . Owners must recognize the principles of management control commonly apply to costs, schedules, quality and productivity are equally applicable to safety and that if properly used, will improve safety performance.

4. American Society of Civil Engineers

Policy Statement 350 on Construction Site Safety adopted by the Board of Directors on July 25, 1998:

The American Society of Civil Engineers (ASCE) believes improving construction site safety requires attention and commitments from all parties involved. It is the ASCE's policy that:

Safety issues be addressed for each project on a project-specific basis.

Role of Owner:

- Assigning overall project safety responsibility and authority to a specific organization or individual.
- Including prior safety performance as a criterion for contractor selection.
- Designating an individual or organization to monitor safety performance during construction and have the responsibility for developing a coordinated project safety plan.
- Designating in contract documents responsibility for final approval of shop drawings and details.

ASCE believes that site safety responsibilities should be assigned to the general contractor, construction manager, or other organization with the required expertise and resources, who is in control of the project site.

Effective improvements in construction site safety can be achieved through a committed, cooperative relationship between owners, contractors, subcontractors, [and] construction managers.

5. American National Standards Institute ANSI/AIHA Z10-2005—Standard for Occupational Health and Safety Management Systems

This national consensus standard was promulgated from input from representatives of many manufacturing industries, insurance representatives, employer associations, the National Safety Council, OSHA and international unions. It defines the minimum requirements for occupational health and safety management systems (OHSMS). It requires companies, corporations, firms and enterprises to establish and implement occupational safety and health programs. It requires assignment of responsibility and accountability as well as other important elements. Relative to contractor safety, it states at 5.1.4. the following:

> **Contractors**. The organization shall establish and implement processes to identify, evaluate and control potential health and safety risks:
>
> A. To the organization's employees from contractor's planned and unplanned activities, operations, and materials on the organization's premise; and,
> B. To the contractor's employees from the organization's activities and operations.
>
> This process shall include appropriate contractor health and safety performance criteria. On multi-employer work sites, the organization shall implement a process for coordinating the relevant portions of its OHSMS with that of other applicable organizations.
>
> Plant contractors may include maintenance, construction, operations, security, landscaping, facility upkeep, janitorial, and a number of other functions. Organizations have a variety of tools for managing contractor health and safety performance, including contract award mechanisms or pre-qualification criteria which considers past health and safety performance, safety training, or health and safety capabilities, as well as direct contract requirements . . . The degree of coordination should depend on factors such as the terms of the contract, the nature of the hazards and risks, the type and size of the operation, and the duration of the work on the site.

The following are other references which show that business executives and owners recognize their responsibility to take reasonable steps to prevent injury performed by contractors on their premise.

1. **Owners Own Up to Contractors' Safety** by Phillip Britt, December 1993, *Safety and Health Magazine* of the National Safety Council. Mr. Britt likewise sets forth the notion that the owner is responsible to manage safety to prevent injury to contractors. He states: "Companies and OSHA agree that companies and contractors benefit most when they work together to promote safety." He quotes the National Safety Council, Health and Safety Management Services' Director, Jim Kaletta as saying: "As companies improve their overall safety and ensure that contracting exposures are controlled, it pays off. It improves their bottom line." This article gives other examples of business owners who have established contractor safety programs to select safe contractors and to monitor their work.
2. **Contractor Safety** by James Roughton published January 1995 in the Journal of the American Society of Safety Engineers, *Professional Safety*. This author gives guidance as previous references. For example, he states:

"Once a responsible contractor has been selected, its management must be held accountable for compliance with safety, health and emergency reporting and response procedures . . . Facility and contractor management must work cooperatively to identify various training needs. Facility management must have a strong presence in this process." He goes on to talk about other specific means to monitor and ensure that the work done by contractors is done safely.

3. **Developing and Implementing a Contractor Safety Program** by Carl Huckaby published August 1994 in the Journal of the American Society of Safety Engineers, *Professional Safety*. This article, like the other references, sets forth specific methods that the owner should take to ensure that workers are not exposed to dangers while working on their premise.
4. **The Importance of Contractor Safety** by James Counts, Ph.D., June 1997, *Occupational Safety and Health Magazine*. Dr. Counts's article points out the responsibility of the host employer relative to safety management. He also talks about the need to select safe contractors and to monitor their work practices and insist upon safe work.
5. **A Construction Safety Program** by Richard Hislop which appeared in the Journal of the American Society of Safety Engineers, *Professional Safety*, September 1991. He too talks about the importance of managing the safety of the contractor. He states, for instance: "Program implementation, operation and monitoring responsibility must be clearly defined at the onset of construction activities . . . The concept also recognizes client's ultimate responsibility for ensuring that all individuals on the site comply with the environmental safety and health program and legal requirements. This responsibility includes continuing oversight function and prerogative to immediately halt subcontractor operation posing serious risk to employees, the public or the environment." He points to OSHA at 1926.16(a) which states that the "prime contractor" cannot be relieved of overall responsibility. He points to 1926.16(c) with respect to the prime contractor and the subcontractors having joint responsibility. He states: "This language is borne out of long-established industry practice as it relates to the hierarchy of controls on construction worksites and in construction with evolving OSHA review comments and civil case law. Who better than the party with 'purse strings authority' can affect compliance with contract provisions for safety and health."

He also states: "Owners ultimately pay for losses on job sites. Following good management practices, owners should oversee subcontractor activities to ensure they too are applying good management and safe work practices . . . Proactively developing a sound program and sensible documentation is by far a better posture than a defensive one."

6. **Specifying Safety in Construction Contracts**, *National Safety Council News*, April 1965. In this article, the National Safety Council points out that Dupont is an example of a conscientious employer who has established a program to manage the safety of contractors on their premise. They point out the language in Dupont's contracts and Dupont's safety philosophy. One example of Dupont's philosophy in 1965 relative to this question is indicated: "An acceptance of the fact that it is good business from the standpoint of both efficiency and economy to prevent personal injuries . . . A conviction that it is reasonably possible to safeguard all construction and operating exposures which may result in occupational personal injury."

   For decades, Dupont has been selling a Contractor Safety Program including manuals and videotapes to industry.

7. **Liability, OSHA and the Safety of Outside Contractors** by Vincent A. Gallagher, *Professional Safety*, January 1993. In this article, Gallagher points out that the need for an owner to be proactive and intimately involved in the safety management of outside contractors is nothing new to safety professionals. Safety authorities are referenced in this regard. There are 32,000 members of the American Society of Safety Engineers who read this Journal. None wrote to the Editor to disagree with anything in this article.
8. **Construction Safety: What Every Business Owner Should Know** by Robert Derocher, August 1998, published in *Health and Safety*, a magazine of the National Safety Council. Mr. Derocher likewise points out the need for the business owner to take reasonable steps to ensure that work performed by contractors is done safely.
9. **Ensure Contractor Safety**, R and D Section, National Safety Council Newsletter March/April, 1992. In this article, the National Safety Council again points out the need to select safe contractors, hold pre-job safety conferences, plan for safety and to monitor to ensure the work is done safely.
10. **Who Is Responsible for Construction Site Safety** by Richard Hislop, which appeared in *Professional Safety*, February 1998. Mr. Hislop likewise indicates the need for the owner to establish contractor safety programs, to select safe contractors, to monitor contractor work, etc.
11. **OSHA's Voluntary Protection Program: A Safety Management Approach for the Nineties** by Frank Burg, *Professional Safety*, July 1991. Mr. Burg likewise points out the need for the host employer to establish a contractor safety program.
12. **Understanding Risk Management** by Harry Borowka, *Occupational Hazards*, November 1991. Mr. Borowka also points out the need for the

owner to ensure the safety of outside contractors' work performed on their premise.

13. **Contractor's Handbook Eases Exchange and Enforcement of Plant Safety Policies** by Jack Daugherty, P.E., *Occupational Health and Safety Magazine*, September 1992. Mr. Daugherty points out the need to establish plant safety and health policies relative to contractors' safe work and to ensure that these policies are given to contractors.
14. The American Petroleum Institute and the Chemical Manufacturers Association published **Improving Owner and Contractor Safety Performance** in September 1991. It gives guidance to the chemical and petrochemical industries relative to principles and practices of injury prevention almost identical to those set forth by the Business Roundtable.

STANDARD OF CARE FOR INJURY PREVENTION OF NON-EMPLOYEES

For several decades, the National Safety Council has been giving guidance to premise owners/corporations relative to reasonable steps that they should take to prevent injury of **non-employees** who perform work on its premise. In 1991, they published their Data Sheet 745 entitled "Safety Considerations for Contractors and Other Non-Employees on Premises." This Data Sheet gives guidance to corporations to establish programs to ensure the safety of business invitees on their premise. The National Safety Council's *Accident Prevention Manual*, 12th Edition, Chapter 25 entitled "Contractor and Non-Employee Safety" also gives guidance regarding non-employee safety:

> Contractor and non-employee safety affect the company's operations, employees and the products or services they perform or sell . . . A company must ensure that its loss control plans include preventing contractor and non-employee incidents or illnesses. Today, many companies hire outside contractors to perform a variety of tasks such as maintenance and repair, clerical duties, construction, computer installation and training. Based on the "General Duty" Clause of the OSHA Act and the 1993 regulation concerning contractor safety performance, employers have a responsibility for the safety of outside employees who either work on the employer's premise or who are sent off site on the employer's business . . . More employers are accepting responsibility not only for the safety performance of their own workers but for the improved safety performance of outside contractors they hire . . . Research shows that concerned employers can do a great deal to improve the on-the-job safety performance of outside workers.

The National Safety Council points out the need for the premise owner to implement an occupational safety and health program for its workers as well as all invited persons including customers, contractors and other non-employees. The customary safe practice is for the employer's safety program to include a section devoted to the management role of the corporate representatives relative to ensuring that contractor and other non-employees performing work on the premise do so safely. The types of non-employees who are invited to the premise owner's business include truck drivers, contract workers, maintenance workers, temporary help, cafeteria workers, and so on. Non-employees work in the same environment as the host employees. The premise owner/host employer should take reasonable steps to ensure that its workers are not injured by outside employees and that outside employees work safely and do not expose its employees to hazards. The National Safety Council has given guidance relative to ensuring that outside workers perform their work safely since at least the publication of their *Accident Prevention Manual*, 6th Edition in 1969.

WRITTEN POLICY FOR CONTRACTORS AND NON-EMPLOYEES PERFORMING WORK ON PREMISE

The customary safe practice is for the corporation's safety program to include policies and procedures for the premise owner/host employer to take to ensure that contractors and non-employees are not exposed to hazards in their contractor safety program. The contractor safety program should require: hiring safe contractors, holding a pre-job safety conference, monitoring and ensuring that contractor and non-employees work safely and in compliance with OSHA.

The customary practice is to assign a liaison representative to attend the pre-job safety conference and to periodically monitor the work of contractors and non-employees. If the defendant does not turn over a copy of the contractor safety program in discovery, your expert can conclude that they do not have one and have therefore violated the customary industry practice of implementing a contractor safety program. Most mid and large size corporations customarily have written policies and procedures related to contractors and non-employees on their premise. They have policies and procedures that they give to the contractor to follow as well as written policies and procedures for host employer representatives to follow when overseeing the safety of the work performed by the contractor or other non-employees. They are often reluctant to turn them over in discovery. You should be persistent in ensuring that they turn them over or make it clear that they have no such documents. The following are questions which may be helpful when deposing the defendant representative most knowledgeable about the safety policies regarding outside contractors and workers.

DEPOSITION QUESTIONS FOR MOST KNOWLEDGEABLE PERSON REGARDING SAFETY POLICY IN PO/HE CASES INVOLVING CONTRACTORS AND NON-EMPLOYEES[1]

1. Before you worked for the defendant company, had you ever worked for a company that had safety policies and procedures for it to follow regarding safety management of contractors and non-employees who perform work on its premise?
2. If so, explain each company and what the safety policy and practice was.
3. Get his/her work history and all of the safety management tasks he/she or a company representative was required to perform relative to safety at all the other companies.
4. Tell me all of the things that your company policy requires your company representatives to do to ensure that contractors or other non-employees on your premise are not injured.
5. Regarding this project, did your company have a policy to ensure that the contractors complied with the contract regarding safety responsibility?
6. What is that policy?
7. What specific steps are your company representatives required to take in order to ensure that the contractors or non-employees work safely?
8. Did your company policy require the contractors at this site to implement safety programs?
9. Did your company policy require contractors to have a pre-job safety conference with representatives of your company to identify hazards and controls before work began?
10. Is it your company policy to monitor the work site to ensure that contractors and other non-employees are working safely?
11. If so, how frequently?
12. Is it your company's policy to require contractors to hold safety meetings?
13. Is it your company policy to attend the contractors' safety meetings?
14. Prior to this project, has your company ever hired other contractors?
15. Approximately how many times?
16. What are some of the types of construction work that has been performed for your company?
17. Were you assigned any safety management tasks for this project?
18. If so, what tasks?
19. Was anyone else at this site assigned safety management tasks?
20. If so, what tasks?
21. Is it your company's policy for representatives who are assigned safety management tasks regarding contractors and non-employees to have their safety performance evaluated?

22. Do you know if there are any written evaluation reports related to the safety performance of any representatives of your company?
23. Has your safety performance ever been evaluated?
24. Have you ever evaluated anyone's safety performance?
25. Has your company ever been sued before because a contractor worker or other non-employee was injured on your premise?
26. Before this deposition, did you give any thought as to what anybody in your company could have done before this incident occurred that would have prevented this injury?
27. Sitting here today, do you know if there was any possible way that somebody from your company could have done something that would have prevented this injury?
28. Have you ever been deposed before?
29. If so, explain.
30. According to your company policy, if you had seen the plaintiff in the moments before this incident exposed to this hazard, would you have been required to do anything?
31. Before this deposition, did you give any thought as to whether or not this exposure to a hazard was foreseeable?
32. Was a pre-job safety conference held before the work involved in this incident was performed?
33. Would it have been possible for exposure to this hazard to have been identified in a pre-job safety conference?
34. Do you know of anyone who anticipated worker exposure to this hazard before this incident occurred?
35. Is it your company's policy to investigate incidents of worker injury to learn how to prevent recurrences?
36. In this case, did your company investigate this incident?
37. If so, were any lessons learned?
38. Would it have been possible for you to have done anything that would have prevented this incident?
39. Does your company have a policy to evaluate the safety performance of contractors in order to use that information when deciding whether or not to hire that contractor in the future?

DEPOSITION OF DEFENSE EXPERT IN PO/HE CASES—CONTRACTOR AND NON-EMPLOYEE INJURY

The following questions are for an expert in cases where a corporation hires a contractor and other non-employees to perform work on its premise. The corporation could also be called a Business Owner, Premise Owner, Host Employer or Company. You could explain to the expert that the defendant could be called any one of these names. However, you are going to use the label Corporation for your questions.

1. Do you know what I mean by the standard of care for a corporation that hires a contractor or other non-employees to perform work on their premise? If so, explain.
2. Do you know of any industry authorities that give guidance to corporations such as the defendant company relative to safety management oversight of contractors or others that they hire to perform work on its premise?
3. Do you know what the National Safety Council is?
4. Do you know what the National Safety Council says with regard to a corporation that hires a contractor or other non-employees to perform on its premise? If so, explain.
5. Do you know what the Business Roundtable is?
6. Do you know what the Business Roundtable says that a corporation should do with regard to safety management and injury prevention of contract workers or others when they hire outside personnel to perform work on its premise? If so, explain.
7. Do you know what the American Society of Safety Engineers is?
8. Do you know what the American Society of Safety Engineers says that a corporation should do with regard to safety management and injury prevention of contract workers when they hire a contractor or others to perform work on its premise? If so, explain.
9. Do you know what the Construction Industry Institute is?
10. Do you know what the Construction Industry Institute says that a corporation should do with regard to safety management and injury prevention of contract workers when they hire a contractor or others to perform work on its premise? If so, explain.
11. Do you know what the American Society of Civil Engineers is?
12. Do you know what the American Society of Civil Engineers says that a corporation should do with regard to safety management and injury prevention of contract workers when they hire a contractor or others to perform work on its premise? If so, explain.
13. Do you know what the American National Standards Institute is?
14. Do you know what the American National Standards Institute says with regard to a corporation or business owner such as the defendant with regard to reasonable steps they should take to prevent injury to contractors or others who perform work on its premise? If so, explain.

15. Did you ever perform an evaluation of a corporation by evaluating whether or not the corporation complied with the steps that the National Safety Council says a corporation should take to prevent contract or other worker injury?
16. Did you ever perform an evaluation of a corporation by evaluating whether or not the corporation complied with the steps that the Business Roundtable says a corporation should take to prevent contract or other worker injury?
17. Did you ever perform an evaluation of a corporation by evaluating whether or not the corporation complied with the steps that the American Society of Safety Engineers says a corporation should take to prevent contract or other worker injury?
18. Did you ever perform an evaluation of a corporation by evaluating whether or not the corporation complied with the steps that the Construction Industry Institute says a corporation should take to prevent contract or other worker injury?
19. Did you ever perform an evaluation of a corporation by evaluating whether or not the corporation complied with the steps that the American Society of Civil Engineers says a corporation should take to prevent contract or other worker injury?
20. Did you ever perform an evaluation of a corporation by evaluating whether or not the corporation complied with the steps that the American National Standards Institute says a corporation should take to prevent contract or other worker injury?
21. In this case, did you perform your evaluation by considering what the National Safety Council says that a corporation should do regarding injury prevention of contractor workers when it hires contractors or others to perform work for them?
22. In this case, did you perform your evaluation by considering what the Business Roundtable says that a corporation should do regarding injury prevention of contractor workers when it hires contractors or others to perform work for them?
23. In this case, did you perform your evaluation by considering what the American Society of Safety Engineers says that a corporation should do regarding injury prevention of contractor workers when it hires contractors or others to perform work for them?
24. In this case, did you perform your evaluation by considering what the Construction Industry Institute says that a corporation should do regarding injury prevention of contractor workers when it hires contractors or others to perform work for them?

25. In this case, did you perform your evaluation by considering what the American Society of Civil Engineers says that a corporation should do regarding injury prevention of contractor workers when it hires contractors or others to perform work for them?
26. In this case, did you perform your evaluation by considering what any American National Standards Institute standard says that a corporation should do regarding injury prevention of contractor workers when it hires contractors or others to perform work for them?
27. Have you ever heard of any "principles of construction safety management"?
28. Do you know what principles are?

    Answer: Principles are fundamental beliefs within a particular society. The following are some construction safety management principles. The industry safety literature is permeated with fundamental agreement with these principles.

    - *Safety begins at the top.*
    - *A proactive rather than a reactive approach is best.*
    - *Assigning specific responsibility and holding people accountable are key to successful management.*
    - *Planning is of the essence.*
    - *Accidents are foreseeable and predictable.*
    - *Safety pays.*

29. You could ask the expert to explain each principle and ask if he/she agrees with those principles and practices.
30. Did you apply those principles in your evaluation of the defendant's conduct in this case? How? Explain each.
31. In your opinion, should a corporation have written policies regarding safety management of contractors or others that they hire to perform work on its premise?
32. In your experience, have you ever come across a corporation that had a policy to oversee the safety of contractors or others that it hires to perform work on its premise?
33. In your experience, do corporations normally have a policy to oversee the safety of contractors or others to ensure that the work performed on its premise is done safely?
34. Do corporations normally have a policy to require contractors or other non-employees to comply with OSHA in their contract?
35. In your experience, do corporations customarily take some steps to see that the contract with contractors and non-employees is complied with?

36. In this case, can you list for me all of the steps that the defendant corporation took to ensure that contractors or non-employees performed their work safely in compliance with the contract?
37. In your opinion, should a corporation take reasonable steps to hire safe contractors?
38. Are you familiar with any industry authorities that give guidance relative to steps to take to ensure that a corporation hires safe contractors?
39. In this case, did the corporation do anything to ensure that the contractor or others that they hired were safe contractors?
40. Do you know of any industry safety authorities that guide the defendant corporation with regard to reasonable steps to take regarding safety management oversight of contractors and other non-employees on its construction projects?
41. If so, what authorities and what steps does each indicate?
42. In the past, have you ever come across a corporation that had a project manager or contract liaison assigned to a construction project?
43. In the past, have you ever known of a project manager or contract liaison of a corporation who took any steps regarding ensuring that the job site safety and health program was being implemented by a contractor or non-employee as required by contract? If so, what steps?
44. Have you ever come across a corporation that monitored the construction site to see that the contractor or non-employee was implementing the job site safety program?
45. Have you ever come across a corporation that had a policy to perform safety inspections on a construction project being performed by a contractor or non-employee on its premise?
46. In this case, did the defendant have anyone assigned to oversee the project to ensure that the contractor or non-employees were working safely?
47. Did a corporation representative do anything to ensure that pre-planning took place with the contractor or non-employee?
48. Did a corporation representative attend safety meetings?
49. Did a corporation representative monitor to ensure that the work was being done safely?
50. Would it have been possible for this injury to have been prevented?
51. Would it have been possible for a representative of the corporation to have done anything that would have prevented this incident?

DISCOVERY REQUESTS

1. Copy of the written safety and health policy and program.
2. Copy of the contractor safety program.
3. Copy of the pre-job safety conference meeting minutes.
4. Copy of all safety inspections reports.
5. Copy of minutes from all safety meetings.
6. Copy of job description of contract liaison representative of PO/HE.
7. Copy of incident investigation report.
8. Copy of all documents related to this project.

NOTE

1. These questions will refer to contractors. However, for other non-employees, you could change the wording of the question to make it appropriate. For example, the first question could refer to truck drivers rather than contractors.

Part IV

PRODUCT SAFETY MANAGEMENT PROGRAMS

Chapter Sixteen

Product Safety Management

SAFETY THROUGH DESIGN

The essence of the product liability case is that at the time of manufacture there was an economically and technologically feasible safe design that would have prevented injury. The late Harry Philo, a prominent trial lawyer who had taught thousands of lawyers about safety and the law, had said that any safety professional worth his or her salt would have to agree with the following principle:

> Any risk of serious injury or death is unreasonable and unacceptable if that risk could be reduced or eliminated through reasonable accident prevention measures. Reasonable accident prevention measures are those which are economically and technologically feasible.

Harry Philo has said that the defense expert should be asked:

- In principle, do you agree that manufacturers should take reasonable steps to prevent catastrophic injury and death?
- Would you agree that if a product contains a hazard that could cause serious injury or death and that hazard could be controlled by means which are not too expensive, the product is unreasonably dangerous and defective?

Accident prevention measures include a wide variety of safety devices, technology and design methods which can be integrated into products to automatically prevent injury. They include a wide variety of safety devices such as:

Interlocks
Pressure sensing devices

Presence sensing devices
Automatic visual alarms
Audible alarms
Deadman controls
Two-hand control
Failsafe devices
Monitors
Pressure relief devices
Restraints
Barriers
Breakaway devices
Tamper proof designs
Retention cables, and so on.

If a product lacks a safety device or design method that is economically and technologically feasible that would likely have prevented injury, there is a theory of liability that is likely to be successful.

> *"To Err Is Human. To Forgive—Design."*
>
> —Alphonse Chapanis, father of human factors engineering

Safety engineering involves designing products that are "forgiving." The interlock on the microwave oven "forgives" the person who would be injured by opening the door with the power on. The interlock on the injection molder automatically prevents injury to the worker who would unjam the machine while it is energized. The smoke alarm "forgives" the person who falls asleep and leaves a cigarette unattended. The guardrail forgives and automatically protects the worker who slips or trips from falling from elevation. The canopy forgives the worker who mistakenly drops material on the worker below. The key question is: Despite any foreseeable uses and misuses of the product by the worker, would the injury have occurred if the product contained an economically and technologically feasible safer design?

The importance of safe design of products is not new. The National Safety Council has been preaching the importance of safe design and the need to follow the Hierarchy of Controls since it first published its *Accident Prevention Manual* in 1946.[1] In 1989, the National Safety Council published *Product Safety Management Guidelines* which also emphasized the importance of design. In 1999, they published *Safety Through Design* which emphasized the primary importance of eliminating hazards by design. These two books are excellent resources for attorneys who handle products cases. Safe design is the most important first step to take to reduce risks of injury.

HOW TO SELECT THE MOST RELIABLE CONTROLS

The American Society of Safety Engineers, OSHA, the American National Standards Institute, the National Safety Council and virtually every safety authority recognizes the importance of following the Hierarchy of Controls, that is, the recognized method of selecting the most reliable ways to control hazards.

HIERARCHY OF CONTROLS

1. Eliminate the hazard altogether when possible.
2. Use engineering methods to reduce the risk of injury.
3. Use training, instructions and warnings to further reduce risk of injury, that is, after exhausting all feasible engineering design techniques.
4. Use personal protective equipment to reduce the risk of injury. Personal protective equipment is the last resort.

The National Safety Council puts highest priority on engineering controls (numbers 1 and 2) because safe design automatically prevents injury and is not dependent upon worker behavior or management for their effectiveness. There is a role for the behavioral controls of training, instructions, warnings and management oversight. But they should be used only after exhausting economically and technologically feasible design techniques to automatically prevent injury.

BLAMING THE WORKER

Alphonse Chapanis challenged safety professionals at the 1986 American Society of Safety Engineers' Professional Development Conference:

> Everyone is at times careless, complacent, overconfident, stubborn. Each of us becomes distracted, inattentive, bored, fatigued. We occasionally take chances, misunderstand, misinterpret, misread. As a result of these and other completely human characteristics, we sometimes do not do or use things in ways expected of us. Because we are human, these traits are fundamental and built into each of us. The equipment, machines and systems that we construct for our use have to be made to accommodate us the way we are and not vice-versa . . . Are you good, ingenuous and dedicated enough to meet the challenge?

STANDARD OF CARE

The **standard of care** is what reasonably could have been done by the product manufacturer to prevent worker injury. The National Safety Council has defined the steps that a reasonable product manufacturer should take in order to manufacture a safe product in their book *Product Safety Management Guidelines*. However, the defense will often argue that the product was reasonably safe because it did not violate any safety standard.

The American National Standards Institute has approved more than 200 safety standards, many related to industrial products. Most OSHA standards were adopted from ANSI standards which were developed before 1970. Many OSHA standards have not been updated and lag behind many ANSI standards. Although there have been many enhancements to ANSI standards, some still lag behind the state of the art. Just because a product does not violate an OSHA or ANSI standard, that does not mean it is therefore safe. It should include state-of-the-art safety devices and designs.

The **state of the art** is the injury prevention method that was economically and technologically feasible at the time of manufacture. It represents what actions could be taken without being cost prohibitive. The state of the art evolves as new technology emerges and as technology costs decrease.

The **state of the industry** is that portion of the state of the art which industry decides to accept. The state of the industry is sometimes called the industry practice. The state of the industry is simply what most decision makers within that industry choose to do.

The industry standard is what ANSI requires. The industry practice and the industry standard may be below the standard of care. If so, the product is unreasonably dangerous because it contains a hazard and risk of injury which could have been eliminated or reduced by reasonable accident prevention measures.

The industry standard may be behind the state of the art due to the lag time between the recognition of the safe design method and when the industry standard is enhanced to require it.

Confusion arises when the industry practice is held to be the standard of care. What the industry **does** and what it **should do** may be two different things. Sometimes, the defense expert says that the state of the industry is the industry standard. These are also two separate concepts and should not be confused.

ANSI standards could be below the state of the art. ANSI standards are minimum standards that change over time as newer technology emerges to control hazards. But some defense experts opine that compliance with OSHA and ANSI standards is all that the product manufacturer should do.

METHODOLOGY OF EVALUATION—PRODUCTS CASES

The method to evaluate the conduct of a manufacturer in products cases is to determine if the manufacturer complied with the standard of care and implemented a **product safety management program**. The hazard is a symptom, not a cause. The essence of a product safety case is that the product is defective because it lacks a design technique or engineering method to automatically prevent injury. The defect could also be related to a failure to provide proper training information, instructions or warnings. The hazard exists because the defendant failed to design and implement a product safety management program. Deposition of the Best Person will show the specific failures in the product safety management system that led to the plaintiff being exposed to a hazard.

PRODUCT SAFETY MANAGEMENT PROGRAM

The National Safety Council has been advocating that manufacturers implement product safety management programs in their *Accident Prevention Manual* since 1969. In 1989, The National Safety Council published *Product Safety Management Guidelines*, First Edition. The National Safety Council is our nation's leading industry advocate for safety and health. It was founded in 1913 and chartered by Congress in 1953. It has established the industry standard or recognized reasonable steps that a product manufacturer should take to manufacture a reasonably safe product. It has more than 35,000 members. Most mid and large sized corporations that manufacture products are members of the National Safety Council.

The following is taken from the National Safety Council's book entitled *Product Safety Management Guidelines*, 2nd Edition published in 1997.

Product Safety Policy Statement

The company policy statements may contain some or all of the following elements:

- A statement of the company's intent to product and market products that are reliable and safe for the user and the environment.
- A statement of the company's intent to comply with all applicable federal, state and local product safety regulations.
- A statement that a company will use all reasonable means to eliminate or minimize all potential hazards related to the development, manufacturing, distribution and use of its products.
- The identification of the Corporate Product Safety Professional by name or title and the person to whom the safety professional reports.

- A detailed list of objectives or goals, including specific product safety responsibilities, organizational descriptions, and administrative procedures for implementing the policy.
- Specific goals for reduction of claims, customer complaints, returned goods, scrap, recall, government agency penalties, failures of products, rework, and accidents or incidents.
- Other considerations such as continuous improvement and environmental safe recycling or disposal.

Responsibilities of Product Safety Professional

The responsibilities of the product safety professional may include some or all of the following:

- Develops policies and procedures.
- Secures and analyzes data from all product safety hazard analyses, product incidents . . . to accurately define the extent of possible future liability.
- Reviews quality assurance, control, and safety procedures, specifications, test records, and sample plans to ensure that existing quality and safety standards are met.
- Submits periodic product reports.
- Studies new developments, new procedures, or changes in procedures and systems.
- Develops communication systems.
- Develops a recording system for product accidents, field failures and customer accidents.
- Acts as chairman or secretary of the product safety committee.
- Reviews recall procedures.

Product Design and Evaluation

Designers must always consider safety as a primary importance in designing a new product or revising an established one. To incorporate safety properly into product design, it should be given comparable priority to function and cost, it should not be subservient to any of the many commercial concerns . . . It is economically desirable to make provisions for safety while the product is in the early conceptual stage to avoid having to redesign significant portions of the product to accommodate later safety provisions. In fact, there is no substitute for designing an acceptable level of safety into the product before the product is piloted for manufacture.

The National Safety Council encourages product manufacturers to have a field information system to collect injury data from customers so that failures can be evaluated. That way, opportunities for making enhancements to the design to prevent further occurrences can be recognized and implemented.

A product safety management program should also include a written recall/retrofit program so that steps to respond to enhance the safety of products in commerce will be already established when opportunities are recognized. The product safety management program also includes a written record retention program.

PRODUCT COMMUNICATIONS DESIGN

Product communications include operator's and safety manuals, advertising, assembly instructions, warnings, signs, stickers, pictures, and so on. The National Safety Council gives criteria relative to when and how to warn. The manufacturer must warn or instruct when:

- The product has significant injury potential, that is, has significant risk of injury.
- The manufacturer knows or should have known of the risk of injury.
- The expected or typical user is unaware of the danger and does not normally guard against it.

Product manufacturers should consider the unintended product uses and misuses and the environment of use. The warning must clearly describe the possible consequences and how to avoid injury. The sign or label must be located on the product so the warning is conspicuous. The sign or label should be able to last for the intended life of the product.[2]

DISCOVERY

The following are documents to request:

1. A copy of your product safety policy.
2. A copy of your product safety management program.
3. Name of the individual who has overall responsibility for the implementation of your product safety program. That is, the person most responsible to ensure that you manufacture reasonably safe products.
4. List of the names and titles of all of the people that have product safety responsibility.
5. Copies of all job descriptions of employees who have been assigned particular tasks to perform with respect to product safety.

6. Any written design guidelines, goals, safe design objectives or criterion that your company has prepared for employees to follow in order to manufacture a reasonably safe product.
7. Any written methods established in your product safety program to identify hazards associated with your products.
8. Any written methods established in your product safety program with regard to performing hazard analysis.
9. Any written method to identify reasonably foreseeable uses and misuses.
10. Any written method to integrate ergonomic principles into the design of your product.
11. Any written procedures relative to the methods to control design changes.
12. Any written documents which guide designers when to warn of hazards associated with the use of your products.
13. Any written documents which guide designers on how to create warnings.
14. Any written documents which guide designers on how to prepare instructions.
15. Any written documents related to a product safety program audit.
16. Any written documents related to a program designed to collect injury data associated with the use of your product.
17. Any written reports of injury analysis data.
18. A copy of your written record retention program.
19. A copy of your written recall/modification program.
20. A written criteria that you have which guides managers how to decide when to have a recall or modification program to enhance the safety of products in the field.
21. All information that you have related to other injuries that you are aware of that resulted from the hazard which caused injury in this case.

DEPOSITION OF THE BEST PERSON

The following are questions to consider when deposing the defendant's Best Person, that is, the person with the most knowledge about the safety policies and procedures taken to manufacture the incident product.

1. What companies did you work for before working for the defendant company?
2. What positions did you hold?
3. What safety responsibilities did you have in each of those positions?
4. Did any of those companies have a written product safety program?
5. Do you have a written job description now?

6. Are there other people in your company that have specific duties related to product safety?
7. Who are they and what are their responsibilities?
8. Have you received any training related to safety?
9. Have you received any training related to product safety?
10. Who put it on? Where? How long did it last? What topics were covered?
11. What is your job title?
12. Do you have a written job description?
13. Could you provide me with a copy?
14. List all of the duties you have including product safety duties.
15. Are you familiar with the National Safety Council?
16. What is it?
17. Is your company a member of the National Safety Council? Since when?
18. Are you familiar with any of the National Safety Council's publications related to product safety?
19. What are some of the publications of the National Safety Council that you are familiar with?
20. How are you familiar with them?
21. When did you first learn of them?
22. Do you have any publications related to product safety at your company in a library or on a shelf someplace?
23. List all of the books that you have related to product safety that you are familiar with.
24. Do you ever refer to any product safety books as references? Which ones?
25. Do you know of any authorities in our country who have written on the subject of product safety?
26. Does your company have a written product safety program?
27. Does your company have any written design guidelines prepared and given to your engineers to follow? Note: They should have generic guidelines for designers to systematically consider the safety of their products during all foreseeable uses and misuses.
28. Does your company have any written design goals, safe design objectives or written criterion established for engineers or others to follow while making decisions relative to the design of your products?
29. Are you familiar with the different methods or models to identify hazards?
30. Which?
31. Is it your company's policy to identify hazards associated with your products?
32. Is it your company's policy to evaluate hazards associated with the use of your products?

33. What are some of the models that your company has used to identify hazards associated with your products?
34. What are some of the models that your company has used to evaluate hazards associated with your products?
35. Has your company ever performed any type of hazard identification of this product?
36. Does your company have a written program related to methods to evaluate hazards?
37. Does your company maintain records of hazards identified?
38. Do you have any records related to hazard evaluations performed?
39. Does your company have a written program related to methods to collect injury data?
40. Does your company ever collect injury data from users?
41. Have you ever seen reports of analyses of injury data?
42. Are you familiar with any of the conclusions of analyses of injury data performed by your company?
43. Does your company maintain ongoing relations with dealers or purchasers?
44. How is that accomplished?
45. Does your company send bulletins out to dealers or users?
46. Has your company sent out any bulletins or other documents to dealers and users of the incident product?
47. Is it your company's policy to design a hazard out of a product when feasible rather than permitting a hazard to exist and then warn of it?
48. Have you ever heard of the hierarchy for selecting the most reliable controls?

    - Eliminate the hazard altogether if possible.
    - Use safety designs and safety devices to reduce the risk of injury.
    - Use training, instructions and warnings to reduce the risk of injury.
    - Use personal protective equipment to control hazards.

49. Is it your company's policy to select hazard controls consistent with this hierarchy?
50. Does your company policy agree that it is more reliable to eliminate the hazard altogether when possible than to permit it to exist and control it through a safety device?
51. Does your company policy agree that it is more reliable to either eliminate or control the hazard through an automatic safety device than it is to permit it to exist and simply warn someone to be careful?
52. Does your company policy recognize the need to consider reasonably foreseeable uses and misuses in the design process? Why?

53. Is part of your company policy that training, instructions and warnings are behavioral controls which should be used to control or address residual hazards which exist after we have used engineering techniques to control the hazard?
54. If there is a hazard associated with one of your products and your company knows of ways to eliminate the hazard or reduce the risk of injury by a safer design, is it your company's policy to do so?
55. Does your company have any written documents which give guidance related to when and how to warn of hazards associated with their products?
56. Do you have any resources at your company which give guidance as to when and how to warn of hazards associated with the products you manufacture?
57. Do you agree in principle that a warning should include the hazard as well as the consequence likely to result from exposure to the hazard?
58. Do you know if any audits have been performed of your product safety program?
59. Does your company have any written documents related to audits of your product safety program?
60. Does your company have a written record retention policy?
61. Does your company have a written recall/modification program?
62. Has your company ever implemented a recall or modified products already in commerce?
63. Is there any established written procedure for decision making relative to when and how to recall/retrofit?
64. With regard to the hazard associated with the product in this case, are you aware of any other injuries which resulted from this hazard?
65. Has your company ever been sued before related to injury caused by this or similar hazards?
66. Did your company ever perform a hazard analysis to identify this hazard?
67. Are there any written documents related to that hazard identification?
68. Have you ever evaluated this hazard or done a risk assessment?
69. Are there any documents retained in that regard?
70. Does your company use the hierarchy of controls to select the most reliable controls related to this hazard?
71. Has this hazard ever been discussed in any meetings?
72. Are there minutes of any meetings related to any discussion of this hazard before this injury occurred?
73. Are there any documents, memos, letters, e-mails or other correspondence related to this hazard retained by your company?
74. Have any changes been made as a result of this injury?

75. Prior to this injury, had your company recognized the foreseeability of this type of injury?
76. Today, does your company recognize that another worker could possibly be injured in the same way as the plaintiff was in this case?
77. Is it now foreseeable to your company that a worker may again suffer injury as the plaintiff did?
78. Would it have been possible for your company to have performed hazard analysis to identify the way this incident occurred?
79. Would it have been possible for your company to have done anything to prevent this incident if the way this incident occurred had been identified beforehand?
80. Tell me all of the steps your company has taken to prevent a similar occurrence.

DEPOSITION OF DEFENSE EXPERT

If the defendant violated the standard of care, the facts will show:

- The product lacked a safe design or warning.
- The defendant failed to perform hazard analysis to identify the defect.

The defendant may also have failed to:

- Create a written product safety program.
- Perform hazard analysis of the incident hazard.
- Follow the hierarchy of controls.
- Have an injury collection system in place to gather injury data to be analyzed to learn of opportunities to enhance the safety of products in commerce.
- Create a written recall/retrofit program.
- Create a written record retention program.

Discovery should have revealed the facts related to product safety management program failures. You could begin the deposition by asking if his/her evaluation took into account each of those failures.

It is likely that the defense expert did his/her evaluation without determining if the defendant violated the principles and practices of product safety management established by the National Safety Council. The following are questions that could be used in deposition of the defense expert:

1. Have you ever heard of the concept "standard of care"?
2. What does that mean to you regarding product safety?
3. Do you know of any industry authorities which establish principles and practices of product safety?
4. Do you know of any books that are authoritative and give guidance to manufacturers relative to safe product design?
5. Do you know any authors who have written on the subject of product safety?
6. Do you know of any journals, texts or organizations which give guidance to manufacturers about reasonable steps to manufacture a safe product?
7. Tell me all of the industry safety authorities that you relied upon—texts, authors, standards and other sources.
8. Are you familiar with any principles of product safety?
9. Tell me all of the principles of product safety that you are familiar with.
10. Have you ever heard the saying: "To err is human. To forgive—design"?
11. When?
12. What does that mean to you?
13. Have you ever heard the expression: "Safety begins on the drawing board" or "Safety begins in the design stages"? What does that mean to you? When did you hear of those expressions?
14. Have you ever heard of the concept "Hierarchy of Controls"? Note: The Hierarchy of Controls establishes the order and preference of hazard control steps. That is, first eliminate the hazard if possible. Second, use safety designs or safety devices to reduce the risk of injury. Three, use training, instructions and warnings. Four, use personal protective equipment
15. Do you know of any authorities which have written about the Hierarchy of Controls?
16. Have you ever heard of the National Safety Council? What is the National Safety Council?
17. Do you know if the National Safety Council gives guidance to manufacturers about ways to manufacture a safe product? How do they do that?
18. Have you ever read any documents of the National Safety Council that give guidance to manufacturers?
19. Are you a member of the National Safety Council?
20. Is the defendant company a member of the National Safety Council?
21. Do you own any books published by the National Safety Council?
22. Does the National Safety Council have a Journal? Have you ever read it? Do you know the name of it?
23. Have you ever attended any conferences of the National Safety Council?
24. Do you know anybody who is a member?

25. Are you familiar with the Human Factors and Ergonomics Society? What is it?
26. Are you a member?
27. Do you read their Journal?
28. Have you ever attended any conferences of the Human Factors and Ergonomics Society?
29. What is human factors and ergonomics?
30. Have you ever commented on questions related to ergonomics and human factors in your role as an expert witness?
31. Have you ever had any training in human factors and ergonomics?
32. Have you ever written on the subject of human factors engineering or ergonomics?
33. Were you ever hired to perform human factors evaluations?
34. Have you ever taught on the subject of human factors engineering and ergonomics?
35. Have you ever heard of the System Safety Society? What is it?
36. Are you a member?
37. Do you read any of their Journals?
38. Do you know of any books published by them?
39. Do they say anything in their publications about the role of the manufacturer as far as you know?
40. Have you ever attended any conferences of the System Safety Society?
41. Do you know anybody who is a member?
42. Are you a member of the American Society of Safety Engineers?
43. Do you read their Journal? What is the name of their Journal?
44. Have you ever read any books, articles or any studies by the American Society of Safety Engineers that gives guidance to product manufacturers relative to safety?
45. Have you ever attended any conferences of the American Society of Safety Engineers?
46. List all of the industry safety authorities which say that the manufacturer and designer have a responsibility to anticipate foreseeable uses and misuses of the product that they manufacture.
47. In your evaluation, did you give any thought to any foreseeable uses and misuses of this product?
48. If so, tell me all of the uses and misuses that you anticipated.
49. Did the defendant identify any foreseeable uses and misuses of this product?
50. I am going to ask you if you agree with a principle. Tell me if you agree or disagree with the following: "Any risk of serious injury or death is unreasonable and unacceptable if that risk can be eliminated or reduced

through reasonable accident prevention measures. Reasonable accident prevention measures are those which are economically and technologically feasible."

51. If the expert dances, you could simplify the question: Do you agree that if we know how to prevent serious injury or death and it doesn't cost too much, that in principle, manufacturers should do what they can that doesn't cost too much to prevent serious injury or death?
52. Do you know what the National Safety Management Society is?
53. Are you a member of the National Safety Management Society?
54. Do you hold any safety certifications?
55. Have you ever published on the subject of product safety?
56. Have you ever published on any topics related to safety?
57. Have you ever taught product safety in any colleges or universities or seminars?
58. Have you ever been hired by a manufacturer to consult in the field of product safety?
59. Have you ever advertised that you are an expert in product safety?
60. Are you qualified as an expert in the principles and practices of product safety management?
61. List for me all of the principles and practices of product safety management that you are aware of.
62. What do you expect conscientious manufacturers who are concerned with preventing injury relating to their product to do relative to identifying reasonably foreseeable uses and misuses of their product?
63. Specifically what do you expect them to do?
64. In your opinion, should a manufacturer put in writing the reasonably foreseeable uses and misuses of your product so that designers can take them in to account?
65. Do you know of any authorities that say that the manufacturer identify and specify reasonably foreseeable uses and misuses of their products?
66. How do you define hazard? Hazard is an unsafe condition or act which can lead to injury.
67. How do you define risk? Risk is the probability or likelihood that a hazard will result from injury.
68. How do you define danger? Danger is the combination of hazard and risk.
69. What is a reasonably safe product? A reasonably safe product is one which does not contain uncontrolled hazards.
70. Should a manufacturer design hazards out of a product? Why?
71. Do you know of any authorities that say a manufacturer should design hazards out?

72. Should a manufacturer warn of the dangers associated with the use of the product? Why?
73. In your opinion, is there a relationship in your opinion between the design of the product and what warnings should be specified?
74. Have you ever heard the term "residual hazard"? What is a residual hazard? (Note: A residual hazard is one that is left after all economically and technologically feasible design methods have been exhausted to reduce the risk of injury. Warnings should be used for residual hazards. It doesn't make sense to leave a hazard in the product and then warn against it when the risk can be reduced or eliminated through engineering means.)
75. Do you know of any safety authorities that say a manufacturer should have a written product safety program?
76. Do you know what a product safety management program should include?
77. On approximately how many cases have you worked as expert for the defendant being a product manufacturer?
78. Did any of those manufacturers have a written product safety program?
79. Have you ever criticized any manufacturer for failure to have a written product safety program?
80. Have you ever seen one?
81. Do you know of a manufacturer that does not have a written product safety program?
82. Have you ever recommended that a manufacturer establish a product safety program?
83. Do you know of any safety authorities that say a product manufacturer should assign responsibilities for product safety management oversight to a particular person?
84. Do you know of any safety authorities that say a manufacturer should assign a product safety coordinator within the organization of the manufacturer?
85. Do you know of any safety authorities that say there be someone designated to coordinate the efforts of the engineering section, the quality control or quality assurance department and the people who design the warnings?
86. Have you ever known an employer to collect injury data related to the products that they have sold? Who? Why would a manufacturer do that?
87. Do you know of any safety authorities that say that manufacturers should establish information systems to systematically collect injury data?
88. Do you know of any safety authorities that say evaluation of injury data should be done to help engineers when designing newer models of a particular product?
89. In your opinion, should injury data be used by engineers when designing newer models? Why?

90. Do you know of any safety authorities that say a manufacturer should establish a written program relative to product recall/modification/retrofit? Why?
91. Do you know of any manufacturers who have written recall/modification/retrofit programs?
92. Do you know of any safety authorities that say a manufacturer should review safety in the design stages?
93. Do you know of any safety authorities that say a manufacturer should perform a design review regarding safety when modifications are made to a product?
94. Should they do it upon review of injury data? Why?
95. Should manufacturers of products retain records?
96. Do you know of any safety authorities that say that manufacturers should have a record retention policy that is in writing?
97. Do you know of any authorities that guide manufacturers to have record retention policies?
98. Have you seen a record retention policy in this case?
99. Do you know of any safety authorities that give guidance to manufacturers about what records should be retained by a product manufacturer?
100. Do you know of any safety authorities that say information related to hazard analysis should be retained? Why?
101. Do you know of any safety authorities that say records should be destroyed while the product is still in service or still being used by some customers?
102. Do you know of any safety authorities that say a product manufacturer should keep written records regarding foreseeable uses and misuses of their products? Why?
103. Do you know of any manufacturer who has determined specifically the uses and misuses of a particular product? Explain.
104. Have you known of any product manufacturers that have developed a product recall/modification/retrofit program? Why did they do that?
105. Do you know of any organizations that guide manufacturers as to when they should implement product recall/modification/retrofit programs?
106. Do you understand what is mean by the term "methodology of evaluation"? What does that mean to you?
107. What is the methodology of evaluation that you use to evaluate the conduct of the product's manufacturer?
108. Have you ever considered the conduct of a manufacturer relative to the principles and practices of product safety management established by the National Safety Council?
109. What method did you use to evaluate the conduct of the plaintiff in this case?

110. Approximately how many products have you evaluated relative to hazards in your career? (This question is not related simply to litigation but all of the products in your entire work career that you have evaluated relative to hazards.)
111. Name some of the types of products that you have evaluated.
112. Name some of the types of products that you have evaluated relative to litigation such as in this case.
113. Approximately how many times have you been hired to work for a manufacturer for a product with an alleged defect and you found that there really was no defect?
114. Have you ever evaluated a product that you found to be defective because it lacked a safe design, safety device, warning or included a hazard that could have been eliminated through design?
115. Explain all of the products that you have found to be defective and all of the reasons why you thought they were defective.
116. Do you agree with me that a worker could operate or work around a machine that is defective and not suffer injury even though exposed to a danger?
117. Would you agree with me that it is by definition not safe to work on or near a product that has a defect in it?
118. Would you agree with me that the unsafe behavior of the designer who doesn't use technologically and economically feasible design techniques to reduce risks *could* be a causative factor in injuries?
119. Would you agree with me that an unsafe design, that is, a defect or uncontrolled hazard associated with a product, necessarily requires the worker using the product to be exposed to a hazard?
120. Do you agree that the unsafe acts of designers can cause unsafe conditions?
121. Do you agree that an unsafe condition can cause an unsafe act when a worker has to work while exposed to the unsafe condition?

CROSS EXAMINATION OF EXPERT WHEN THERE IS COMPLIANCE WITH A MINIMAL ANSI STANDARD YET EXPOSURE TO A HAZARD—PRODUCTS CASES

Some ANSI standards like some OSHA standards are unreasonably permissive. Sometimes workers will be injured because of exposure to a product hazard for which there is an ANSI standard but it is not addressed by the ANSI standard. When an expert opines that exposure to a hazard is acceptable because it does not violate the ANSI standard, they could be cross examined with the following questions:

1. Are you familiar with ANSI standards?
2. Do you agree with me that over the years, many ANSI standards have changed?
3. Would you agree that when we compare the ANSI standards that were in effect 20 or 30 years ago to today's ANSI standards, we find significant enhancements in many standards?
4. Do you know if manufacturers of products for which there is an ANSI standard usually have representatives on the committee which promulgates the standard?
5. Would you agree with me that most major manufacturers of a particular product have representatives on the ANSI committee?
6. Are you familiar with the rules making process and voting by ANSI committees relative to proposed changes to improve safety?
7. Would you agree with me that the ANSI standards are by definition "consensus standards"?
8. Have you ever heard that ANSI standards are considered to be "minimal" standards, that is, the minimum that the committee could agree upon?
9. Have you ever read an ANSI standard that you thought should have included a safety requirement which did not?
10. In litigation, have you ever opined that a manufacturer was not negligent as evidenced by the fact that their product complied with an ANSI standard in effect at the time the product was manufactured?
11. Have you ever been involved in cases where the opposing expert said that the ANSI standard should have included a particular safety requirement where you argued for some reason that it should not?
12. Have you ever argued that a product was defective even though it complied with ANSI?
13. Do you expect that eventually, many ANSI standards will change in some ways to require greater protection than they do today?
14. Is it possible that today, there is an ANSI standard that does not require a feasible safer design?
15. Do you know of any ANSI standards that, in your opinion, should be made safer today because there is an economically and technologically feasible way to enhance the safety of the product addressed by the ANSI standard?
16. Is it your opinion that manufacturers should do what is economically and technologically feasible to prevent serious injury and death regardless of whether the ANSI standard requires it?
17. Have you ever opined that an ANSI standard need not be upgraded relative to safety because the injury data does not indicate a need for such an improvement?

18. Do you think that manufacturers should justify expenses related to safety devices by cost benefit analysis? That is, to show that the cost of the device is less than the costs associated with the injuries?
19. Are you a member of any ANSI committee?
20. If so, have you ever voted?
21. Do you know if one manufacturer who is a member of the ANSI committee is against a particular change, can block the passage of a proposed safer change?
22. Have you ever voted for a proposed change that was blocked by other members?
23. Would you agree with me that there is a time lag that exists from the time new technology becomes available to prevent injury and the time when that new technology is required by the ANSI standard?
24. In your expert opinion, is it possible that there could be excessive time lag between the time when new technology becomes available and is cost effective and the time before an ANSI standard requires the safer design?
25. Have you ever seen a time lag in this regard which you thought was too long?
26. Is it possible for workers to be injured while working on products manufactured in compliance with ANSI standards which could have been made safer?
27. Do you know of any ANSI standards that you think could be improved in some way?
28. Would you agree that ANSI standards are continually improving and becoming safer?

NOTES

1. *Safety Through Design*, Wayne C. Christensen and Fred A. Manuele, National Safety Council, 1999, p. ix.

2. National Safety Council, *Product Safety Management Guidelines*, Chapter 4, 1997, pp. 65–73.

Part V

OTHER IMPORTANT TOPICS

Chapter Seventeen

Standards for Hiring of Safe Contractors

The construction project owner, general contractor, construction manager, and premise owner/host employer who hires construction contractors should take reasonable steps to ensure that they hire safe contractors. The standard for selecting safe contractors has been established by leading industry safety authorities such as:

- The American Society of Safety Engineers—an association of over 36,000 safety professionals, most of whom work for mid and large sized corporations.
- The National Safety Council—an association of over 35,000 members, mostly from mid and large sized corporations.
- The Business Roundtable—an association of the 200 largest corporations in America.
- Construction Industry Institute—an association representing leading owners, contractors and suppliers in both public and private sectors.

AMERICAN SOCIETY OF SAFETY ENGINEERS

The following statement was made by the American Society of Safety Engineers in their book entitled CONSTRUCTION SAFETY MANAGEMENT AND ENGINEERING and was also published in the Business Roundtable's document entitled "Improving Safety Performance, A Construction Industry Cost-Effective Project Report A-3, January 1982." This statement applies to CPOs, corporations, business owners/employers who act as GC/CM and who hire general contractors, construction managers and contractors.

> *Owners must recognize and honor the moral and legal obligations to provide a safe work environment to minimize injuries. Owners have, in addition to the moral and legal obligations, an* ***economic*** *incentive to help reduce the number of accidents that occur on their construction sites . . . One way that an owner (business owner/employer) can carry out this responsibility (that is, to prevent injury on a construction site) is to hire contractors who have a record of good safety performance. This requires attention during the process of qualifying contractors for bidding work and selecting contractors for a contract award. A prospective contractor with a history of good safety performance is more likely to perform safely in the future than a contractor with a poor, or less-than-average, safety record.*
>
> *Selecting the right contractor is crucial in today's competitive business environments. The safety performance of an outside contract workforce can influence not only the cost and quality of the outsourced project, but many other areas of business operations as well—from regulatory compliance to community relations . . . Owners have a direct economic stake in the safety performance of their contractors because accident costs are an expense to the contractor and are subsequently passed on, one way or another, to the owner . . . The selection and eventual hiring of a contractor to provide a service or construct a major facility should be managed with a process that ensures the selected contractor meets the basic qualification criteria set by the owner's management. A contractor selection or screening committee created by the owner should set the qualification specifications . . . The criterion should include provisions to verify that the contractor has a successful safety and environmental compliance record.*[1]

The aforementioned industry authorities agree that there are three sources of information for owners to evaluate the probable safety performance of prospective contractors:

- Experience Modification Rate for Workers Compensation Insurance[2]
- OSHA Total Incidence Rates
- Contractor's Safety Program/Safety Attitudes and Practices

THE NATIONAL SAFETY COUNCIL

In their ACCIDENT PREVENTION MANUAL, 11th Edition 1997, the National Safety Council stated the following with regard to selection of safe contractors:

> Examine contractor's previous accident records and workers compensation records when selecting a contractor. Along with the data from the contractor's OSHA 200 Form, the safety and health professional would request the Experi-

ence Modification Rate (EMR) from the company's insurance carrier agent, which lists the EMR for the past three years . . . One of the safety and health professional's strongest tools may be the prequalification form. This form, sent to the contractor, requests a list of data to be received and an overview of their safety and health program. A prequalification form is a list of questions in an organized format which should offer a relevant, accurate, timely, and complete history of the company's safety and health history. Example questions or requests:

Please provide the following:

- The OSHA 200 Form for the three previous years
- The EMR for the previous three years
- A copy of the company's safety manual
- A copy of the written hazard communication program
- A brief outline of safety and health training provided to supervisors

BUSINESS ROUNDTABLE

The following is taken from the Business Roundtable's publication entitled "Improving Construction Safety Performance":

SELECTION OF SAFE CONTRACTORS

Findings

This part of the study deals with reducing the number and severity of construction accidents by choosing a safe contractor.

Three sources of information provide ways for owners to evaluate the probable safety performance of prospective contractors:

- Experience modification rates for workers compensation insurance
- OSHA incidence rates for recordable injuries and illnesses
- Contractor safety attitudes and practices

Experience Modification Rates for Workers' Compensation Insurance

The insurance industry has developed experience rating systems as an equitable means of determining premiums for workers compensation insurance. These rating systems consider the average worker's compensation losses for a given firm's type of work and amount of payroll and predict the dollar amount of expected losses to be paid by that employer in a designated rating period, usually three years. Rating is based on comparison of firms doing similar types of work, and the employer is rated against the average expected performance in each work classification. Losses incurred by the employer for the rating period are then compared to the expected losses to develop an experience rating.

Workers compensation insurance premiums for a contractor are adjusted by this rate, which is called the experience modification rate (EMR). Lower rates, meaning that fewer or less severe accidents had occurred than were expected, result in lower insurance costs. A contractor's EMR is adjusted annually by using the rate for the first three of the last four years.

OSHA Incidence Rates

The Occupational Safety and Health Act (1970) requires employers to record and report accident information on Occupational Injuries and Illnesses Annual Survey Form No. 200. The employer must retain completed forms for five years. Information available from a contractor's OSHA Form No. 200 includes:

- Number of fatalities
- Number of injuries and illnesses involving lost workdays
- Number of injuries and illnesses involving restricted workdays
- Number of days away from work
- Number of days of restricted work activity
- Number of injuries and illnesses without lost workdays

A contractor, having the number of hours his employees worked during the year, can compute incident rates for any or all of the items above using the following formula:

$$\frac{\text{No. of incidents} \times 200{,}000 \text{ hours}}{\text{No. of hours worked}} = \text{Incidence Rate}$$

(The 200,000 hours in the formula represents the equivalent of 100 employees working 40 hours per week, 50 weeks per year, and is the standard base for incidence rates.)

In calculating the OSHA recordable incidence rate, the number of incidents in the formula are the total of the numbers of fatalities, injuries and illnesses involving lost and restricted workdays, and injuries and illness without lost workdays. The Bureau of Labor statistics compiles construction industry incidence-rate averages each year for 14 separate classifications of construction work and various employee size groupings.

Contractor Safety Attitudes and Practices

Management accountability for safety performance is a very important factor in determining a company's safety record. Companies which hold their project management accountable for accidents along with productivity, schedules, quality, etc., are the ones which have the best safety records.[3] Based on the results from the research on the effects of top management on safety in construction, the following five measures of managerial accountability for safety were suggested by Stanford:[4]

1. The recipients of accident reports and frequency distribution of the reports (field superintendent, vice president of construction, president of firm).
2. The frequency of project safety inspections and the degree to which they include project and field superintendents.
3. The frequency of safety meetings for field supervisors.
4. The compilation method for accident records and the frequency of reporting. (Those contractors who subtotal their accidents by superintendent and foreman, rather than just by company, have a more detailed accountability system.)
5. The compilation method for accident costs and the frequency of reporting. (Again, great accountability comes from a more detailed system, so that individual foremen and superintendents are measured in terms of their accident costs on the job.)

Conclusions

The experience modification rate is a widely used indicator of a contractor's past safety performance. Owners should request, from prospective contractors, EMRs for the three most recent years, which will show the firm's trend in safety performance. Interstate EMRs, intrastate EMRs and monopolistic state ratings should not be compared with each other because different data bases are used for each system. Interstate EMRs of different contractors can be compared, as can intrastate EMRs of different contractors operating in the same state.

The OSHA incidence rates also show past safety performance. Since these are uniform national statistics, there are no limitations in comparing rates in one part of the country with those in another. Moreover, OSHA incidence rates reflect more recent experience than EMRs. Owners should request, from contractors, OSHA incidence rates for recordable injuries and illnesses for the three most recent years.

The reliability of OSHA incidence rates is solely dependent on judicious reporting by the employer, while the EMRs are established by independent rating bureaus. Although the EMR is a more objective measure than the OSHA incidence rate, there is a correlation between them. Both will indicate past safety performance.

The safety attitudes and practices of a contractor are helpful in evaluating his safety and health capabilities. Owners should look for:

- Management accountability
- A qualified staff
- Written safety and health programs
- Regular orientation of foremen and new workers
- Frequent, effective tool-box safety meetings
- On-the-job discipline
- Management commitment

Past research on effective safety performance in construction indicates that the comparative measures, such as the experience modification rate and OSHA incidence rate, are more reliable and objective than the management accountability items.

A questionnaire for the use of owners in obtaining safety information from prospective contractors was developed for the task force by Stanford University (See Appendix E). Use of the questionnaire will give owners a way to evaluate safety as they consider contractor qualification and selection.

CONSTRUCTION INDUSTRY INSTITUTE

The following is from the Construction Industry Institute's Study RR190-11—The Owner's Role in Construction Safety:

> Careful selection of safe contractors: Owners aggressive in safety use proactive criteria to evaluate and select contractors. This criteria includes the contractor's total recordable injury rate (TRIR) on past projects, qualifications of the contractor's safety staff, qualifications of the contractor's project management team, and the assessed quality of the contractor's overall safety program.

DEPOSITION OF CPO, CORPORATE REP, GC/CM REGARDING HIRING SAFE CONTRACTORS

1. Is it your company's policy to take reasonable steps to hire safe contractors?
2. According to your company policy, what are all of the steps that are taken to ensure that your company hires a safe GC or contractor?
3. Do you know who made the decision to hire contractors for this project?
4. Prior to working for the defendant company, had you ever worked for a company that had a policy to consider the safety performance of contractors during the bid evaluation process? If so, explain.
5. How many times has your current employer hired contractors or general contractors?
6. What were some of the types of contractors that your current employer has hired?
7. How long have you worked for the defendant?
8. List for me all of your safety responsibilities.
9. Do you know what documents should be requested from a contractor in order to have information to evaluate a contractor's past safety performance?
10. Does your company prepare documents which are sent to bidders soliciting bids?

11. Does your company require bidders to provide your company with any information related to the bidder's safety performance that your company then uses in the bid evaluation process?
12. What information regarding safety does your company require contractors to send in order for your company to perform bid evaluation?
13. Has your company ever required a bidder to submit a copy of their safety program?
14. Has your company ever required a contractor to submit information about their Experience Modification Rate related to workers compensation?
15. Has your company ever required bidders to submit documents related to their OSHA Incidence Rates?
16. Has your company ever required contractors to submit copies of their OSHA inspection history?
17. Has your company ever selected a contractor based solely on the fact that it was the low bidder?
18. Do you know if anyone required bidders to send your company a copy of their occupational safety and health program?
19. Do you know if anyone from your company required bidders to send your company a copy of their occupational safety and health plan?
20. Do you know if anyone from your company required the bidder to submit to your company their workers compensation experience modification rate?
21. Do you know if anybody required contractors to submit copies of their OSHA records and OSHA incidence rate?
22. Do you know if anyone required contractors to submit any other safety performance documents?
23. Does your company have any written guidelines that are sent to contractors giving guidance on what to include in their bids?
24. In the past, has your company ever given bidders documents to explain what must be submitted with their bid relative to evidence of their past safety performance?
25. Tell me all of the steps that your company took to ensure that they hired safe contractors for this project.
26. How many bidders were there for this job?
27. Does your company use any documents to evaluate the bids of contractors?
28. Do you know if your company created any documents during the bid evaluation process, that is, documents that they use to perform the evaluation?
29. Have you seen any documents developed in the bid evaluation process for selection of contractors for this project?

DEPOSITION OF EXPERT REGARDING HIRING OF SAFE CONTRACTOR

The following are questions which could be used when deposing an expert over the question of whether or not the CPO, corporate representative, business owner/employer, general contractor, and construction manager took reasonable steps to hire a safe contractor:

1. Is it possible that a contractor would submit a bid lower than others because that contractor did not include costs regarding safety?
2. Do you know of any industry authorities that have established standard ways to evaluate the safety performance of contractors who bid to do construction work for a business owner, general contractor or construction manager?
3. If so, list all of those authorities.
4. Do you know what reasonable steps could be taken by a business owner/employer, general contractor or construction manager when trying to determine whether or not a bidder is a safe contractor?
5. When you performed your evaluation of responsibility in this case, did you consider whether or not the defendant complied with any industry standards relative to accepted ways to evaluate a contractor's past safety performance?
6. Do you know what the American Society of Safety Engineers says should be done in order to select safe contractors?
7. Do you know what the Business Roundtable says?
8. Do you know what the National Safety Council says?
9. In any case that you have worked on in the past, have you ever evaluated a defendant's role in selecting safe contractors, that is, according to what industry authorities say should be done?
10. Do you know what an experience modification rate is?
11. Have you ever asked for a defendant's experience modification rate when performing any evaluation in the past?
12. Did you ever consider OSHA records when considering the safety performance of any defendant in any case at all?
13. Do you know how to calculate OSHA incidence rates?
14. Do you know of any industry authorities that say that bid documents should make it clear that safety costs should be included?
15. In this case, did the defendant say in bid documents to bidders that they should make clear their costs related to performing the work safely?

16. Would you agree that it would be easier to select a safe contractor if, during the bid evaluation process, the bid selectors could see the specific costs allocated for safety among bidding contractors?
17. Have you ever had the responsibility to select construction contractors?
18. Did you ever evaluate the safety performance of contractors?
19. Did you ever perform a final evaluation of a contractor's performance to use as a basis to understand their performance for future bids that they may make?
20. Have you ever worked for a company that selected contractors for construction projects?
21. Did they have any method to select safe contractors?
22. Have you ever recommended to any company that they establish a method to select safe contractors?
23. Have you ever read any articles, books, standards or any documents that give guidance relative to methods to select safe contractors? If so, explain.
24. Have you ever written on the subject of selecting safe contractors?
25. Do you consider yourself to be expert on the method that the GC/CM should use when selecting safe contractors?
26. In your opinion, should a company such as the defendant evaluate bidders' past safety performance?
27. In this case, did the defendant evaluate the safety performance of bidders?

NOTES

1. Improving Safety Performance, A Construction Industry Cost-Effectiveness Project Report A-3, January 1982, The Business Roundtable, Washington D.C.

2. The EMR is a number assigned to a contractor by their workers compensation insurance company which is a measure of their safety performance relative to companies in their industry. A 1.0 EMR would be assigned to a company who has an experience of injury costs equal to the average company in that industry. A 2.0 EMR would show a loss rate of double the industry. A 0.5 EMR would show a company's losses are half of the average in that industry.

3. Based on Stanford University Department of Civil Engineering *Technical Report No. 196.*

4. Based on Stanford University Department of Civil Engineering *Technical Report No. 260.*

Chapter Eighteen

The Uses of OSHA

The Occupational Safety and Health Law passed in 1970 empowered Congress to promulgate and adopt occupational safety and health standards. Many of the OSHA general industry standards in 29CFR1910 were adopted from American National Standards (ANSI) which existed prior to 1970. Most construction safety standards in 29CFR1926 were adopted from prior construction safety standards that were applicable to federally funded construction projects or were adopted from ANSI standards. Since 1971, OSHA has promulgated new standards and has modified some standards. However, the majority of the standards in 29CFR1910 and 29CFR1926 come from standards which existed before 1970. The majority of OSHA standards are good, safe standards. However, there are many serious hazards to which workers could be exposed for which there are no OSHA standards. Some of the existing standards are dangerous because they permit workers to be exposed to hazards that can cause serious injury or death. We cannot always say that because there was no OSHA violation, the workplace was reasonably safe.

DANGEROUS OSHA STANDARDS

We have seen in Chapters 8 and 9 that some OSHA standards related to scaffolds and steel erection are unreasonably permissive and dangerous. Another deficiency in OSHA standards is their machine guarding standards. Some require interlocks on guards of specific machines to automatically prevent exposure to moving parts if the guard is lifted or removed. However, there is no general standard for interlocks for all machine guards which can be lifted or removed. So some machine guards without interlocks comply with OSHA standards.

Another example is OSHA's requirement for backup alarms on vehicles on construction sites. OSHA permits vehicles with an obstructed view to the rear to be operated without a reverse signal alarm (backup alarm) above surrounding noise level if there is a spotter or observer. All vehicles with obstructed views to the rear should have backup alarms, vision systems or other technology to reduce the risk of workers being run over. It is unreasonable to expect that there will always be a spotter or observer available.

OSHA also has no standard for heat, cold, ergonomics and literally hundreds of chemicals which could cause serious illness and death to workers. Safety professionals know that we cannot say that because it complies with OSHA, it is therefore safe.

SECTION 5(A)(1) OF THE OCCUPATIONAL SAFETY AND HEALTH ACT—THE GENERAL DUTY CLAUSE

For hazards likely to lead to serious injury or death for which OSHA has no standard, OSHA could apply the General Duty Clause, or Section 5(a)(1) of the Occupational Safety and Health Act. It requires the employer to provide a workplace free of recognized hazards. If OSHA can prove that the hazard is recognized, likely to lead to serious injury or death and that the employer had knowledge of the hazard (actual or constructive), then OSHA is required to issue an allegation of a violation of the General Duty Clause to the employer of the employees exposed to the hazard. However, OSHA cannot issue a General Duty violation if there is an existing OSHA standard which addresses the hazard but does not require feasible hazard controls for exposure to a particular hazard. OSHA's fall protection standards related to ironworkers and scaffolds as discussed in Chapters 8 and 9 are examples of such standards. They permit some workers on scaffolds and some ironworkers to be exposed to fall hazards greater than six feet above ground.

OSHA policy prevents it from issuing citations of violations of the General Duty Clause to GCs or CMs. In that case, the plaintiff's expert could opine that the GC/CM "permitted" a violation of the General Duty Clause rather than opining that the GC/CM violated the General Duty Clause. OSHA would not be able to cite the GC/CM for permitting contractor employees to violate OSHA standards as Controlling Employer under OSHA's Multi-Employer Citation Policy. OSHA could cite the GC/CM for General Duty violations if the GC/CM employees were exposed to the hazard.

OSHA—MULTI-EMPLOYER CITATION POLICY—WHO CAN OSHA CITE?

According to their Field Inspection Reference Manual (FIRM) (see Appendix F), OSHA's policy is to allege violations, not only to the employer of the employee exposed to the hazard (exposing employer), but also to three other types of employers:

- Creating Employer. For example, the employer whose employee removes the cover over the floor hole.
- Correcting Employer. That is, the employer who, by the rules on the job, would be required to install the hazard control. For example, the carpenter is required to put up guardrails.
- Controlling Employer.

CONTROLLING EMPLOYER

The GC/CM or Premise Owner/Host Employer (PO/HE) should be considered by OSHA to be the Controlling Employer. In order to determine if a GC/CM or (PO/HE) is a Controlling Employer, OSHA first looks to see if the contract assigns safety responsibility to the GC/CM or (PO/HE). If so, it is the Controlling Employer.

OSHA looks at the exercise of control by the GC/CM or PO/HE. In order to be a controlling employer, the GC/CM or PO/HE must exercise reasonable care to prevent and detect violations.

It is usually easy to show that the GC/CM or (PO/HE) had control over the contract work. Their primary function is to control the project. They often negotiate, select contractors and purchase materials. They also tell contractors and subcontractors:

- What work to do
- Where to work
- When to work
- They coordinate with contractors and subcontractors
- They schedule contractors
- They monitor the job site to ensure the work is done according to specifications
- They authorize payment

Premise Owners/Host Employers usually have the same control over the construction projects on their premise as general contractors and construction managers have in new construction. They often have their own Contractor Safety Program which is part of their overall safety program. The Contractor Safety Program documents the need for the PO/HE to provide safety management oversight of the GC/CM or contractor that they hire. In most construction injury cases and premise cases, the GC/CM or PO/HE should be considered by OSHA to be the Controlling Employer.

OSHA'S ENFORCEMENT POLICY: MULTI-EMPLOYER CITATION POLICY

The Code of Federal Regulations sets forth OSHA's philosophy with regard to responsibility on a construction site in 29CFR1926.16(a) through (d). OSHA recognizes that all tiers of management have safety responsibilities and that the prime contractor has overall responsibility for compliance with OSHA standards.

> 29CFR1926.16(a) . . . In no case shall the prime contractor be relieved of **overall responsibility** (emphasis added) for compliance with the requirements of this part for all work to be performed under the contract.
>
> 29CFR1926.16(b) . . . The prime contractor assumes all obligations prescribed as employer obligations under the standards contained in this part, whether or not he contracts any part of the work.
>
> 29CFR1926.16(c) . . . Thus, the prime contractor assumes the entire responsibility under the contract and the subcontractor assumes responsibility with respect to his portion of the work. With respect to subcontracted work, the prime contractor and any subcontractor or subcontractors shall be deemed to have joint responsibility.
>
> 29CFR1926.16(d) . . . Where joint responsibility exists, both the prime contractor and his subcontractor or subcontractors, regardless of tier, shall be considered subject to the enforcement provisions of the Act.

The above language in 1926.16 (a) through (d) has appeared in every Federal Register published by OSHA since 1971. It gives a philosophical basis for their Multi-Employer Citation Policy. Regulations 1926.16 (a) through (d) are not safety standards. They cannot be cited by OSHA. OSHA can only issue citations related to hazards to which workers were permitted to be exposed. 1926.16 (a) through (d) explains OSHA's understanding of the overall responsibility for compliance with OSHA standards by the prime contractor as well as a shared responsibility by all contractors and subcontractors. All industry safety authorities as indicated in Chapter 5 also agree that the GC/CM has overall responsibility for implementation of the job site safety program. They all agree that safety is a shared responsibility, that is, at all tiers of management.

WHY OSHA WOULD NOT CITE A CONTROLLING EMPLOYER

OSHA should cite the exposing employer and the Controlling Employer in cases where they can prove actual or constructive knowledge. However, during incident investigation, OSHA frequently does not cite the GC/CM when a contractor worker is injured. Some of the reasons that OSHA would not cite a GC/CM when the facts indicate that they should are:

Area Directors would rather not have cases contested before the Occupational Safety and Health Review Commission. In a serious injury or death case, the Area Director realizes that a citation issued to the GC/CM or PO/HE is more likely to lead to a contest than a citation issued only to the employer of the injured worker. If the GC/CM or PO/HE is cited as Controlling Employer, it will most likely contest because it has much more at stake economically from a third party lawsuit than it would have from an OSHA violation. The GC/CM or PO/HE knows that it is harder to defend a third party lawsuit when they have been cited by OSHA. OSHA also realizes that because of this, the GC/CM or PO/HE is more likely to contest.

OSHA sometimes decides not to cite the GC/CM or PO/HE and to use their representative's testimony against the exposing employer. That way, OSHA has less chance of a contest from the exposing employer.

Another reason OSHA might not cite a GC/CM or PO/HE is because it is harder to get information to prove knowledge on the part of the GC/CM or PO/HE than the employer. It is easier to impute knowledge to the supervisor of the exposed employee who assigns the task or who works in the same environment as the exposed employer than it is to impute knowledge to the GC/CM or PO/HE who makes periodic walks through the work site.

OSHA may not cite the GC/CM or PO/HE because OSHA does not always get all the information. They sometimes get incorrect information. Witnesses sometimes do not fess up to what they know. They sometimes protect the GC/CM or PO/HE because they want to get more work from them. Some, although well intentioned, give incorrect information. Some deliberately lie.

OSHA does not have the resources to get all of the information which can be obtained through discovery. They gather enough information to support an allegation of a violation of a standard. During incident investigation, OSHA does not put people under oath and rarely conducts depositions. They get a narrow view of a big picture. Discovery in litigation reveals much more information. In retrospect, with the information obtained in discovery, it may be clear that OSHA did not cite the GC/CM because OSHA did not have all of the facts. Often after discovery and depositions of many witnesses, it is sometimes easy to conclude that the GC/CM or PO/HE should have known of the danger and that OSHA should have cited them had OSHA had all of the information.

Other reasons that OSHA would not cite a GC/CM or PO/HE is because sometimes the inspector is incompetent or lazy. Some just do not pursue investigations to show that the GC/CM knew or should have known of the hazard because it simplifies their life. However, all OSHA enforcement personnel take an oath to enforce the law and standards as Congress intended. They are not granted the authority to make decisions contrary to their directives as set forth in their Field Operations Manual, any more than a police officer has the authority to decide which criminals to arrest for certain crimes.

GETTING INFORMATION FROM OSHA

OSHA's policy requires investigation of all fatal accidents. They have discretion to decide whether or not to investigate serious injury incidents. Serious injury incidents are usually investigated when reported to them by police or emergency medical technicians, when there is significant publicity or when a worker, union rep, family member or a worker's lawyer notifies them and requests it. The sooner the request made to OSHA, the more likely they will respond.

To find out if OSHA has investigated a particular incident, you could call the local area office and ask. The file will be under the name of the employer of the injured employee as well as other companies which were cited. If there is an investigative file, you should write and ask for all information releasable under the Freedom of Information Act. Ask for copies of photos. They may have a video tape. Their charges are minimal. You may have to prod them to respond in a timely fashion. Some Area Offices have a significant backlog of Freedom of Information requests. After you send a letter, call and speak to the person who does the Freedom of Information requests. Get a name and ask how long they expect it will take. You will probably have to follow up.

After OSHA investigates, they will give you only a copy of the citation. The cited employer has fifteen working days from the date they receive the violation to contest. If they do not contest the entire file can be released subject to redactions due to confidentiality laws. If they do contest, OSHA will release the file only after the contest has been settled or been decided by the Occupational Safety and Health Review Commission.

The OSHA file can supply important information. However, confidentiality laws require OSHA to delete some information. They will not give you the names of employee witnesses but should provide witness statements. They may provide notes that paraphrase what witnesses have said. They sometimes give the names of management reps, sometimes not. Sometimes they give the OSHA inspector's notes. They should not give the opinions of the OSHA inspector, but sometimes they do. Often the person who performs the redaction is a clerk with little or no legal training. Unfortunately, the philosophy of OSHA regarding Freedom of Information requests is—when in doubt, do not release it. Challenges can be made but the process can be time consuming.

If you want to have the OSHA inspector deposed or to testify in court, expect OSHA to make a federal case about it. OSHA argues that if their inspectors were required to testify in litigation, they would perform far fewer inspections. It is **extremely** rare for an OSHA inspector to testify in deposition or at trial relative to third party litigation.

For every citation issued, the OSHA inspectors must be able to show to their supervisor and area director that the cited employer knew or should have known of the hazard or violation on the citation. If OSHA has issued an allegation of a violation to the employer, they have concluded that there was "employer knowledge" of the hazard, that is, actual or constructive. The extent of exposure and how or why the employer knew may be deleted from the inspector's report. But OSHA should not have issued a citation if they did not have evidence which they believed would prove knowledge, actual or constructive, on the part of the citation recipient.

OSHA can also be helpful by giving you the enforcement history of a defendant. You can access OSHA's website at www.osha.gov. To get the enforcement history, follow the link to statistics/inspection data. This will give you information about inspections that have taken place and what citations were issued. It will give the number of the standard cited and the proposed fine. You can look up the standard in the Code of Federal Regulations, 29CFR1926 or 1910, to see the wording of the standard that was cited by OSHA. You could also write to the particular Area Office that issued the citation and ask for a copy of all of the files of OSHA inspections of the defendant under the Freedom of Information Act.

It might be helpful to know the OSHA history of the employer of the plaintiff. You should know that when OSHA inspectors investigate an accident, they are required to recommend citations for all apparent hazards, not just hazards or standards related to the cause of injury. It sometimes happens that they have no basis to allege a violation of a standard related to the cause of injury or death, and they cite a violation that had nothing to do with the cause of injury.

If you have a question about whether OSHA has a standard related to a particular hazard, you could call the OSHA office and ask. You could also access the OSHA site to search for interpretations or compliance directives which explain enforcement policy related to particular standards.

Chapter Nineteen

Evaluation of the Role of the Employer of the Plaintiff

The injured worker's employer has a responsibility to implement an occupational safety and health program and to comply with OSHA regulations. In most cases, the injury would have been prevented had the injured worker's employer complied with OSHA standards. However, a key question is: Why did the defendant permit the employer to work unsafely and in violation of OSHA standards?

Some attorneys think that because the conduct of the injured worker's employer was so egregious that they simply should not pursue a third party case. However, the more egregious the conduct of the employer, the more egregious it is for the defendant to permit such dangerous work. Often the reason the dangerous work was permitted is because the defendant could save money. For example:

EXCAVATION SAFETY

Consider the case where an excavation contractor blatantly violates OSHA standards by failing to shore, slope or use a trench box. Most likely the excavation contractor got the job because they submitted the low bid which excluded the significant costs related to sloping, shoring and the use of a trench box.

The CPO, GC or CM that contracts with the excavation contractor can save a lot of money if he/she awards the contract to the lowest bidder and then turns a blind eye to how the excavation work is performed, that is, if injury does not occur. Contractors who realize that the CPO, GC or CM is not concerned with safety and who know that the work will go to the lowest bidder will be inclined to cut safety costs in order to get work.

The CPO, GC or CM then designs their contracts with the excavating contractor requiring indemnification for costs associated with worker injury. The primary culprit in this arrangement is not the excavator contractor who performs the work unsafely in violation of OSHA standards. The primary culprit is the CPO, GC or CM which selected the lowest bid while not ensuring that the bid included the costs to do the work safely. The primary problem is that they participate in a deal which consciously risks the lives of workers to save money. They consciously protect their economic risk but fail to require protection for workers. They monitor to ensure that the work was performed according to specifications but fail to monitor with regard to safety. They stacked the deck against the workers.

IRONWORKER FALLS FROM ELEVATION

A steel erector contractor blatantly violates OSHA standards by failing to provide fall protection during steel erection. Most likely the contractor got the job because of a low bid which excluded the costs for fall protection. As with the excavation contractor, the CPO, GC or CM can save money if they award the contract to the contractor who submits the lowest bid and then turns a blind eye to safety.

ROOFER OR FRAMER FALLS FROM ELEVATION

Consider a case where a roofer or framer contractor blatantly violates OSHA standards by not training workers and by not requiring workers to be protected from falls. In this case, the GC/CM that hired the roofer/framer did nothing to verify that workers were properly trained and certified as required by OSHA standards. Nor did they do anything to ensure that workers actually installed fall protection. The GC/CM saves the time and the money because the roofer/framer can do the work for less money if they are not required to train workers, provide safety equipment and take the time to work safely.

One way to make clear to the jury the relative responsibilities of the CPO, GC or CM is to ask the plaintiff's safety expert a final line of questions to end direct testimony:

- Didn't the plaintiff's employer have a responsibility to comply with OSHA regulations?
- Isn't it true that we would not be here today if the employer had complied with OSHA regulations?

- Why do you still say that the GC/CM's conduct was the primary cause of Mr. Plaintiff's injury?

The expert will then be able to summarize his/her testimony and say, for example,

> It is true that safety is a shared responsibility and that the plaintiff's employer had safety management responsibility. However, the primary overall responsibility to ensure that the job site safety program is implemented lies with those at the **top**. A fundamental principle of safety management is that "safety begins at the top."
>
> Here the defendant company (GC/CM) is the top. It created the environment in which all of the contractors worked. It created the environment wherein safety was ignored. According to industry and government safety authorities and standards, they had the **primary, overall responsibility** to prevent injury at this site. The GC/CM had more power, control, authority and influence than the contractors and subcontractors. They ran the job. They created the relationship which excluded safety. They are the entity that can save money by allowing the contractor to cut corners to get the job done sooner. Time is money. They were the company with the responsibility to implement the job site safety program. They simply should not have permitted this hazard to exist.

The expert could then briefly summarize the most important facts, such as defendant failed to:

- Have a written safety program
- Hold a pre-job safety conference
- Conduct safety inspections
- Have weekly safety meetings

To end expert testimony, a PowerPoint list of key facts could be shown again to the jury.

Sometimes plaintiff attorneys want to exclude or try to minimize the role of the employer. My experience is that the conduct of the employer is always brought up by the defense in depositions and is almost always brought up in trial. If the employer's role is not addressed by the plaintiff's expert in direct testimony, the defense attorney will surely try to bring it up in their case through their expert. Despite legal possibilities in some jurisdictions of excluding testimony related to the conduct of the employer, I believe it should be brought up and discussed by the plaintiff's expert in direct testimony. One reason is because it would be better for the jury to hear the explanation of the employer responsibility first of all from the plaintiff's expert. Another reason is because after listening to the plaintiff's expert's qualifications and testimony, the jury will know that the employer is responsible to comply with OSHA. If it is not brought up and explained to the jury by the plaintiff expert, the jury will be on their own and/or influenced by the defense attorney's arguments. Another reason to bring the employer's role up in direct testimony is that the jury may think that the plaintiff's expert was holding back and not forthright in addressing it in direct testimony.

Chapter Twenty

Evaluation of the Role of the Injured Worker

Sometimes defense experts with little understanding of OSHA and safety opine that the plaintiff violated OSHA's General Duty Clause, Section 5(b) of the Occupational Safety and Health Act. However, it is not possible for a worker to violate Section 5(b) or any OSHA standard because the standards address the conduct of employers and not employees.

Section 5(b) of the Act states: "Each employee shall comply with Occupational Safety and Health Standards and all rules, regulations, and orders issued pursuant to this Act which **are applicable to his own actions and conduct** (emphasis added)."

It is also not possible for a worker to violate an OSHA standard because Congress did not grant OSHA the authority to cite or fine any worker. OSHA standards address the responsibility of employers, not workers. The employer has the responsibility to provide a workplace free of recognized hazards that are causing or are likely to cause serious injury or death [Section 5(a)(1)].

Workers do not create safety policies nor do they have the responsibility to implement safety programs. Their role is to follow safe instructions. Nevertheless, all safety professionals agree that safety is a shared responsibility and that workers should act reasonably and not needlessly expose themselves to risks of injury. However, if a worker disobeys safety instructions, it does not necessarily mean the worker is responsible for his/her own injury. It depends on the facts.

In some instances, the employer's written safety program may prohibit unsafe behavior, the worker may have been properly trained and instructed, but the employer actually only pays "lip service" to safety. That is, sometimes the "de facto policy" is to permit unsafe behaviors. In many environments in the construction industry workers would risk losing their jobs if they were to complain or to refuse to work every time they were exposed to a hazard.

Workers should not be put in a position where they must choose between risking their lives or risking their jobs. They should be provided with an environment free of recognized hazards. That is why OSHA was passed.

Not all employers are so unscrupulous as to permit uncontrolled hazards in their work environment. Many do indeed make reasonable efforts to prevent worker injury. Even with reasonable efforts on the part of the employer, GC and CM, injury will sometimes occur because of the unsafe conduct of the worker. What is a fair way to evaluate the conduct of the worker?

The following method is essentially the method that OSHA uses when deciding whether or not to issue a citation to an employer when there is apparent unsafe behavior or a "rules violation" on the part of the worker exposed to the hazard. It is also consistent with decisions of the Occupational Safety and Health Review Commission as to when alleged violations should be vacated because of workers' rules violation.

Factors to consider when evaluating the behavior of the injured worker:

- **Instruction**. Did the employee violate safety instructions?
- **Training**. Was the worker trained to recognize the hazard and the risk that led to injury?
- **Environment**. What was the safety management environment? What was the physical environment?

Consideration of these three factors will give a basis to form opinions about the conduct of the plaintiff.

SAFETY INSTRUCTION

Workers should be instructed regarding safety procedures and should follow their instructions. If a worker violated safety instructions, the employer had no knowledge of the violation, and the employer had been diligently implementing a safety program, there is no basis for liability. However, sometimes employers have safety programs with rules that they permit to be violated. The "de facto" or actual policy is then to permit workers to work unsafely. It is not fair to fault a worker for unsafe behavior when it was a standard accepted procedure and was permitted by all levels of management. Workers are often permitted to work in violation of safety policy because it gets the job done quicker and it saves time and money. Sometimes workers do work unsafely because if they were to complain every time that they were required to work while exposed to a hazard, they would be fired or wouldn't get calls for work from the union hall.

TRAINING OF HAZARD AND RISK

The next factor to evaluate is what the worker knew about the hazard and the risk. Was the worker trained to recognize the hazard and the risk of injury? The hazard is the unsafe condition or procedure which led to injury. Risk is related to those factors (risk factors) which make it more likely that the hazard will result in injury.

We recognize risk factors relative to heart disease such as high cholesterol, lack of exercise, obesity, alcohol use, smoking, etc. Risk factors related to breast cancer include environment, family history, diet, etc. Likewise there are risk factors related to injury.

Usually the worker will recognize the hazard that led to injury. For example, the worker at elevation knows he/she is exposed to a fall hazard. We can assume the worker was not trying to get injured. He/she likely was not aware of the particular **risk factor** that led to injury. In the moments just before the fall, the worker most likely did not realize that exposure to the hazard would result in a fall. For instance:

- A worker on a sloped roof of a residence under construction knows a slip can result in a fall (that is, he/she recognizes the hazard), but did not realize that the plywood was **wet** and **slippery** (risk factor).
- An ironworker knows that a misstep could result in a fall but did not realize that the crane operator was going to **overshoot the load** (risk factor) that he/she was guiding.
- A worker in a trench knows that the trench could collapse but did not know the **type of soil, compaction or moisture content** (risk factors) of the bank was so loose.
- A worker knows the forklift truck could run over him/her but did not know it was reversing (risk factor) toward him/her at the time of injury because he/she did not see or hear it. A backup alarm would have reduced the risk by warning the worker. Lack of a backup alarm is a risk factor.

It is unfair to blame a worker who did not or who could not be expected to know of the hazard or risk that led to injury. However, if the worker was aware of the hazard and the risk, we should still look at other factors before assigning fault.

Management can be expected to communicate, plan, monitor and inspect to verify compliance. However, management reps cannot be expected to be everywhere, all the time, watching everybody do everything. It essentially comes down to whether or not the employer knew or should have known of the unsafe behavior. Knowledge of the hazard (actual or constructive) is the key factor in every case.

ENVIRONMENT

The next factor to consider is the environment in which the employee works. Workers should not be permitted to work in environments which are unreasonably dangerous, such as on a roof without fall protection, in a trench without protection, around floor holes without guardrails or covers, etc. They also should be working in an environment where safety is being managed at all levels, that is, one where management has required fall protection on roofs, safe trenches and excavations and protection around holes, etc. Important questions to consider when evaluating the behavior of a worker relative to the environment are:

- Is the physical environment reasonably safe?
- Is the management system taking reasonable steps to prevent injury?

If the worker who performs an unsafe act is properly trained regarding hazard and risk, has been given adequate safety instruction, is in an environment that is reasonably safe and the management system is conscientiously managing safety, his or her lawyer should not be looking for a defendant to sue. However, if the worker was not trained, did not realize the risk that led to injury, did not violate any safety instructions, worked in an environment which was unsafe and within a management system that did not implement a safety program, he or she should not be faulted for his/her injury. Of course, in most cases, the facts are somewhere between these two extremes.

You might end direct testimony of your expert by asking:

1. In your evaluation, did you consider the conduct of the plaintiff?
2. How did you evaluate the conduct of the plaintiff?
3. What did your analysis find? Answer: The plaintiff did not violate safety instructions. The plaintiff was not trained as required by OSHA nor aware of risk factors. The plaintiff had to work in a physically dangerous environment where there was no hazard control and within a management system that failed. Based on these facts, I find no basis to fault the plaintiff for causing his/her own injury.

Chapter Twenty-One

Challenging the Defense Expert—Qualifications and Method of Evaluation

Often in a worker injury case, there is no engineering question regarding how the incident occurred or what caused the injury. The primary expert to use to explain the standard of care to the judge and jury should be a safety professional. A safety professional is a person who has dedicated his/her professional life to worker injury prevention. A safety expert will have applied the principles and practices of safety management and will have performed the functions of hazard identification, evaluation and control for many years. He/she will have worked for organizations such as an insurance company in loss control, manufacturing companies, construction companies, consulting companies, government agencies, universities and so on. The safety professional should be a member of the American Society of Safety Engineers. Most members of the American Society of Safety Engineers are not graduate engineers. In most worker injury cases, there is no engineering question. The essential question is—Who is supposed to do what to prevent worker injury? Do the facts show that the defendant failed to take reasonable steps to prevent injury? Were those failures a cause of the worker's injury?

The defense often hires an engineer with little background in safety management. The engineer may have taken a few OSHA courses. That does not make one an OSHA safety expert. An engineering expert will likely not have performed a scientific engineering evaluation. The engineer will likely not have tested materials, applied formulas or performed calculations. Often the only safety management experience that the engineer has is as performing safety management as an auxiliary function while serving as a project manager on construction projects. They are vulnerable to challenges to their qualifications and their methodology of evaluation.

Engineering experts' evaluations often ignore the industry standards established by the American Society of Safety Engineers, the National Safety Council, the American National Standards Institute and others. They often focus on OSHA as the only indicator of negligence. They can and should be challenged.

You could ask the expert to give you his/her last five plaintiff reports and last five defense reports related to construction worker injury cases or five of each related to cases which have settled or have been adjudicated. You can then see if he/she shifts the methodology of evaluation depending upon who pays.

The defense expert may be a civil engineer or mechanical engineer who performs evaluations and forms opinions based on his/her experience and what they believe to be the industry standard. They often confuse the industry practice with the industry standard. While they may be competent to look at the hazard and to read the OSHA standards to form opinions about whether or not the hazard was controlled as required by the standard, that is far short of an evaluation of the industry standard of care and policies and procedures that OSHA uses to decide if there is a basis to allege a violation of a standard.

My experience has been that engineers who are not safety professionals perform evaluations based solely on whether or not there was a violation of an OSHA standard that led to injury. OSHA compliance is one important indicator of the standard of care but not the only one.

When there is no engineering question involving causation, engineers who have little safety background and expertise with OSHA are particularly vulnerable to a Daubert or Daubert-type challenge.[1] In most construction injury cases, the essential question is related to "why" there was exposure to a hazard such as an unprotected hole, a floor opening without a guardrail, a truck without a backup alarm, etc. The expert should be a safety professional, OSHA expert, and an expert in the principles and practices of construction safety management.

Answers to the following questions during deposition will give you facts to use when deciding whether or not to bring a Daubert-like challenge.

CHALLENGING THE "OSHA EXPERT"

1. Have you ever worked as an employee of OSHA?
2. Have you ever worked as a consultant to OSHA?
3. Have you ever performed services for OSHA?
4. What is the Occupational Safety and Health Review Commission?
5. Have you ever testified before the Occupational Safety and Health Review Commission?
6. Have you ever been hired as a consultant for companies in any matters before the Occupational Safety and Health Review Commission?

7. Have you ever taught anywhere on the subject of the policies and procedures for law enforcement for OSHA?
8. Have you ever published on the subject of the policies and procedures that OSHA follows to enforce the law?
9. Have you ever advertised as having competency as an OSHA expert?
10. According to OSHA's Field Operations Manual, can you tell me the four elements that OSHA has to prove in order to sustain an allegation of a serious violation before the Occupational Safety and Health Review Commission? Answer:

    - There was a standard that was violated.
    - There was exposure, that is, actual or potential exposure, to the hazard.
    - There was knowledge, actual or constructive, on the part of the employer.
    - Serious injury is the likely result if exposure to the hazard results in injury.

11. According to the OSHA Field Operations Manual, can you tell me what OSHA's definition is of "constructive knowledge"? (Answer: Constructive knowledge is imputed when "with reasonable diligence" the employer should have known of the exposure to the hazard in violation of the OSHA standard.)
12. Can you tell me the three elements that OSHA considers when deciding if an employer had constructive knowledge that an employee was exposed to a hazard in violation of an OSHA standard? Answer:

    - The duration of the hazard. The longer the exposure time, the more likely the employer should have known of its existence.
    - The number of workers exposed to the hazard, the more likely that the employer would know of the exposure.
    - The size of the job. The smaller the job, the more likely the employer would know of the exposure.

13. Do you know what OSHA's Field Operations Manual says about when to issue citations for "potential exposure" to a hazard? (Answer: OSHA will interview workers about work that has been done in the area where the hazard exists. They will consider what future work has to be done in those areas. A classic example is a trench with no one in it but there is a shovel on the excavation floor. There is potential exposure because somebody was in there and someone would have to go in to get it.)
14. Do you know what OSHA's Field Operations Manual says about how to determine if a citation should be issued for a "rules violation" on the part

of an employee? (Answer: If the exposure is an "isolated incident" within an environment where safety was being competently managed, OSHA wouldn't cite the employer for a "rules violation" that the employer couldn't reasonably have been expected to identify and be aware of.)

15. Can you tell me the difference between a vertical standard and a horizontal standard as defined by OSHA? (Answer: A horizontal standard covers the entire construction industry, such as fall hazards [1926.500]. A vertical standard covers one particular hazard, such as trenches or steel erection standards. OSHA's policy is to cite the vertical standard rather than the horizontal standard when there are two standards covering the same exposure.)
16. Can you give me an example of a horizontal standard? (1926.501, fall protection, is a horizontal standard because it covers all exposures.)
17. Can you give me an example of a vertical standard? (1926.451 related to scaffolds is a vertical standard.)
18. Do you know the factors that OSHA considers when deciding when a violation should be classified as "willful" as opposed to being a serious violation?
19. Do you know what OSHA means by an Affirmative Defense? (Answer: Some affirmative defenses are: unpreventable employee misconduct, unpreventable supervisory misconduct, isolated incidents, greater hazards, infeasibility.)
20. Can you tell me some of the affirmative defenses that OSHA considers to allegations of violations of OSHA standards?
21. Do you know what OSHA's General Duty Clause is?
22. Do you know how OSHA uses the General Duty Clause? (Answer: OSHA uses the General Duty Clause to cite when there is a serious hazard that is recognized and is likely to cause serious injury or death.)
23. Can you tell me the ways that OSHA shows "industry recognition" of a hazard related to an allegation of a violation of the General Duty Clause, Section 5(a)(1) of the Occupational Safety and Health Act? Answer: OSHA looks to see if the industry recognized the hazard. That is,

    - Is there an ANSI standard?
    - Does the National Safety Council recognize it?
    - Do industry publications recognize it?
    - Do manufacturers warn of the hazard?
    - Has NIOSH recognized it?
    - Is there common sense recognition of the hazard?

24. Do you own a copy of the OSHA Field Operations Manual?

25. Have you ever referred to the OSHA's Field Operations Manual before forming opinions about violations of OSHA?
26. Can you tell me what the OSHA's Field Operations Manual says regarding an isolated incident as an affirmative defense?
27. Can you tell me what the OSHA's Field Operations Manual says regarding "preventable employee misconduct" as an affirmative defense?
28. Can you tell me what the OSHA's Field Operations Manual says regarding "greater hazard" as an affirmative defense?
29. Do you know what the Occupational Safety and Health Act specifies with regard to statute of limitations?
30. Do you know what the Occupational Safety and Health Act says about "coverage," that is, which employees are specified as covered and which employees are exempt from the Occupational Safety and Health Act?
31. Can you tell me what the Occupational Safety and Health Act says about OSHA's authority to **adopt** national consensus standards? (Answer: From 1970 to 1972 only OSHA had authority to adopt national consensus standards.)
32. Do you know what the Occupational Safety and Health Act says about OSHA's authority to **promulgate** standards? (Answer: The Act gives OSHA authority to promulgate standards.)
33. Do you know what the Occupational Safety and Health Act says with regard to the relationship between OSHA and common law? (Answer: The law says OSHA was not meant to affect common law or workers comp.)
34. Do you know if the Occupational Safety and Health Act grants OSHA the authority to cite a worker for a violation of an OSHA standard? (The Act doesn't give OSHA the authority to cite a worker.)
35. Do you know if in the Occupational Safety and Health Act Congress gave OSHA the authority to stop work being performed on a construction site because of hazardous conditions? (The Act doesn't give OSHA the authority to stop any work.)
36. Do you know the method that OSHA uses to determine whether or not a violation is a willful violation?
37. Do you know what a Variance is relative to compliance with OSHA standards?
38. Do you know the reasons why OSHA would grant a variance from a standard?
39. Can an OSHA inspector grant a variance?
40. Can an Area Director grant a variance?
41. Can a Regional Administrator grant a variance? Answer: Only the National Office can grant a variance.

42. Have you ever participated in an informal conference with OSHA after OSHA issued an employer a citation?
43. Have you ever presented testimony to OSHA during any standards promulgation processes?
44. Have you ever written to OSHA about your opinions of any proposed standards?
45. Can you tell me the names of any safety journals or magazines or any news service which provides updates of information on changes which occur in OSHA's policies and standards?
46. Have you ever had anything published on the subject of OSHA standards?
47. Have you ever taught on construction safety in any colleges or universities regarding OSHA regulations?
48. Were you ever qualified as expert in OSHA's policies and procedures for enforcing standards?
49. Do you hold yourself out as expert in the policies and procedures that OSHA uses when enforcing the standards?
50. Have you ever been qualified as an expert in any particular OSHA standard?

CHALLENGE TO EXPERT'S CONSTRUCTION SAFETY MANAGEMENT EXPERIENCE

1. Are there any industry organizations which you consider to be authoritative regarding what they say relative to reasonable steps that a GC/CM should take to prevent contractor and subcontractor worker injury?
2. Are there any safety journals that you consider to be authoritative in the field of construction safety management?
3. Are there any books that you consider to be authoritative in the field of construction safety management?
4. Are there any authors that you consider to be authoritative in the field of construction safety management?
5. Who are some of the most respected construction safety professionals in the United States?
6. Have you ever written a safety manual?
7. Have you ever been hired to design a safety program?
8. Have you ever written any manuals, brochures or books on construction safety?
9. Have you ever held a job where your primary function was safety management?

10. Are you a member of the American Society of Safety Engineers?
11. Are you a member of the National Safety Council?
12. Are you a member of the National Safety Management Society?
13. Are you a member of the Human Factors Society?
14. Are you a member of the System Safety Society?
15. Are you a member of the Construction Safety Institute?
16. Have you ever taught in any colleges or universities on any safety subject?
17. Have you ever taught safety anywhere at all?
18. Have you ever published any article regarding construction safety management?
19. Have you ever published any article regarding any aspect of safety?
20. Have you ever had any articles published on any subject at all?
21. Have you ever advertised services related to construction safety management in any trade journals?
22. Have you ever published in any journal or anywhere on the subject of construction safety management?
23. Have you ever attended any construction safety conference of any of these construction safety management societies?
24. Do you subscribe to any safety journals?
25. Did you ever work full time in safety management?
26. Have you ever been trained in safety management?
27. Were you ever hired to perform a safety audit?
28. Were you ever hired to evaluate a company's safety program?
29. Are you expert in the principles and practices of construction safety management?
30. List for me all of the principles and practices of construction safety management that you are aware of.
31. Were you ever qualified as expert in the principles and practices of construction safety management?

PRINCIPLES AND PRACTICES OF ACCIDENT INVESTIGATION AND CAUSATION ANALYSIS

1. Have you ever taught on the subject of the principles and practices of accident investigation and causation analysis?
2. Have you ever attended any course devoted to the subject of the principles and practices of accident investigation and causation analysis?
3. Have you ever done any research related to the principles and practices of accident investigation and causation analysis?

4. Have you ever published on the subject of the principles and practices of accident investigation and causation analysis?
5. Have you ever advertised as having expertise in the principles and practices of accident investigation and causation analysis?
6. Have you ever been qualified in litigation as an expert in the principles and practices of accident investigation and analysis?
7. Have you ever advertised that you have competency in the area of the principles and practices of accident investigation and analysis?
8. Do you consider yourself to be expert in the area of the principles and practices of accident investigation and causation analysis?

PRINCIPLES AND PRACTICES OF FALL HAZARD CONTROL

1. Have you ever taught on the subject of the principles and practices of fall hazard control in any colleges or universities?
2. Have you ever published on the topic of the principles and practices of fall hazard control in the construction industry?
3. Have you ever advertised as an expert with competency in the principles and practices of fall hazard control in any trade journals?
4. Have you ever advertised in any publications purchased by lawyers that you have expertise in the principles and practices of fall hazard control?
5. Have you ever been qualified in any court as an expert in the principles and practices of fall hazard control?
6. Do you know the names of the authorities which establish the principles and practices of fall hazard control?
7. Are you a member of the International Fall Protection Society?
8. Do you consider yourself to be an expert in the principles and practices of fall hazard control?

NO ENGINEERING EVALUATION PERFORMED

1. Am I correct that you are a civil/mechanical engineer?
2. In this case, did you use any engineering methods to test materials?
3. Did you perform any calculations?
4. Did you use any formulas or perform any quantitative analysis?
5. Did you perform any engineering reliability studies?
6. Would you agree with me that there is no engineering question involved in the question of responsibility for this injury?

At this point, the expert may agree that he/she is not an OSHA expert nor a safety management expert and did no engineering evaluation. You may then ask:

7. Do you understand your role to be one to clarify and simplify for the jury the responsibilities of the defendant for injury prevention in this case?
8. Since you are not an OSHA expert and you are not a safety management expert and there is no engineering question involved and you are an engineer, how is it that your background qualifies you to help the jury understand questions of safety management responsibility and OSHA compliance?

EVALUATING THE CONDUCT OF THE PLAINTIFF

1. In approximately how many cases have you performed evaluations of the conduct of an injured construction worker?
2. Do you know of any safety authorities that give guidance related to how to evaluate the conduct of a worker who is injured?
3. In your report, did you express the particular method that you used to evaluate the conduct of the plaintiff?
4. Do you know how OSHA considers the behavior of workers when deciding whether or not to allege violations of their standards?
5. Have you ever been qualified as an expert with competency to evaluate the conduct of the worker in the injury causation process?
6. List for me all the factors that you normally consider when evaluating the conduct of an injured worker.
7. Did the worker violate specific safety instructions?
8. What was the worker trained about the hazard and risk to which he/she was exposed just before this incident occurred?
9. Was the environment in which the worker was required to work reasonably safe?
10. Was the worker working in an environment where safety was being managed?

CROSS EXAMINATION OF EXPERT WHO FAILS TO CONSIDER ANSI IN CONSTRUCTION/PREMISE CASES

ANSI standards are national consensus industry standards. They are part of the standard of care. They are considered to be "minimal" standards, that is, the minimum that could be agreed upon by the majority of the members of the committee. They should be considered by the expert in his/her evaluation.

1. Do you know what the American National Standards Institute is?
2. Do you own any publications of the American National Standards Institute?
3. Do you know if the American National Standards Institute has approved any construction safety standards?
4. Do you know how ANSI standards are promulgated?
5. Do you know which types of organizations participate in the development of ANSI standards?
6. Do you know if ANSI standards are national consensus standards?
7. What are national consensus standards?
8. Have you ever performed an evaluation where you have relied on an ANSI standard for your evaluation and opinions? Explain which standards. Were you working for the plaintiff or the defendant?
9. Prior to this case, did you ever rely upon ANSI A10.33—Safety and Health Program Requirements for Multi-Employer Projects?
10. Prior to this case, did you ever rely upon ANSI A10.38—Basic Elements of an Employer's Program to provide a safe and healthful work environment?
11. Prior to this case, did you ever rely upon ANSI A10.32—Fall Protection Systems?
12. Prior to this case, did you ever rely upon ANSI A10.1—Pre-Project and Pre-Task Safety and Health Planning?
13. When you performed your evaluation in this case, did you rely upon ANSI A10.33?
14. If not, why not?
15. When you performed your evaluation in this case, did you rely upon ANSI A10.38?
16. If not, why not?
17. When you performed your evaluation in this case, did you rely upon ANSI A10.32?
18. If not, why not?
19. When you performed your evaluation in this case, did you rely upon ANSI A10.1?
20. If not, why not?
21. Do you know in general what ANSI A10.33 says about the safety role of a CPO, GC, CM and PM?
22. Do you know in general what ANSI A10.38 says about the requirements of a safety program?
23. Do you know in general what ANSI A10.32 says about fall protection?
24. Do you know in general what ANSI A10.1 says about planning for safety?
25. Do you own a copy of ANSI standard A10.33? A10.38? A10.32? A10.1?
26. Have you ever read any of those ANSI standards?

CROSS EXAMINATION OF EXPERT WHO OPINES THAT COMPLIANCE WITH A DANGEROUS OSHA STANDARD IS REASONABLE

Sometimes workers will be injured because of exposure to a hazard for which there is no OSHA standard or the standard which applies is permissive and dangerous. Ironworkers exposed to falls less than 15 feet is one example. OSHA does not require any fall protection at all for any ironworker working less than 15 feet above ground despite the fact that it is entirely feasible to provide fall protection. Workers on scaffolds exposed to falls less than 10 feet is another example. OSHA permits workers on scaffolds less than 10 feet to be without fall protection. There are many other hazards to which workers are exposed and there is no OSHA standard. The following are general questions for experts who opine that compliance with a dangerous OSHA standard is acceptable:

1. Are you familiar with OSHA's standards promulgation process?
2. If so, explain.
3. Have you ever participated in any way in the promulgation of an OSHA standard?
4. If so, explain.
5. Can the standards promulgation process result in new standards?
6. Can the standards promulgation process cause changes or enhancement in current standards?
7. Do you know of any OSHA standards that have been changed or enhanced by the standards promulgation process? Answer: Steel erection, fall protection in construction, scaffold standards, ladder standards and many others.
8. Would you agree with me that changes can result in enhancements or improvements to make the standard more safe and protective?
9. Would you agree with me that new standards are promulgated because there were hazards for which there were no OSHA standards to protect workers?
10. Do you agree that over time, OSHA promulgates some new standards and improves some existing standards because there were hazards to which workers were exposed and OSHA did not require those workers to be protected with feasible hazard controls?
11. Do you agree that in the future, OSHA will promulgate new standards regarding hazards which can cause serious injury for which there is no current OSHA standard?
12. Do you agree that OSHA will enhance some existing standards to make them safer and provide workers with greater protection?

13. Do you agree that there are many proposed standards in various stages of the standards development process?
14. Do you agree that the standards development process is somewhat political?
15. If so, explain.
16. Do you agree that the standards promulgation process of OSHA is influenced by the industry organizations and labor organizations which are affected by the proposed standard?
17. Would you agree that compromises are sometimes made in the standards promulgation process?
18. Would you agree that compromises can result in standards which are minimal?
19. Have you ever heard the expression that OSHA standards are "minimal" standards achieved through the standards promulgation process?
20. Is it possible that today a worker could be injured because of a hazard for which there is no OSHA standard but there are economically and technologically feasible ways to control that hazard?
21. Is there an OSHA standard that requires standard fall protection on scaffolds nine feet above ground level? (NOTE: The OSHA fall protection standard requires fall protection beginning at ten feet. OSHA used to require fall protection on scaffolds to begin at four feet. However, they "raised" it to ten feet. It does not make sense.)
22. Would you agree with me that a worker falling nine feet could suffer quadriplegia, brain damage or death?
23. Is there an OSHA standard that requires fall protection for ironworkers working less than 15 feet above ground? (NOTE: OSHA does not require fall protection for ironworkers until they are 15 feet above ground level. That also does not make sense.)
24. Could brain damage, quadriplegia and death result from a fall of less than 15 feet?
25. Does OSHA have standards related to cold temperatures?
26. Does OSHA have standards related to heat?
27. If a worker was required to work near a furnace with temperatures above 120 degrees, is there any OSHA standard that would apply?
28. If workers were required to work in freezers with temperatures well below freezing, is there any OSHA standard that applies?
29. Would you agree that OSHA does not have standards related to ergonomics or cumulative trauma?
30. Would you agree that serious injury could and has resulted from repetitive tasks due to cumulative trauma?

31. Would you agree that there are hundreds of chemicals which OSHA has no standard for relative to permissible exposure levels in the atmosphere?
32. If there is a hazard that could result in serious injury or death and there are economically and technologically feasible ways to control the hazard and there is no OSHA standard, is it reasonable to permit a worker's life to be exposed to that hazard?
33. Is it acceptable to you (as a profession) to allow workers to be exposed to risks that could result in serious injury or death when the risk could be eliminated or controlled through reasonable accident prevention measures, that is, those which are economically and technologically feasible?
34. Do the ethics of engineering societies say that the members should hold safety to be paramount?

CROSS EXAMINATION OF EXPERT WHO OPINES THAT BECAUSE OSHA DID NOT CITE A DEFENDANT, THE DEFENDANT THEREFORE DID NOT VIOLATE AN OSHA STANDARD

My experience is that judges do not permit experts to testify as to which company OSHA cited. However, in their reports, defense experts sometimes will express an opinion that the defendant GC/CM did not violate OSHA and is not a controlling employer based on the fact that OSHA did not cite them. The following are questions which can be used to show that this presumption could be false.

1. Have you ever been trained by OSHA as to when to cite or not cite according to the OSHA Multi-Employer Workplace Policy?
2. Have you ever made recommendations to an OSHA Area Director about whether or not to cite an employer relative to OSHA's Multi-Employer Workplace Policy?
3. Have you ever testified before the Occupational Safety and Health Review Commission regarding issues of OSHA's Multi-Employer Workplace Policy?
4. Is it possible for an OSHA representative to make mistakes by failing to cite employers who should have been cited?
5. If a GC/CM is actually a controlling employer according to OSHA's definition, do you know of any good reason why OSHA would choose not to issue a citation to that controlling employer?
6. In your experience, are all OSHA inspectors of equal competence?

7. Are some OSHA inspectors very well qualified and conscientious while others are not well qualified nor conscientious?
8. Would you expect that some Area Directors are more courageous and others more timid?
9. Would you expect some Area Directors to be more conscientious than others?
10. Would you expect some Area Directors to be more politically astute than others?
11. Would you expect some Area Directors to be more legally astute than others?
12. Isn't it true that when you perform evaluations in worker injury cases, much of the information you review is from the deposition of people who are under oath?
13. Information that you receive to evaluate responsibility is after depositions and discovery, isn't that true?
14. Isn't it true that the discovery process and sworn depositions will often reveal much more detailed information and facts about a particular incident than an OSHA inspector can typically get?
15. Isn't it true that OSHA inspectors do not put people under oath when they perform investigations?
16. Do you realize that sometimes management officials will not voluntarily give the OSHA inspector information which may be detrimental to them?
17. Do you recognize that sometimes it is possible that management representatives will give misleading information to OSHA inspectors?
18. Do you recognize that sometimes witnesses will give not only misleading information but will actually give false information?
19. Do you know of any circumstance where OSHA failed to cite a controlling employer when they should have?
20. Is it possible that there could be times when OSHA would fail to cite a controlling employer that they should have?
21. Is it possible that OSHA would not cite a GC/CM as a controlling employer when they should have because they were trying to keep the number of contested cases low?
22. Is it possible that OSHA Area Directors recognize the probability of a contest being greater when the general contractor is cited and therefore do not cite the general contractor to keep contested cases low?
23. Could it be that OSHA did not issue a citation to a controlling employer when they should have because they were just not able to obtain enough information to prove an allegation even though that employer was really a controlling employer?

24. Would you agree with me that just because OSHA does not cite a GC/CM as controlling employer, that doesn't mean that the facts show that the GC/CM was not a controlling employer?
25. In order to determine whether or not an employer is a controlling employer under OSHA's Multi-Employer Workplace Policy, is it important to consider the following factors: (NOTE: These are the factors that OSHA says must be considered when determining whether or not an employer is a controlling employer.)
    - Whether or not they negotiated contracts
    - Whether or not they set schedules
    - Whether or not they determined the sequence that crafts work
    - Whether or not they are able to resolve disputes between contractors
    - Whether or not the contract assigns safety responsibility
26. In this case, did you consider whether or not the GC/CM negotiated contracts?
27. Did you consider whether or not the GC/CM set schedules?
28. Did you consider whether or not the GC/CM determined the sequence of work?
29. Did you determine whether or not the GC/CM resolved disputes between contractors?
30. Did the GC/CM determine where the work was going to be done by contractors?
31. Did the GC/CM determine when the work would be done?
32. Did the GC/CM inspect to see if the work was done properly according to specifications?
33. Did the GC/CM determine whether contractors would be paid because the work was completed properly?
34. Did the GC/CM run the job and control the work?

NOTE

1. *Daubert vs. Merrell Dow* 509US579 (1993) requires the expert to be qualified in his/her area of expertise and to use a generally accepted methodology of evaluation to form opinions.

Chapter Twenty-Two

Working with Your Expert

Every workers compensation case with significant losses should be evaluated for third party possibilities, not only by lawyers but by an expert or experts. No one sees it all. I must admit that I have turned down more than one case because I did not think there was a viable theory of liability only to learn later that an attorney successfully litigated the case. When you are not sure if there is a viable theory of liability, it helps to know an expert or experts to consult to see what they see. Most experts will give you an initial free evaluation to see if he/she will likely be able to help.

Once you have a pretty good idea of where you are going, you should hire the expert. It can be a mistake to do all of the discovery and then look for an expert. An expert could be helpful in giving input into discovery requests. The expert may suggest representatives to be deposed that you wouldn't have thought of. For example, there may be a local safety representative of the defendant but also a regional or corporate level safety manager that could be exposed. In my experience, that corporate level safety manager can be very important to establish what the local level management should have done. They are usually dedicated safety professionals who indeed have tried their best to prevent worker injury. They may have performed root cause analysis of the incident and shared their findings with other company location managers so they too could make appropriate changes to prevent recurrences.

The expert should be helpful in creating lists of proposed deposition questions for you to ask of deponents such as superintendents of the general contractor, construction manager, construction project owner, corporate safety manager, division safety manager, local safety manager, best person in products cases, and the opposing expert.

Your expert could do research in areas such as:

- Magnitude and severity of injuries suffered from the hazard to which your client was exposed as reported by OSHA, NIOSH, the National Safety Council and other organizations. That is, such injury data relative to:
  - Trench collapse
  - Trucks reversing and running over pedestrians
  - Falls from roofs
  - Crane boom contact with overhead power line
- OSHA history of employer and defendants
- Publications of the opposing expert
- Qualifications of opposing expert. Sometimes experts embellish, exaggerate or provide false or misleading information. Your expert may be able to detect false qualifications.
- Past history of the defendant relative to litigation. The expert may have participated in litigation against the defendant before.
- Your expert or his or her expert friends may have reports of the expert used in cases involving the defendant.
- Sometimes experts retain their expert reports and depositions of opposing experts.
- Sometimes reports show an expert changes his or her methodology of evaluation depending on the needs of the case.
- Sometimes reports show that the expert relied on a particular authority in one case and did not include that authority in a case where it would have been detrimental.

PREPARATION FOR TRIAL

You could ask your expert to propose questions for qualifications and direct testimony. If the expert is experienced, he/she probably knows a clear, simple ways to present questions so that the jury understands exactly what was supposed to be done by whom, what was done or not done, and what opinions and conclusions flow from those facts. Trial testimony could follow the plaintiff's expert report. The **cornerstone** of the report and the basis of liability is the key facts obtained through discovery.

The key deposition will likely be that of the superintendent of the GC, the CM, the safety manager, the person most knowledgeable regarding product safety management in products cases or in premise cases, or the contractor liaison representative. The following is an example of facts obtained from the deposition of the superintendent of the general contractor:

DEPOSITION OF SUPERINTENDENT OF GENERAL CONTRACTOR

- He has been a superintendent for this company for 20 years (6-4).
- He scheduled contractors, coordinated contractors, held weekly meetings, inspected the work of contractors, authorized payments, and ran the job (7-20).
- He has had no OSHA or safety training (9-15).
- He did not require contractors to attend a pre-job safety meeting (12-8).
- He did not hold weekly safety meetings with contractors (15-22).
- He did not perform daily inspections (22-1).
- No one from his company performed daily safety inspections (23-7).
- He did not require any workers exposed to falls to have the OSHA required safety training (29-12).
- He never did anything to verify if forklift operators had the OSHA required safety training (31-6).
- He never did anything to verify that workers on scaffolds received the OSHA required scaffold safety training (32-4).
- He never verified that any workers received any OSHA required training (33-10).
- He never evaluated the safety performance of any contractor (41-5).
- His safety performance was never evaluated by anyone in his company (43-1).
- He has no written assigned safety management tasks (44-2).
- He does take reasonable steps to make sure that the contract is implemented with regard to quality of work or specification compliance (47-8).
- He does not do anything to ensure that contractors comply with OSHA as required by his company's contract with them (49-13).
- If he had seen the plaintiff exposed to this hazard prior to this incident, he would have told him to stop working (54-3).
- The plaintiff and co-workers had been performing their work in the same way for several days prior to this incident (59-9).
- The exposure of the plaintiff and co-workers to the fall hazard was conspicuous, that is, was easy to identify.

SAMPLE EXPERT REPORT

See Appendix G for a Sample Expert Report.

DIRECT TESTIMONY OF SAFETY EXPERT

Direct testimony of the expert could follow the outline of the report. The following is an example of questions for direct testimony of the plaintiff's expert:

1. Did I give you an assignment?
2. What did you do to prepare for that assignment?
3. Explain to the jury how you performed your evaluation? Answer: I considered the following:

METHODOLOGY OF EVALUATION

- Industry Standard—Principles and Practices of Safety Management
- OSHA Standards
- ANSI Standards
- Contract
- Safety and Health Program of General Contractor

PRINCIPLES AND PRACTICES OF SAFETY MANAGEMENT

4. What do you mean by the principles and practices of safety management? Answer: Industry safety authorities have established customary reasonable steps that general contractors should take to prevent contractor worker injury. Those industry safety authorities are:

INDUSTRY SAFETY AUTHORITIES—STANDARD OF CARE

- The Associated General Contractors of America
- The National Safety Council
- Construction Industry Institute
- American National Standards Institute

5. What is the Associated General Contractors of America?

ASSOCIATED GENERAL CONTRACTORS OF AMERICA

- Founded in 1927.
- The U.S. leading authority in the construction industry with more than 30,000 members.
- Has published the *Manual of Accident Prevention in Construction* since 1927
- Has guided general contractors regarding ways to prevent construction worker injury for more than 80 years

6. What is the National Safety Council?

THE NATIONAL SAFETY COUNCIL

- Leading industry advocate for worker injury prevention in the United States.
- Founded in 1917 and chartered by the United States Congress.
- 36,000 members including representatives of corporations, unions, government agencies, insurance companies, academia and consultants
- Has published *Accident Prevention Manual* and *Core Safety Materials for the Construction Professional* which give guidance related to ways to prevent worker injury.
- Founded in 1917 to standardize ways to prevent worker injury. They give guidance in their *Accident Prevention Manual* about construction safety management and the responsibilities of both general contractors and contractors.

7. What is the Construction Industry Institute?

CONSTRUCTION INDUSTRY INSTITUTE

- A non-profit consortium of more than 100 leading general contractors, owners and engineers.
- Publication—*Managing Subcontractor Safety*, i.e. how to prevent construction worker injury.

8. What is the American National Standards Institute?

> **AMERICAN NATIONAL STANDARDS INSTITUTE**
>
> The American National Standards Institute is an industry consensus standard that establishes minimum procedures for general contractors on a construction site regarding safety management.
>
> - Has promulgated more than 200 industry safety standards.
> - Members include representatives from industry, government, unions, academia and consultants.
> - Publication—*Safety and Health Program Requirements for Multi-Employer Projects*; i.e., how to prevent construction worker injuries.

9. Do those industry safety authorities essentially say the same thing with regard to reasonable steps that a general contractor should take to prevent contractor and subcontractor worker injury?
10. What do they say?

> **SAFETY MANAGEMENT ROLE OF GENERAL CONTRACTORS**
>
> All of the above are in agreement that the general contractor should:
>
> - Implement the job safety and health program and take reasonable steps to ensure that contractor and subcontractor workers are not exposed to hazards.
> - Hold a pre-job safety meeting to plan to identify hazards before work begins so controls are in place before exposure to danger.
> - Train project manager, superintendent, construction manager, foremen regarding safety and OSHA compliance.
> - Verify that workers are trained as required by OSHA.
> - Conduct weekly safety meetings with contractors.
> - Monitor the job site to ensure that controls are indeed implemented.

11. Were there facts that were important for your evaluation?
12. What facts? Answer: Here, the expert could list the key facts from the deposition testimony of the superintendent and other representatives that show management failures and violations of OSHA standards. This

could be an exhibit. The exhibit could be used in cross examination of the defense expert.

13. Would you be able to express all of your opinions within a reasonable degree of certainty as a safety professional?
14. From your evaluation, did you form an opinion whether or not the defendant general contractor's conduct violated the principles and practices of safety management established by industry safety authorities?
15. And what is that opinion?
16. What is the basis of that opinion? Answer: The expert could briefly summarize the facts just listed.
17. Did you form an opinion whether or not the violation of the industry standard was a cause of Mr. Plaintiff's injury?
18. Why do you say that? Answer: Because had the defendant managed safety and required the work to be done safely, this hazard would have been controlled and this incident would not have occurred.

OSHA STANDARDS

19. Were there OSHA standards that were important for your evaluation?
20. What OSHA standards? EXHIBIT—Relevant OSHA standards
21. Were there facts that were important for your evaluation of whether or not OSHA standards were violated?
22. What facts?
23. Did you form an opinion whether or not the defendant violated any OSHA standards?
24. What is the basis of your opinion? Answer: The expert could explain OSHA's Multi-Employer Citation Policy and why the defendant was a controlling employer and violated OSHA standards.
25. Did you form an opinion whether or not the violation of the OSHA standard by the defendant was a cause of Mr. Plaintiff's injury?
26. And what is that opinion? Answer: The injury would have been prevented if the general contractor required compliance with OSHA because there would have been no exposure to this hazard.

CONTRACT BETWEEN CPO AND GC

27. Were there provisions of the contract between the construction project owner and the general contractor regarding safety that were important for your evaluation?

28. What contract provisions? EXHIBIT—Contract safety language.

CONTRACT

Article 10.1. Safety Programs and Precautions:

10.1.1. The Contractor shall be responsible for initiating, maintaining and supervising all safety precautions and programs in connection with the performance of the contract.

10.2.1. The Contractor shall take all necessary precautions for safety of, and shall provide all necessary protection to prevent damage, injury and loss to:

.1. Employees on the work and other persons who may be affected thereby.

10.2.2. The Contractor shall give notices and comply with applicable laws, ordinance, rules, regulations and lawful orders of public authorities bearing on the safety of persons or property or their protection from damage, injury or loss.

10.2.3. Contractor shall erect and maintain, as necessary by existing conditions and performance of the contract, all necessary safeguards for safety and protection.

10.2.6. The Contractor shall designate a responsible member of the contractor's organization at the site whose duties shall be the prevention of accidents.

29. Did you evaluate to determine whether or not the general contractor complied with its contract with the construction project owner?
30. What did you find?
31. What facts were important for your evaluation?
32. Did you form an opinion whether or not the general contractor violated its contract with the construction project owner?
33. And what is that opinion?
34. Did you form an opinion whether or not the violation of the contract was a cause of Mr. Plaintiff's injury?
35. And what is that opinion?

GENERAL CONTRACTOR'S SAFETY PROGRAM AND POLICY

36. Did you review the general contractor's safety program?
37. Were there provisions of the general contractor's safety program that were important for your evaluation?

38. What provisions? EXHIBIT—excerpts from general contractor's safety program.
39. Did you perform an evaluation to determine whether or not the defendant complied with its own safety and health program?
40. And what did you find?
41. Did you form an opinion whether or not the defendant general contractor violated its own safety program?
42. And what is that opinion?
43. Did you form an opinion whether or not the defendant's failure to comply with its own safety program was a cause of Mr. Plaintiff's injury?
44. And what is that opinion?

EVALUATION OF PLAINTIFF

45. Did you evaluate the conduct of Mr. Plaintiff?
46. How did you perform your evaluation of Mr. Plaintiff? Answer: I considered three factors:
    - Did he/she violate safety instructions?
    - Was he/she trained as required about hazard and risk?
    - What was the environment in which he/she was working? That is, the physical environment as well as the safety management environment.
47. What did you find?
48. Did Mr. Plaintiff's employer have any responsibility for safety at this job site? Answer: He had a responsibility to work safely and in compliance with OSHA regulations.
49. Did the plaintiff's employer comply with OSHA standards? Answer: No.
50. Why then do you say that the general contractor's conduct was a cause when the employer was also responsible? Answer: A fundamental principle of safety management is that safety begins at the top. Here, the top was the defendant general contractor. It had more power, control and authority than any contractor on the job site. They were the entity required to implement the job site safety program. They were the entity that sets the stage and communicates with contractors whether or not safety is going to be really enforced or whether they just pay lip service to safety. There is a perennial conflict between safety and the time and costs associated with working safely. Sometimes unscrupulous general contractors will allow contractors and subcontractors to work unsafely to save time and money. That is why OSHA was passed. Each contractor and subcontractor should comply with OSHA. But it is only the general contractor that has the primary overall responsibility for making sure that contractors and subcontractors do indeed work safely and in compliance with OSHA.

Appendix A

Safety Management Standards in Construction

SAFETY AND HEALTH PROGRAM

29CFR1926.20(b)—Initiate and maintain accident prevention programs as may be necessary to comply with this Part.

Management Commitment to Safety and Health:

29CFR1926.20(a)—Provide employees with sanitary and safe working conditions.

29CFR1926.20(b)—Assign safety and health responsibilities.

29CFR1926.32(f)—Give safety and health designees authority to correct hazards.

29CFR1926.1903.11(d)—Ensure employees that they may voice safety and health concerns without fear of reprisal.

29CFR1926.21(b), 29CFR1926.33, 29CFR1926.59, 29CFR1926.454, 29CFR1926 Subpart Z—Inform employees of hazards.

29CFR1926.59, 29CFR1926.65, 29CFR1926.652—Coordinate hazard communication with other employers on site.

29CFR1903.2(a)—Post the OSHA State or Federal Poster

Hazard Identification and Determination:

29CFR1926.20(a), 29CFR1926.21(b)—Evaluate operations, procedures, facilities, and equipment to identify hazards.

29CFR1926.55, 29CFR1926.62, 29CFR1926 Subpart Z, 29CFR1926.1101—Monitor exposure levels.

29CFR1926.20(b)(2), 29CFR1926.703(b), 29CFR1926.1081—Ensure regular safety and health inspections.

29CFR1904.4—Conduct accident investigations.

29CFR1926.103, 29CFR1926.951—Determine if engineering or administrative controls or personnel protective equipment are to be used.

Hazard Elimination and Control:

29CFR1926.20(b)(3), 29CFR1926.1417(a), 29CFR1926.951—Ensure machines and tools are in safe working order and in compliance with relevant standards.

29CFR1926.55, 29CFR1926.103, 29CFR 1926 Subpart Z—Institute engineering and work practice controls to eliminate health hazards.

29CFR1926.25, 29CFR1926.852, 29CFR1926.152(c)(5), 29CFR1926.900(k)(5)—Perform housekeeping to remove hazards posed by scrap and debris in work areas.

29CFR1926.28(a), 29CFR1926 Subpart E—Provide appropriate personal protective equipment when other controls are infeasible.

29CFR1926.34—Guarantee safe means of egress.

Training:

29CFR1926.21(b)(2), 29CFR1926.65, 29CFR1926.302(e), 29CFR1926.1060—Train employees to recognize hazards.

29CFR1926.21(b)(2), 29CFR1926.65, 29CFR1926.454, 29CFR1926.901(c)—Train workers to recognize and avoid unsafe conditions.

29CFR1926.21(b)—Provide training on safe work practices and applicable standards.

29CFR1926.20(b)(4), 29CFR1926.302(e)—Provide training on safe operation of equipment and machinery.

29CFR1926.1060(a), 29CFR1926.454, 29CFR1926.800(b) and (c)—Provide training on hazards of access ladders and stairways.

29CFR1926.21(b)(6), 29CFR1926.353(b), 29CFR1926.801—Provide training on confined and enclosed space entry hazards and precautions.

Appendix B

Safety and Health Program for Small Business

Introduction

This sample program follows the Occupational Safety and Health Administration's (OSHA) "Safety and Health Program Management Guidelines," published on January 26, 1989, in the *Federal Register*. These guidelines were drawn from the experience obtained enforcing the OSHA Act, from the Voluntary Protection Programs (VPP), OSHA programs to recognize excellence in worksite safety and health, from OSHA's Consultation Program, and from public commentary. This sample program is especially written for the small, independent business owner, but the outline can be applied to any size business.

This management system contains four basic program elements:

- Management Leadership and Employee Involvement;
- Worksite Analysis;
- Hazard Prevention and Control;
- Training.

Under each element are numerous sub-elements. This program contains descriptions of how the program elements and sub-elements are designed and implemented. Specific documents resulting from program implementation will need to be kept in an organized fashion.

WORKSITE GOODFELLOW'S SAFETY AND HEALTH PROGRAM

Management Leadership and Employee Involvement

Management commits the necessary resources of staff, money, and time to ensure that all persons on the worksite are protected from injury and illness hazards. In addition, management visibly leads in the design, implementation, and continuous improvement of the site's safety and health activities. Specifically, the highest level management establishes and reviews annually the site's safety and health policy and ensures that all employees know, understand, and support that policy. All management levels, with input from hourly employees, develop an annual safety and health goal with objectives and action plans to reach that goal. At the end of each year all management levels, with input from hourly employees, evaluate progress in accomplishing the action plans, achieving all objectives, and meeting the annual goal. This evaluation, which also includes an evaluation of the overall safety and health program, results in a written report that includes the next year's goal, objectives, and action plans, including any remaining action needed to accomplish the current year's goal.

Management ensures that all employees, including themselves, have clearly written safety and health responsibilities included within their job description, with appropriate authority to carry out those responsibilities. Also, management ensures that all employees, including all levels of management, receive performance evaluations that include a written evaluation of the accomplishment of assigned safety and health responsibilities.

Management ensures that all visitors to the site, including contract and temporary labor, co-op students, interns, vendors, and sales people, have knowledge of site hazards applicable to them and how to protect themselves against those hazards, including emergency alarms and procedures. Management also ensures that these visitors do not introduce to the site hazards that can be prevented or that are not properly controlled.

Management ensures that at least several avenues exist for employee involvement in safety and health decision making and problem solving. These avenues may include serving on committees and ad hoc problem solving groups, acting as safety observers, assisting in training other employees, analyzing hazards inherent in site jobs and how to protect against those hazards (writing JHAs), and planning activities to heighten safety and health awareness. Management encourages employees' involvement and devises appropriate recognition for outstanding employee participation.

Suggested documents to implement this element.

- Worksite policy (note how this policy is communicated to the workforce and visitors);
- Current year's goals, objectives, action plans, and program evaluation;
- Job descriptions that include safety and health responsibilities;
- Performance evaluations that include an evaluation of safety and health responsibilities;
- Budget showing money allocated to safety and health;
- Contractor bidding proposal sheets showing all contractors' prior safety and health record;
- Orientation outline for all site visitors, including contractors;
- Evidence of employee involvement, such as committee minutes or other records of employee participation in safety and health program decisions.

Worksite Analysis

Management hires outside consultants as necessary to conduct baseline surveys that identify all safety and health hazards at the site at the time of the survey. All hazards found during these surveys are eliminated whenever possible or controlled. All employees who may encounter the controlled hazards are trained in appropriate job procedures to follow to protect themselves from these hazards.

Management establishes change procedures to follow whenever the site experiences changes in equipment, material, or processes. To ensure employee protection, these change procedures include consideration of safety and health in the selection of the change, equipment and process shut down procedures, start up procedures, and phase hazard analysis. Appropriate employees are trained to follow these procedures.

Management and employees work together to analyze safety and health hazards inherent in each job site and to find means to eliminate those hazards whenever possible, and otherwise to protect persons against those hazards. These job hazard analyses (JHAs) are revised as appropriate, for example, following a change in the job, the reappearance of a hazard, or an accident at this job.

All employees at this site are trained to recognize hazards and to report any hazard they find to the appropriate person so that the hazard can be corrected as soon as possible. In addition to taking immediate action to report a hazard orally and to provide interim protection, if necessary, including stopping the work causing the hazard, employees may submit a safety work order to the maintenance department, or they may submit a safety suggestion form. Safety work orders take priority over any other work order. Safety suggestions will be considered each week during the site inspection by the site inspection team. All employee reports of hazards must be eventually written, with the correction date recorded. These reports are posted in the lunch room until the hazard is corrected and then are kept on file in the owner's office for three years. During that time they are available for employee review.

Site management, with input from an hourly employee chosen by lot, organizes the monthly site inspection team. Membership on these teams rotates each month with the goal that all site employees serve one month each year. Teams consist of four people, two managers or supervisors and two hourly employees. Each week, at the beginning of work on Wednesday morning, the team inspects the entire worksite, in writing describing all hazards found, including their location. The team assigns appropriate persons responsible for seeing that the hazard is corrected and documenting the date of the correction. These inspection reports are posted in the lunch room, in the maintenance shop, and in the owner's office. A hazard remains on the monthly report until it is corrected.

Any near miss, first aid incident, or accident is investigated by the trained team selected each year by the owner and an hourly employee. The team consists of two managers or supervisors and two hourly employees, each of whom has received training in accident investigation. All investigations have as a goal the identification of the root cause of the accident, rather than assigning blame. All accident reports are posted in the lunch room and are open to comment by any employee. The accident investigation team assigns responsibility to appropriate employees for correcting any hazards found and for assigning a date by which the correction must be completed.

As part of the annual safety and health program evaluation, the site owner, a manager, and an hourly employee review all near misses, first aid incidents, and entries on the OSHA 300 Log, as well as employee reports of hazards, to determine if any pattern exists that can be addressed. The results of this analysis are considered in setting the goal, objectives, and action plans for the next year.

Suggested documents to implement this element.

- Results of baseline safety and health surveys, with notation of hazard correction;
- Forms used for change analyses, including safety and health considerations in the purchase of new equipment, chemical, or materials;
- JHAs;
- Employee reports of hazards;
- Site safety and health inspection results, with hazard corrections noted;
- Accident investigation reports, with hazard corrections noted;
- trend analyses results.

Hazard Prevention and Control

Management ensures that this priority is followed to protect persons at this site: (1) Hazards will be eliminated when economically feasible, such as replacing a more hazardous chemical with a less hazardous one; (2) Barriers will protect persons from the hazard, such as machine guards and personal protective equipment (PPE); (3) Exposure to hazards will be controlled through administrative procedures, such as more frequent breaks and job rotation.

Management ensures that the worksite and all machinery is cared for properly so that the environment remains safe and healthy. If maintenance needs exceed the capability of the worksite employees, contract employees are hired to do the work and are screened and supervised to ensure they work according to the site's safety and health procedures.

All employees, including all levels of management, are held accountable for obeying site safety and health rules. The following four step disciplinary policy will be applied to everyone by the appropriate level of supervisor:

- oral warning;
- written reprimand;
- three day's away from work;
- dismissal.

Visitors, including contractors who violate safety and health rules and procedures, will be escorted from the site. Should the disciplined person request a review of the disciplinary action, an ad hoc committee of six people, three managers and three hourly workers, chosen by their respective colleagues, will review the situation and make a recommendation to the owner, who reserves the right for final decision. If his decision differs from the committee, he may, within confidentially strictures, make public his reasons.

The site works with appropriate outside agencies, such as the fire department, the police department, and the hospital to write emergency plans for all potential emergencies, including fire, explosion, accident, severe weather, loss of power and/or water, and violence from an outside source. Desk top drills are conducted monthly so that all employees experience a drill on each type of emergency once a year. A total site evacuation drill focusing on one emergency type, with all work shut down and coordinated with the appropriate agency, is conducted once a year. Each drill, whether table top or actual evacuation, is evaluated by the drill planning committee, constituted each year with two managers or supervisors and two hourly employees who volunteer. This committee's written report is posted in the lunch room, and supervisors ensure that all employees know the results. When necessary, the emergency procedures are revised as a result of the evaluation report.

Persons needing emergency care are transported by company van or community ambulance to the hospital, located five miles from the site. Usually that trip can be made in less than ten minutes. Onsite during all shifts designated persons fully trained in cardiac pulmonary resuscitation (CPR), first aid, and the requirements of OSHA's Bloodborne Pathogen Standard, are the first responders to any emergency. These persons are trained by qualified Red Cross instructors. One of these designated persons' safety and health responsibilities is to ensure that first aid kits are stocked and readily accessible in the marked locations throughout the plant. Appropriate personal protective equipment (PPE) is provided for the different types of accidents possible at the site. All emergency responders have been offered the Hepatitis B vaccine.

Management maintains a proactive occupational health program that provides for occupational health professionals from the local hospital to participate in worksite analyses to find and protect employees against all health hazards. This plan provides initial health screening for each employee, appropriate to the hazards with which each employee will be working, and for tracking of any health changes in each employee through periodic physical examinations, post-exposure exams, and exit exam. Certified industrial hygienists conduct periodic air and noise monitoring.

The doctor and occupational health nurse, working on contract for the site, examine health surveillance data to discern changes in overall employee health screening results to discern any trends that need to be addressed. Health professionals, appropriately trained and knowledgeable about site hazards, immediately treat employees for occupational health problems and follow each case until the individual can return full time to all aspects of his assigned job. These professionals ensure that employee medical records are kept confidentially so that diagnosis and treatment are not divulged, but management does have information about the employee under treatment as to:

- ability to perform job tasks;
- job limitations or accommodations needed;
- length of time the limitations must be implemented.

Management ensures that supervisors honor these restrictions. This health care is provided free of charge for all employees. The total plan is reviewed annually to assess its effectiveness.

Through consultants, management has assessed all work at this site and determined that the following OSHA standards apply to the site's work. Individual safety and health programs for each of these standards have been written and implemented. Employees affected by these standards have been trained to understand them and to follow the programs' directions. These standards are:

Hazard Communication
Confined Space Program
Hearing Conservation
Lockout/Tagout
Bloodborne Pathogens Program
Emergency Evacuation Program
Required PPE, Including Respiratory Protection

Suggested Documents to Implement This Element

- Preventive Maintenance Schedule
- Disciplinary program and records
- Site Rules
- Written Programs mandated by OSHA
- Maintenance records
- Emergency drill procedures and critiques
- Health surveillance and monitoring records
- Reports and investigations of near misses, first aid, and OSHA 300 logs

Training

Management believes that employee involvement in the site's safety and health program can only be successful when everyone on the site receives sufficient training to understand what their safety and health responsibilities and opportunities are and how to fulfill them. Therefore, training is a high priority to ensure a safe and healthy workplace. Finding time and knowledgeable personnel to do effective training is vital. Each year management pays special attention to the evaluation of the year's training efforts to look for methods of improvement.

Currently, all new employees receive two hours of safety and health orientation before they begin work. When they have learned this material, they begin their assigned job with a trained buddy. For the first day the employee only observes the buddy doing the job and reads the appropriate JHAs. The second day the new employee does the job, while the buddy observes him/her. For the first six months on the job a new employee is considered a probationer and may not work beyond the line of vision of another employee. Supervisors are strictly charged to ensure that this training process is followed for all new employees and for any employee beginning a new job at the worksite.

All employees are paid for one full day's work (eight hours) beyond their production schedule each pay period. This time is usually split into several sections to attend training classes. A list of training topics, by week, is published each year. Each topic is offered at least twice. Each employee is responsible for ensuring that he/she masters the year's training topics. Completing the year's training is a significant portion of each employee's performance evaluation, including all levels of management, and training records are kept by the personnel manager and are available for employee review, upon request.

All employees are encouraged to suggest qualified trainers, including themselves. Management is responsible for ensuring that all training offered at the site is conducted by qualified persons.

Suggested Documents to Implement This Element

- List of yearly training topics with name of trainer and his/her qualifications;
- Yearly training class schedule with attendance lists;
- Individual employee training records with evidence of subject mastery.

Appendix C

OSHA Construction Industry Training Requirements

Many standards promulgated by the Occupational Safety and Health Administration (OSHA) explicitly require the employer to train (or instruct, or communicate, or inform . . .) employees in the safety and health aspects of their jobs. Other OSHA standards make it the employer's responsibility to limit certain job assignments to employees who are "certified," "competent," or "qualified"—meaning that they have had special previous training, in or out of the workplace. Also, the term "designated" personnel means selected or assigned by the employer or the employer's representative as being qualified to perform specific duties.

The OSHA training requirements listed below have been excerpted from Title 29, Code of Federal Regulations (CFR), Part 1926 for Construction. Some Administrative standards (Parts 1903 and 1904) and General Industry standards (Part 1910) apply to the Construction Industry as well. Note that additional training requirements may appear in certain other consensus standards (ANSI, NFPA, etc.) incorporated by reference in the various parts of the OSHA CFR, and are therefore mandatory.

NOTICE—IMPORTANT INFORMATION:

- The OSHA training requirements listed on this website are only intended to provide users with a generic, non-exhaustive overview of the OSHA training requirements for specific standards-related topics. Most requirements for posting information, warning signs, labels, and the like are excluded from this information, as are most references to the qualifications of people assigned to test workplace conditions or equipment.
- This website is not the official or final authority to determine OSHA compliance responsibilities, which are set forth in OSHA standards themselves,

and the Occupational Safety and Health Act of 1970. Because OSHA regulations are constantly being added, deleted, and/or revised, you must not rely on this website as the official or final authority of OSHA training requirements; refer to the official OSHA regulations available on OSHA's website (osha.gov).

- Moreover, because interpretations and enforcement policy may change over time, the reader should consult administrative interpretations and decisions by the Occupational Safety and Health Review Commission and the courts. This information is also available on the OSHA website (osha.gov).
- Some states have implemented their own OSHA-approved state plan OSHA program with regulations affecting employee training that could differ from Federal OSHA's, so consult your state regulations where applicable.
- In the absence of applicable training requirements for a particular work activity, hazardous substance, tool or piece of equipment or machinery, employers are encouraged to refer to manufacturers' recommendations for safety training, where available, as well as those listed in applicable voluntary consensus standards.
- The information contained in this website is for informational purposes only, and should not be used to replace professional advice. Users of this website and their employers are responsible for how they choose to utilize this content, and OSHA Training Services Inc. assumes no liability for the use or misuse of the information contained herein.

Construction Industry Training Requirements (click topic to view)

1926.20—General Safety and Health Provisions
1926.21—Safety Training and Education
1926.33—Access to Employee Exposure and Medical Records*
1926.35—Employee Emergency Action Plans
1925.50—Medical Services and First Aid
1926.53—Ionizing Radiation
1926.54—Non-ionizing Radiation
1926.55—Gases, Vapors, Fumes, Dusts, and Mists
1926.59—Hazard Communication*
1926.60—Methylenedianiline
1926.62—Lead
1926.64—Process Safety Management
1926.65—Hazardous Waste Operations and Emergency Response
1926.101—Hearing Protection
1926.103—Respiratory Protection*

1926.150—Fire Protection
1926.201—Signaling
1926.202—Barricades
1926.302—Powder-Operated Hand Tools
1926.304—Woodworking Tools
1926.350–1926.354—Welding and Cutting
1926.404—Wiring Design and Protection
1926.451–1926.454—Scaffolding
1926.500–1926.503—Fall Protection
1926.551—Helicopters
1926.552—Material Hoists, Personnel Hoists, and Elevators
1926.602—Material Handling Equipment
1926.604—Site Clearing
1926.650–1926.652—Excavations
1926.700–1926.706—Concrete and Masonry Construction
1926.750–1926.761—Steel Erection
1926.800–1926.804—Underground Construction, Caissons, Cofferdams, and Compressed Air
1926.850–1926.860—Demolition
1926.900–1926.914—Blasting and the Use of Explosives
1926.950–1926.960—Power Transmission and Distribution
1926.1050–1926.1060—Ladders (and Stairways)
1926.1071–1926.1091—Commercial Diving Operations*
1926.1101—Asbestos
1926.1103–1926.1016—Thirteen Carcinogens*
1926.1117—Vinyl Chloride*
1926.1118—Inorganic Arsenic*
1926.1126—Chromium (VI)
1926.1127—Cadmium
1926.1128—Benzene*
1926.1129—Coke Oven Emissions*
1926.1144—1,2-dibromo-3-chloropropane*
1926.1145—Acrylonitrile*
1926.1147—Ethylene Oxide*
1926.1148—Formaldehyde*
1926.1152—Methylene Chloride*
1926.1200–1926.1013—Confined Spaces in Construction
1926.1400–1926.1442—Cranes & Derricks in Construction
1926.1500–1926.1501—Cranes and Derricks Used in Demolition and Underground Construction

*The OSHA Construction standards listed above that have been marked with an asterisk (*) are identical to those set forth in the General Industry standard with the same name in Part 1910.

ADMINISTRATIVE REQUIREMENTS

1903.2—Posting of Notice; Availability of the Act, Regulations and Applicable Standards
1904.35—Injury and Illness Recordkeeping Requirements—Employee involvement

GENERAL INDUSTRY STANDARDS APPLICABLE TO CONSTRUCTION INDUSTRY

The following General Industry standards also apply to the Construction industry:

1910.179(1)—Operator Training for Powered Industrial Trucks (forklifts)
1910.1020—Access to Employee Exposure and Medical Records
1910.1030—Bloodborne Pathogens

ADDITIONAL NOTE: The OSHA Construction standards listed above that have been marked with an asterisk (*) are identical to those set forth in the General Industry standard with the same name in Part 1910.

Appendix D

Construction Users Roundtable

CURT MEMBERSHIP ROSTER

Construction Owners

ABBOTT LABORATORIES
AIR PRODUCTS & CHEMICALS, INC.
ALLIANT ENERGY
AMEREN
AXIALL CORPORATION
BARRICK GOLD CORPORATION
BASF CORPORATION
BAXTER HEALTHCARE CORP.
BAYER TECHNOLOGY SERVICES
BLUESCOPE
BOEING COMPANY (THE)
CATERPILLAR INC
CHEVRON
DEERE & COMPANY
DOW CHEMICAL COMPANY (THE)
DTE ENERGY
DUKE ENERGY CORPORATION
DUPONT
ELI LILLY AND COMPANY
ENTERGY
EXELON CORPORATION
EXXONMOBIL CHEMICAL CO.
GENERAL ELECTRIC

GENERAL MOTORS
HONDA OF AMERICA MFG., INC.
HONEYWELL
INTEL CORPORATION
INTERNATIONAL PAPER
JOHNSON & JOHNSON
KOCH INDUSTRIES, INC.
LINDE PROCESS PLANTS
MARATHON PETROLEUM
MERCK & CO., INC.
MITSUBISHI NUCLEAR ENERGY SYSTEMS
NRG ENERGY
NV ENERGY
ONTARIO POWER GENERATION
OWENS CORNING
PENTAIR LTD
PHILLIPS 66 COMPANY
PRAXAIR, INC.
PROCTER & GAMBLE CO. (THE)
SANDIA NATIONAL LABORATORIES
SHELL GLOBAL SOLUTIONS (U.S.), INC.
SIEMENS ENERGY
SOUTHERN COMPANY
SUNCOR ENERGY SERVICES, INC.
TENNESSEE VALLEY AUTHORITY
THYSSENKRUPP INDUSTRIAL SOLUTIONS (USA), INC.
TOYOTA
UNIVERSITY of WASHINGTON—CAPITAL PROJECTS
U.S. ARCHITECT OF THE CAPITOL
U.S. ARMY CORPS OF ENGINEERS
U.S. DEPARTMENT OF STATE—OBO
U.S. GENERAL SERVICES ADMINISTRATION
WESTINGHOUSE ELECTRIC COMPANY
ZURICH INSURANCE GROUP

Contractor Associates

AECOM TECHNOLOGY CORPORATION
ALBERICI CONSTRUCTORS, INC.
AMEC FOSTER WHEELER
BECHTEL CORPORATION

BMWC CONSTRUCTORS, INC.
CB&I (Fmr. THE SHAW GROUP, INC.)
CIANBRO COMPANIES (THE)
EMCOR GROUP INC.
FLUOR CORPORATION
ISC CONSTRUCTORS, LLC
JACOBS
KBR
MATRIX NAC, INC.
RUDOLPH/LIBBE COMPANIES (THE)
SKANSKA USA
TURNER CONSTRUCTION
URS CORPORATION
YATES COMPANIES (THE)

Associations

ABC (Associated Builders & Contractors)
AGC (Associated General Contractors of America)
AIA (American Institute of Architects)
AISC (American Institute of Steel Construction)
ASC (Alliance Safety Council)
FCA INTERNATIONAL (Finishing Contractors Association)
IMPACT (Ironworkers Management Progressive Action Cooperative Trust)
MILLWRIGHT INDUSTRY TRUST
NACA (North American Contractors Association)
NAWIC (National Association of Women in Construction)
NECA (National Electrical Contractors Association)
NCCER
TAUC (The Association of Union Constructors)

Subscribers

Areva
Barnhart Crane & Rigging
Boldt Company (The)
Brand Energy Solutions, LLC
Brandenburg Industrial Service Company
Brock Group (The)
Century 3, Inc.
Construction Safety Experts, Inc.

Day & Zimmermann
E-J Electric Installation Co.
Gilbane
Global Project Management Partners
Graycor Industrial Constructors
Gribbins Insulation Company
Hargrove Engineers + Constructors
HazTek, Inc.
Holder Construction Company
Integrated Project Services, Inc.
JV Driver Group
Kelchner, Inc.
Kokosing Construction Co., Inc.
Kwest Group
Lauren Engineers & Constructors, Inc.
LPR Construction Co.
Mammoet USA Inc.
McAbee Construction, Inc.
Messer Construction
PCL Industrial Construction Co.
Robins & Morton Power & Industrial
Rosendin Electric, Inc.
S & B Engineers and Constructors, Ltd.
SpawGlass
The Industrial Company (TIC)
Turner Industries Group
United Group Services
Vulcan Industrial Contractors
Zachry Industrial, Inc.

Appendix E

Contractor Safety Evaluation Questionnaire

ITEMS FOR INCLUSION IN CONTRACTOR SAFETY EVALUATION QUESTIONNAIRE

1. List your firm's Interstate Experience Modification Rate for the last 3 years:

   20 ____ 20 ____ 20 ____

2. Please use your last year's OSHA no. 200 log to fill in:
   Number of injuries and illnesses:

   (a) number of lost workday cases ____
   (b) number of restricted workday cases ____
   (c) number of cases with medical attention only ____
   (d) number of fatalities ____

3. Employee hours worked last year (do not include any nonwork time, even though paid) ____
4. Check your type of work:

   Nonresidential building____
   Heavy (nonhighway) construction____
   Plumbing, heating, and air conditioning ____
   Other____

5. Are accident reports (OSHA 200) and report summaries sent to the following? How often?

	No	*Yes*	*Monthly*	*Quarterly*	*Annually*
Field superintendent	____	____	____	____	____
Vice president of construction	____	____	____	____	____
President of firm	____	____	____	____	____

6. Do you hold site safety meetings for field supervisors?

   Yes ____ No ____ How often? Weekly ____ Biweekly ____

   Monthly ____ Less often, as needed ____

7. Do you conduct project safety inspections? Yes ____ No ____

   If yes, who conducts this inspection (title)? ______________________

   ______________________ And how often? ______________________

8. How are accident records and accident summaries kept? How often are they reported?

	No	*Yes*	*Monthly*	*Annually*
Accidents totaled for all company	____	____	____	____
Accidents totaled by project	____	____	____	____
Subtotaled by superintendent	____	____	____	____
Subtotaled by foreman	____	____	____	____

9. How are the costs of individual accidents kept? How often are they reported?

	No	*Yes*	*Monthly*	*Annually*
Costs totaled for all company	____	____	____	____
Costs totaled by project	____	____	____	____
Subtotaled by superintendent	____	____	____	____
Subtotaled by foreman	____	____	____	____

10. List key personnel planned for this project. Please list names, expected positions, and safety performance on last three projects worked on.
11. Do you have a written safety program? Yes _____ No _____
12. Do you have an orientation program for new hires? Yes _____ No _____

13. If yes, does this include instruction on the following?

	Yes	*No*
a. Head protection	_____	_____
b. Eye protection	_____	_____
c. Hearing protection	_____	_____
d. Respiratory protection	_____	_____
e. Safety belts and lifeline	_____	_____
f. Scaffolding	_____	_____
g. Perimeter guarding	_____	_____
h. Housekeeping	_____	_____
i. Fire protection	_____	_____
j. First aid facilities	_____	_____
k. Emergency procedures	_____	_____
l. Toxic substances	_____	_____
m. Trenching and excavation	_____	_____
n. Signs, barricades, flagging	_____	_____
o. Electrical safety	_____	_____
p. Rigging and crane safety	_____	_____

14. Do you have a training program for newly hired or promoted foremen?

    No ______ Yes _____

    If yes, does it include instruction on the following?

	Yes	*No*
a. Safe work practices	_____	_____
b. Safety supervision	_____	_____
c. Toolbox meetings	_____	_____
d. Emergency procedures	_____	_____
e. First aid procedures	_____	_____
f. Accident investigation	_____	_____
g. Fire protection and prevention	_____	_____
h. New-worker orientation	_____	_____

15. Do you hold craft toolbox safety meetings? Yes _____ No _____

    How often? Weekly _____ Biweekly _____ Monthly ______

    Less often, as needed _____

Appendix F

OSHA—Multi-Employer Citation Policy

DIRECTIVE NUMBER:	**EFFECTIVE DATE:**
CPL 2-0.124	December 10, 1999

SUBJECT: Multi-Employer Citation Policy

ABSTRACT

Purpose:	To clarify the Agency's multi-employer citation policy
Scope:	OSHA-wide
References:	OSHA Instruction CPL 2.103 (the FIRM)
Suspensions:	Chapter III, Paragraph C. 6. of the FIRM is suspended and replaced by this directive
State Impact:	This Instruction describes a Federal Program Change. Notification of State intent is required, but adoption is not.
Action Offices:	National, Regional, and Area Offices
Originating Office:	Directorate of Compliance Programs

Contact: Carl Sall (202) 693-2345
Directorate of Construction
N3468 FPB
200 Constitution Ave., NW
Washington, DC 20210

By and Under the Authority of
R. Davis Layne
Deputy Assistant Secretary, OSHA

TABLE OF CONTENTS

I. Purpose. This Directive clarifies the Agency's multi-employer citation policy and suspends Chapter III. C. 6. of OSHA's Field Inspection Reference Manual (FIRM).

II. Scope. OSHA-Wide

III. Suspension. Chapter III. Paragraph C. 6. of the FIRM (CPL 2.103) is suspended and replaced by this Directive.

IV. References. OSHA Instructions:

- CPL 02-00.103; OSHA Field Inspection Reference Manual (FIRM), September 26, 1994.
- ADM 08-0.1C, OSHA Electronic Directive System, December 19,1997.

V. Action Information

A. Responsible Office. Directorate of Construction.
B. Action Offices. National, Regional and Area Offices
C. Information Offices. State Plan Offices, Consultation Project Offices

VI. Federal Program Change. This Directive describes a Federal Program Change for which State adoption is not required. However, the States shall respond via the two-way memorandum to the Regional Office as soon as the State's intent regarding the multi-employer citation policy is known, but no later than 60 calendar days after the date of transmittal from the Directorate of Federal-State Operations.

VII. Force and Effect of Revised Policy. The revised policy provided in this Directive is in full force and effect from the date of its issuance. It is an official Agency policy to be implemented OSHA-wide.

VIII. Changes in Web Version of FIRM. A note will be included at appropriate places in the FIRM as it appears on the Web indicating the suspension of Chapter III paragraph 6. C. and its replacement by this Directive, and a hypertext link will be provided connecting viewers with this Directive.

IX. Background. OSHA's Field Inspection Reference Manual (FIRM) of September 26, 1994 (CPL 2.103), states at Chapter III, paragraph 6. C., the Agency's citation policy for multi-employer worksites. The Agency has determined that this policy needs clarification. This directive describes the revised policy.

A. Continuation of Basic Policy. This revision continues OSHA's existing policy for issuing citations on multi-employer worksites. However, it gives clearer and more detailed guidance than did the earlier description of the policy in the FIRM, including new examples explaining when citations should and should not be issued to exposing, creating, correcting, and controlling employers. These examples, which address common situations and provide general policy guidance, are not intended to be exclusive. In all cases, the decision on whether to issue citations should be based on all of the relevant facts revealed by the inspection or investigation.

B. No Changes in Employer Duties. This revision neither imposes new duties on employers nor detracts from their existing duties under the OSH Act. Those duties continue to arise from the employers' statutory duty to comply with OSHA standards and their duty to exercise reasonable diligence to determine whether violations of those standards exist.

X. Multi-employer Worksite Policy. The following is the multi-employer citation policy:

A. Multi-employer Worksites. On multi-employer worksites (in all industry sectors), more than one employer may be citable for a hazardous condition that violates an OSHA standard. A two-step process must be followed in determining whether more than one employer is to be cited.

1. Step One. The first step is to determine whether the employer is a creating, exposing, correcting, or controlling employer. The definitions in paragraphs (B)–(E) below explain and give examples of each. Remember that an employer may have multiple roles (see paragraph H). Once you determine the role of the employer, go to Step Two to determine if a citation is appropriate (NOTE: only exposing employers can be cited for General Duty Clause violations).
2. Step Two. If the employer falls into one of these categories, it has obligations with respect to OSHA requirements. Step Two is to determine if the employer's actions were sufficient to meet those obligations. The extent of the actions required of employers varies based on which category applies. Note that the extent of the measures that a controlling employer must take to satisfy its duty to exercise reasonable care to prevent and detect violations is less than what is required of an employer with respect to protecting its own employees.

B. The Creating Employer

1. Step 1: Definition: The employer that caused a hazardous condition that violates an OSHA standard.
2. Step 2: Actions Taken: Employers must not create violative conditions. An employer that does so is citable even if the only employees exposed are those of other employers at the site.

a. **Example 1**: Employer Host operates a factory. It contracts with Company S to service machinery. Host fails to cover drums of a chemical despite S's repeated requests that it do so. This results in airborne levels of the chemical that exceed the Permissible Exposure Limit.

Analysis: **Step 1**: Host is a creating employer because it caused employees of S to be exposed to the air contaminant above the PEL. **Step 2**: Host failed to implement measures to prevent the accumulation of the air contaminant. It could have met its OSHA obligation by implementing the simple engineering control of covering the drums. Having failed to implement a feasible engineering control to meet the PEL, Host is citable for the hazard.

b. **Example 2**: Employer M hoists materials onto Floor 8, damaging perimeter guardrails. Neither its own employees nor employees of other employers are exposed to the hazard. It takes effective steps to keep all employees, including those of other employers, away from the unprotected edge and informs the controlling employer of the problem. Employer M lacks authority to fix the guardrails itself.

Analysis: **Step 1**: Employer M is a creating employer because it caused a hazardous condition by damaging the guardrails. **Step 2**: While it lacked the authority to fix the guardrails, it took immediate and effective steps to keep all employees away from the hazard and notified the controlling employer of the hazard. Employer M is not citable since it took effective measures to prevent employee exposure to the fall hazard.

C. The Exposing Employer

1. Step 1: Definition: An employer whose own employees are exposed to the hazard. See Chapter III, section (C)(1)(b) for a discussion of what constitutes exposure.
2. Step 2: Actions Taken: If the exposing employer created the violation, it is citable for the violation as a creating employer. If the violation was created by another employer, the exposing employer is citable if it (1) knew of the hazardous condition or failed to exercise reasonable diligence to discover the condition, and (2) failed to take steps consistent with its authority to protect is employees. If the exposing employer has authority to correct the hazard, it must do so. If the exposing employer lacks the authority to correct the hazard, it is citable if it fails to do each of the following: (1) ask the creating and/or controlling employer to correct the hazard; (2) inform its employees of the hazard; and (3) take reasonable alternative protective measures. In extreme circumstances (e.g., imminent danger situations), the exposing

employer is citable for failing to remove its employees from the job to avoid the hazard.

a. **Example 3**: Employer Sub S is responsible for inspecting and cleaning a work area in Plant P around a large, permanent hole at the end of each day. An OSHA standard requires guardrails. There are no guardrails around the hole and Sub S employees do not use personal fall protection, although it would be feasible to do so. Sub S has no authority to install guardrails. However, it did ask Employer P, which operates the plant, to install them. P refused to install guardrails.

   Analysis: **Step 1**: Sub S is an exposing employer because its employees are exposed to the fall hazard. **Step 2**: While Sub S has no authority to install guardrails, it is required to comply with OSHA requirements to the extent feasible. It must take steps to protect its employees and ask the employer that controls the hazard—Employer P—to correct it. Although Sub S asked for guardrails, since the hazard was not corrected, Sub S was responsible for taking reasonable alternative protective steps, such as providing personal fall protection. Because that was not done, Sub S is citable for the violation.

b. **Example 4**: Unprotected rebar on either side of an access ramp presents an impalement hazard. Sub E, an electrical subcontractor, does not have the authority to cover the rebar. However, several times Sub E asked the general contractor, Employer GC, to cover the rebar. In the meantime, Sub E instructed its employees to use a different access route that avoided most of the uncovered rebar and required them to keep as far from the rebar as possible.

   Analysis: **Step 1**: Since Sub E employees were still exposed to some unprotected rebar, Sub E is an exposing employer. **Step 2**: Sub E made a good faith effort to get the general contractor to correct the hazard and took feasible measures within its control to protect its employees. Sub E is not citable for the rebar hazard.

D. The Correcting Employer

1. Step 1: Definition: An employer who is engaged in a common undertaking, on the same worksite, as the exposing employer and is responsible for correcting a hazard. This usually occurs where

an employer is given the responsibility of installing and/or maintaining particular safety/health equipment or devices.

2. Step 2: Actions Taken: The correcting employer must exercise reasonable care in preventing and discovering violations and meet its obligations of correcting the hazard.

   a. **Example 5**: Employer C, a carpentry contractor, is hired to erect and maintain guardrails throughout a large, 15-story project. Work is proceeding on all floors. C inspects all floors in the morning and again in the afternoon each day. It also inspects areas where material is delivered to the perimeter once the material vendor is finished delivering material to that area. Other subcontractors are required to report damaged/missing guardrails to the general contractor, who forwards those reports to C. C repairs damaged guardrails immediately after finding them and immediately after they are reported. On this project few instances of damaged guardrails have occurred other than where material has been delivered. Shortly after the afternoon inspection of Floor 6, workers moving equipment accidentally damage a guardrail in one area. No one tells C of the damage and C has not seen it. An OSHA inspection occurs at the beginning of the next day, prior to the morning inspection of Floor 6. None of C's own employees are exposed to the hazard, but other employees are exposed.

   Analysis: Step 1: C is a correcting employer since it is responsible for erecting and maintaining fall protection equipment. **Step 2**: The steps C implemented to discover and correct damaged guardrails were reasonable in light of the amount of activity and size of the project. It exercised reasonable care in preventing and discovering violations; it is not citable for the damaged guardrail since it could not reasonably have known of the violation.

E. The Controlling Employer

1. Step 1: Definition: An employer who has general supervisory authority over the worksite, including the power to correct safety and health violations itself or require others to correct them. Control can be established by contract or, in the absence of explicit contractual provisions, by the exercise of control in practice. Descriptions and examples of different kinds of controlling employers are given below.

2. Step 2: Actions Taken: A controlling employer must exercise reasonable care to prevent and detect violations on the site. The extent of the measures that a controlling employer must implement to satisfy this duty of reasonable care is less than what is required of an employer with respect to protecting its own employees. This means that the controlling employer is not normally required to inspect for hazards as frequently or to have the same level of knowledge of the applicable standards or of trade expertise as the employer it has hired.
3. Factors Relating to Reasonable Care Standard. Factors that affect how frequently and closely a controlling employer must inspect to meet its standard of reasonable care include:

    a. The scale of the project.
    b. The nature and pace of the work, including the frequency with which the number or types of hazards change as the work progresses.
    c. How much the controlling employer knows both about the safety history and safety practices of the employer it controls and about that employer's level of expertise.
    d. More frequent inspections are normally needed if the controlling employer knows that the other employer has a history of non-compliance. Greater inspection frequency may also be needed, especially at the beginning of the project, if the controlling employer had never before worked with this other employer and does not know its compliance history.
    e. Less frequent inspections may be appropriate where the controlling employer sees strong indications that the other employer has implemented effective safety and health efforts. The most important indicator of an effective safety and health effort by the other employer is a consistently high level of compliance. Other indicators include the use of an effective, graduated system of enforcement for non-compliance with safety and health requirements coupled with regular jobsite safety meetings and safety training.

4. Evaluating Reasonable Care. In evaluating whether a controlling employer has exercised reasonable care in preventing and discovering violations, consider questions such as whether the controlling employer:

    a. Conducted periodic inspections of appropriate frequency (frequency should be based on the factors listed in G.3.);

b. Implemented an effective system for promptly correcting hazards;
c. Enforces the other employer's compliance with safety and health requirements with an effective, graduated system of enforcement and follow-up inspections.

5. Types of Controlling Employers

a. Control Established by Contract. In this case, **the Employer Has a Specific Contract Right to Control Safety**: To be a controlling employer, the employer must itself be able to prevent or correct a violation or to require another employer to prevent or correct the violation. One source of this ability is explicit contract authority. This can take the form of a specific contract right to require another employer to adhere to safety and health requirements and to correct violations the controlling employer discovers.

(1) **Example 6**: Employer GH contracts with Employer S to do sandblasting at GH's plant. Some of the work is regularly scheduled maintenance and so is general industry work; other parts of the project involve new work and are considered construction. Respiratory protection is required. Further, the contract explicitly requires S to comply with safety and health requirements. Under the contract GH has the right to take various actions against S for failing to meet contract requirements, including the right to have non-compliance corrected by using other workers and back-charging for that work. S is one of two employers under contract with GH at the work site, where a total of five employees work. All work is done within an existing building. The number and types of hazards involved in S's work do not significantly change as the work progresses. Further, GH has worked with S over the course of several years. S provides periodic and other safety and health training and uses a graduated system of enforcement of safety and health rules. S has consistently had a high level of compliance at its previous jobs and at this site. GH monitors S by a combination of weekly inspections, telephone discussions and a weekly review of S's own inspection reports. GH has a system of graduated enforcement that it has applied to S for the few safety and health violations that had been committed by S in the past

few years. Further, due to respirator equipment problems S violates respiratory protection requirements two days before GH's next scheduled inspection of S. The next day there is an OSHA inspection. There is no notation of the equipment problems in S's inspection reports to GH and S made no mention of it in its telephone discussions.

Analysis: Step 1: GH is a controlling employer because it has general supervisory authority over the worksite, including contractual authority to correct safety and health violations. **Step 2**: GH has taken reasonable steps to try to make sure that S meets safety and health requirements. Its inspection frequency is appropriate in light of the low number of workers at the site, lack of significant changes in the nature of the work and types of hazards involved, GH's knowledge of S's history of compliance and its effective safety and health efforts on this job. GH has exercised reasonable care and is not citable for this condition.

(2) **Example 7**: Employer GC contracts with Employer P to do painting work. GC has the same contract authority over P as Employer GH had in Example 6. GC has never before worked with P. GC conducts inspections that are sufficiently frequent in light of the factors listed above in (G)(3). Further, during a number of its inspections, GC finds that P has violated fall protection requirements. It points the violations out to P during each inspection but takes no further actions.

Analysis: **Step 1**: GC is a controlling employer since it has general supervisory authority over the site, including a contractual right of control over P. **Step 2**: GC took adequate steps to meet its obligation to discover violations. However, it failed to take reasonable steps to require P to correct hazards since it lacked a graduated system of enforcement. A citation to GC for the fall protection violations is appropriate.

(3) **Example 8**: Employer GC contracts with Sub E, an electrical subcontractor. GC has full contract authority over Sub E, as in Example 6. Sub E installs an electric panel box exposed to the weather and implements an assured equipment grounding conductor program, as required un-

der the contract. It fails to connect a grounding wire inside the box to one of the outlets. This incomplete ground is not apparent from a visual inspection. Further, GC inspects the site with a frequency appropriate for the site in light of the factors discussed above in (G)(3). It saw the panel box but did not test the outlets to determine if they were all grounded because Sub E represents that it is doing all of the required tests on all receptacles. GC knows that Sub E has implemented an effective safety and health program. From previous experience it also knows Sub E is familiar with the applicable safety requirements and is technically competent. GC had asked Sub E if the electrical equipment is OK for use and was assured that it is.

Analysis: Step 1: GC is a controlling employer since it has general supervisory authority over the site, including a contractual right of control over Sub E. **Step 2**: GC exercised reasonable care. It had determined that Sub E had technical expertise, safety knowledge and had implemented safe work practices. It conducted inspections with appropriate frequency. It also made some basic inquiries into the safety of the electrical equipment. Under these circumstances GC was not obligated to test the outlets itself to determine if they were all grounded. It is not citable for the grounding violation.

b. <u>Control Established by a Combination of Other Contract Rights</u>: Where there is no explicit contract provision granting the right to control safety, or where the contract says the employer does <u>not</u> have such a right, an employer may still be a controlling employer. The ability of an employer to control safety in this circumstance can result from a combination of contractual rights that, together, give it broad responsibility at the site involving almost all aspects of the job. Its responsibility is broad enough so that its contractual authority necessarily involves safety. The authority to resolve disputes between subcontractors, set schedules and determine construction sequencing are particularly significant because they are likely to affect safety. (NOTE: citations should only be issued in this type of case after consulting with the Regional Solicitor's office.)

(1) **Example 9**: Construction manager M is contractually obligated to: set schedules and construction sequencing, require subcontractors to meet contract specifications, negotiate with trades, resolve disputes between subcontractors, direct work and make purchasing decisions, which affect safety. However, the contract states that M does not have a right to require compliance with safety and health requirements. Further, Subcontractor S asks M to alter the schedule so that S would not have to start work until Subcontractor G has completed installing guardrails. M is contractually responsible for deciding whether to approve S's request.

Analysis: **Step 1**: Even though its contract states that M does not have authority over safety, the combination of rights actually given in the contract provides broad responsibility over the site and results in the ability of M to direct actions that necessarily affect safety. For example, M's contractual obligation to determine whether to approve S's request to alter the schedule has direct safety implications. M's decision relates directly to whether S's employees will be protected from a fall hazard. M is a controlling employer. **Step 2**: In this example, if M refused to alter the schedule, it would be citable for the fall hazard violation.

(2) **Example 10**: Employer ML's contractual authority is limited to reporting on subcontractors' contract compliance to owner/developer O and making contract payments. Although it reports on the extent to which the subcontractors are complying with safety and health infractions to O, ML does not exercise any control over safety at the site.

Analysis: **Step 1**: ML is not a controlling employer because these contractual rights are insufficient to confer control over the subcontractors and ML did not exercise control over safety. Reporting safety and health infractions to another entity does not, by itself (or in combination with these very limited contract rights), constitute an exercise of control over safety. **Step 2**: Since it is not a controlling employer it had no duty under the OSH Act to exercise reasonable care with respect to enforcing the subcontractors' compliance with safety; there is therefore no need to go to Step 2.

c. Architects and Engineers: Architects, engineers, and other entities are controlling employers only if the breadth of their involvement in a construction project is sufficient to bring them within the parameters discussed above.

(1) **Example 11**: Architect A contracts with owner O to prepare contract drawings and specifications, inspect the work, report to O on contract compliance, and to certify completion of work. A has no authority or means to enforce compliance, no authority to approve/reject work and does not exercise any other authority at the site, although it does call the general contractor's attention to observed hazards noted during its inspections.

Analysis: Step 1: A's responsibilities are very limited in light of the numerous other administrative responsibilities necessary to complete the project. It is little more than a supplier of architectural services and conduit of information to O. Its responsibilities are insufficient to confer control over the subcontractors and it did not exercise control over safety. The responsibilities it does have are insufficient to make it a controlling employer. Merely pointing out safety violations did not make it a controlling employer. NOTE: In a circumstance such as this it is likely that broad control over the project rests with another entity. **Step 2**: Since A is not a controlling employer it had no duty under the OSH Act to exercise reasonable care with respect to enforcing the subcontractors' compliance with safety; there is therefore no need to go to Step 2.

(2) **Example 12**: Engineering firm E has the same contract authority and functions as in Example 9.

Analysis: **Step 1**: Under the facts in Example 9, E would be considered a controlling employer. **Step 2**: The same type of analysis described in Example 9 for Step 2 would apply here to determine if E should be cited.

d. Control Without Explicit Contractual Authority. Even where an employer has no explicit contract rights with respect to safety, an employer can still be a controlling employer if, in actual practice, it exercises broad control over subcontractors at the site (see Example 9). NOTE: Citations should only be issued in this type of case after consulting with the Regional Solicitor's office.

(1) **Example 13**: Construction manager MM does not have explicit contractual authority to require subcontractors to comply with safety requirements, nor does it explicitly have broad contractual authority at the site. However, it exercises control over most aspects of the subcontractors' work anyway, including aspects that relate to safety.

Analysis: Step 1: MM would be considered a controlling employer since it exercises control over most aspects of the subcontractor's work, including safety aspects. **Step 2**: The same type of analysis on reasonable care described in the examples in (G)(5)(a) would apply to determine if a citation should be issued to this type of controlling employer.

F. Multiple Roles

1. A creating, correcting or controlling employer will often also be an exposing employer. Consider whether the employer is an exposing employer before evaluating its status with respect to these other roles.
2. Exposing, creating and controlling employers can also be correcting employers if they are authorized to correct the hazard.

Appendix G

Safety Expert Report

SAFETY EXPERT REPORT

January 2, 2016

INJURED EMPLOYEE vs. ABC GENERAL CONTRACTORS, INC.

I. ASSIGNMENT:

This case was assigned by attorney John Doe to review various documents and to render an opinion regarding the conduct of the defendants relative to the injury suffered by Injured Worker.

II. PREPARATION:

By way of preparation, I reviewed the following:

- Deposition transcripts of . . .
- Various photos of the area where this incident occurred.
- Plaintiff's Certified Answers to Form A Interrogatories.
- Defendant's Demand for Response to Notice to Produce.
- Defendant's Answers to Interrogatories
- Defendant's Response to Plaintiff's Notice to Produce
- Drawings

III. BACKGROUND:

This incident occurred on January 27, 2014 at a residence under construction at 8 Polazzo Grande in Morganville, New Jersey. At the time of this incident, Injured Worker working for His Employer was installing electrical wiring and high-hat lights on the first floor. He was working in the Grand Salon area.

IV. DESCRIPTION OF INCIDENT:

Just prior to this incident, Injured Worker had been working on the second floor. He came downstairs to see where to run the wires. He was walking and looking to see where he had to run the wires. There was a circular stairway leading to the basement which was not protected by a standard guardrail. There were no stairs installed at the time of this incident. As he was walking, he inadvertently stepped into the stairway opening. He fell and was seriously injured.

V. METHODOLOGY OF EVALUATION:

The method to evaluate the conduct of ABC General Contractors, Inc. in this case is to compare their conduct to the principles and practices of construction safety management established by industry safety authorities as well as compliance with OSHA regulations. It will also consider whether ABC General Contractors, Inc. complied with its own safety program and its contract.

VI. MAGNITUDE AND SEVERITY OF FALLS IN THE CONSTRUCTION INDUSTRY:

OSHA has found that, between 1985 and 1989, the leading cause of fatal injury in the construction industry has been falls from elevation. Falls account for 33 percent of all construction fatal injuries in the United States.

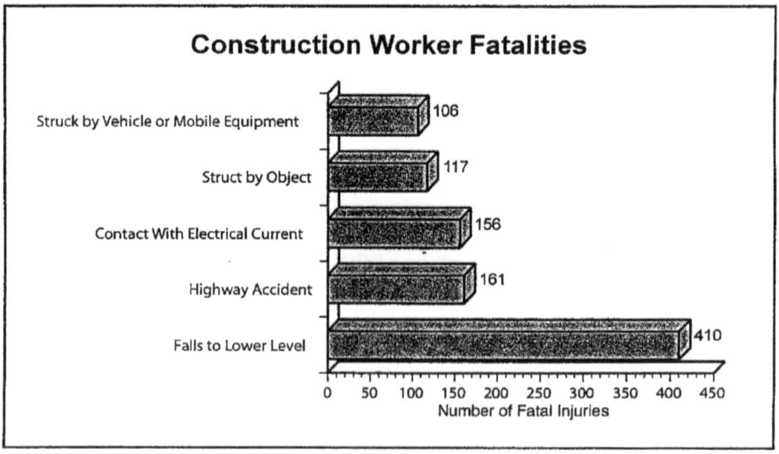

Fatal Falls in the Construction Industry

Source: Centers for Disease Control (CDC), National Institute for Occupational Safety and Health, *Worker Health Chartbook, 2004.*

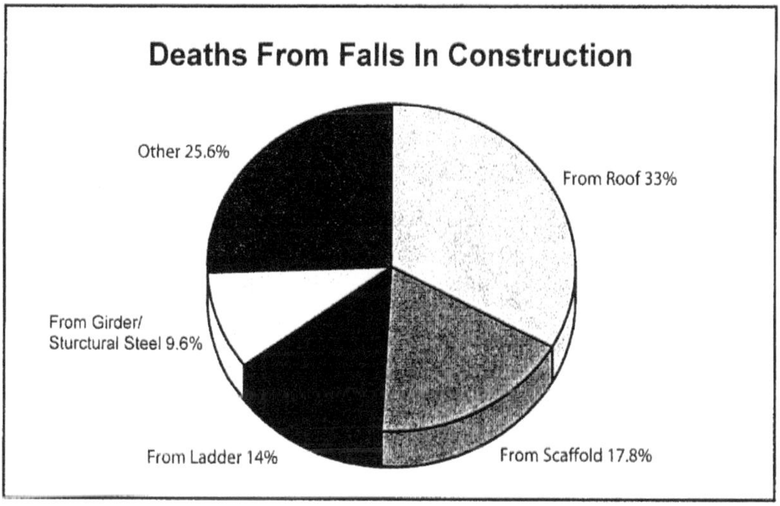

Deaths from Falls in Construction

Source: The Center to Protect Workers' Rights (CPWR), *The Construction Industry Chart Book,* 2002. Bureau of Labor Statistics (BLS), National Census of Fatal Occupational Injuries Summary 2004, http://stats.bls.gov/news.release/cfoi.nr0.htm.

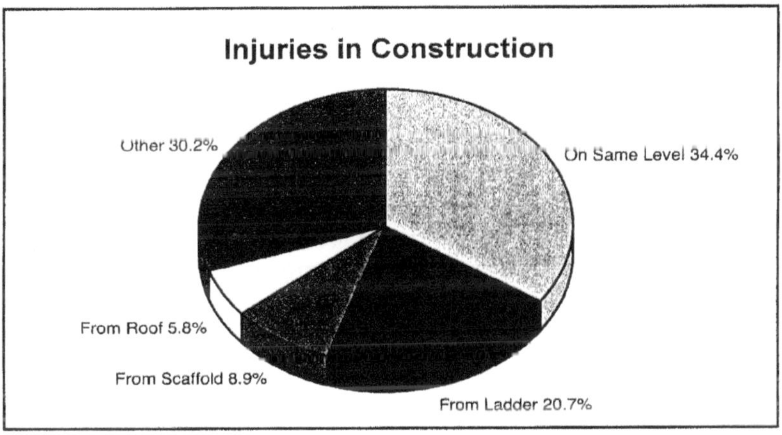

Injuries in Construction

Source: The Center to Protect Workers' Rights (CPWR), *The Construction Industry Chart Book,* 2002. Bureau of Labor Statistics (BLS), National Census of Fatal Occupational Injuries Summary 2004, http://stats.bls.gov/news.release/cfoi.nr0.htm.

VII. INDUSTRY STANDARD FOR INJURY PREVENTION IN THE CONSTRUCTION INDUSTRY: SAFETY MANAGEMENT PRINCIPLES AND PRACTICES

The following is a brief review of the industry standard or standard of care relative to injury prevention in the construction industry. For decades, both industry authorities and government authorities have been in agreement with regard to the steps that a general contractor/ construction manager/contractor should take in order to ensure that work performed on their behalf is done safely and in compliance with OSHA.

a. **Principles and Techniques of Construction Safety Management**

A review of the construction safety management literature will find fundamental agreement with the following principles:

1. Safety begins at the top.
2. Assignment of specific responsibility and accountability are key to successful construction safety management.
3. Safety begins in the design stages—on the drawing board.
4. Safety is a shared responsibility.
5. A proactive rather than reactive approach is best.
6. Accidents are foreseeable and predictable.
7. Controls can be anticipated and put in place before exposure to the hazard takes place.
8. Planning is essential.
9. It is irresponsible to allow the evolution of a hazard and hope that safety inspection discovers the hazard before injury results.

I have applied these principles and techniques of injury prevention for thirty-five years. I have evaluated over 200 construction safety programs, investigated over one thousand construction injury incidents and have applied the techniques of hazard identification, evaluation and control for thirty-five years. Likewise, over 36,000 members of the American Society of Safety Engineers, that is, representatives from the construction industry, general industry, the insurance industry, government, and labor are also in agreement with these principles and techniques of safety management and have been applying them for decades. I have written on the subject of the appropriate methodology of evaluation in construction industry cases in peer-reviewed articles in the Journal of the American Society of Safety Engineers. There is no disagreement regarding these principles and techniques of construction safety management among construction safety experts.

b. **American National Standard for Construction and Demolition Operations—Safety and Health Program Requirements for Multi-Employer Projects ANSI A10.33-1992.**

The Secretariat for this standard is the National Safety Council. It was promulgated in 1992. It establishes the minimum procedures that responsible owners and general contractors are required to comply with on a multi-employer construction site. The provisions contained in the ANSI standard are a composite of the most effective policy and program elements taken from examples provided by industry. The organizations represented by this standard are many of the most important organizations involved in the construction industry in the United States. They come from construction companies, insurance companies, labor organizations, governmental organizations, construction safety consultants and many major construction contractors.

ANSI has found that investigation of major construction failures and individual injuries indicate that in a majority of instances, the lack of coordination between owner, construction manager, general contractor and/or subcontractor was a primary contributing factor. The ANSI standard points out: "In addition, studies by Stanford University and the Business Roundtable (an association of the 200 largest corporations in America) have established that designation of a single individual to have overall authority and responsibility for the execution of a construction project is essential to ensure the safety of the employees and quality of workmanship." The requirements of this standard are essentially the same as those requirements established by previous authorities, such as the Associated General Contractors of America, the National Safety Council, the Construction Industry Institute and the Business Roundtable.

The Forward of this standard states: "Investigation of major construction failures and individual injuries indicate that in a majority of instances, a lack of coordination between the owner, construction manager, general contractor and/or subcontractor was a primary contributing factor. . . . This standard is a basis for each owner and contractor to use as a minimum program in developing and implementing safe, cost effective construction projects. . . . It is expected that this standard will find a major application in industry, serving as a guide to contractors, labor and equipment manufacturers." The organizations represented include safety organizations, many major contractors, international unions, employer organizations and representatives of the federal government agencies. The following are some of the provisions of this standard:

2. Definition. Project Constructor. A person, firm, or corporation, i.e., the construction manager, general contractor, prime contractor, or other entity, designated in the project documents, responsible for supervising and controlling all construction work performed on the project.

   This standard requires the Project Constructor to implement an occupational safety and health program. This includes pre-work planning including hazard analysis before work begins. It requires training of supervisory personnel as well as monitoring of the job site by a competent person to identify hazardous conditions. It sets forth specific responsibilities of the Project Constructor which include developing, implementing, monitoring and enforcing the job site safety and health program.

c. **The National Association of Home Builders**

The National Association of Home Builders gives guidance to literally tens of thousands of residential construction companies relative to ways to ensure that work is done in ways that contractors and subcontractors' workers are not needlessly injured and killed. They have provided several publications to guide this industry. The following are some examples:

- The Model Safety and Health Program for the Building Industry, Second Edition, 1995
- Construction Management—The Superintendent's Job, Second Edition, 1990
- How to Hire and Supervise Subcontractors, 1991
- Fall Protection Compliance Manual—An Employer's Compliance Manual for OSHA's Fall Protection Regulations, 1995
- An Ounce of Prevention—Job Site Safety and Ensurance for Builders and Remodelers, 1995
- An Occupational Safety and Health Program for Builders: Guidelines for Residential and Commercial Construction, 1990

In their publication, "An Ounce of Prevention," the National Association of Home Builders gives guidance to the builder to prevent injuries to subcontractors or their employees. They state: "It's just not **your own employees** you have to worry about. You can also be held responsible for injuries of subcontractors or their employees . . . If you are doing business as a . . . builder, you have a legal obligation to provide your subcontractors and their employees with a safe place to work. If you do not, you are being negligent. The law requires you to supervise the project to ensure the safety of **all** the workers on the site, including the employees of subcontractors. Moreover, this is one of those **nondelegable** duties we mentioned in Chapter 2. The responsibility to supervise and inspect your job sites to ensure that safety practices meet the requirements for your industry is yours. If you assign that task to someone else, and they do not do it right, you are liable for the consequences of their mistakes."

Throughout these publications, the National Association of Home Builders guides general contractors and builders to implement a job site occupational safety and health program. That is, they exhort the builders in this industry to design and implement safety programs by requiring contractors and subcontractors to implement their own safety and health programs. They exhort the builder to manage safety, just as they manage all other aspects of construction such as scheduling, quality assurance, coordination, etc. The National Association of Home Builders recognizes the moral responsibility of the builder to take reasonable steps to manage safety to ensure that contractor and subcontractor employees are not needlessly exposed to hazards and risks which could cause catastrophic injury or death.

The National Association of Home Builders specifically addresses the relationship between general contractor and subcontractors when they state: "More and more, builders are finding out that when an OSHA inspection takes place on their job site, they can be held responsible for the violations of their subs. Since March 1992, when OSHA increased their penalties by seven-fold, the affect of a subcontractor's violations can have an even greater impact on the builder's bottom line . . . One of the best ways a builder can avoid OSHA citations that result from a subcontractor's violations is to only utilize subs who have effective safety and health programs and policies that aggressively attempt to comply with OSHA standards. Builders should share information about developing a safer work site with the sub. Having a safe, OSHA-compliant job site is good business for everyone on the site. If there are no injuries, then workers compensation rates go down and the concern for third party lawsuits is lessened . . . Remember, OSHA currently wants the builder or general contractor to ensure that all employers under contractual control comply with all requirements."

d. **Associated General Contractors of America**

Since 1927, the Associated General Contractors of America have published their MANUAL OF ACCIDENT PREVENTION IN CON-

STRUCTION. The primary objective of the Manual is to ensure effective control of accidents in the construction industry. They point out in their 1972 Edition of this Manual the following: “There must be recognition of the fact that control of accidents is the result of management and employees working together for a common objective. The leadership for such an effort must, however, originate with management. The degree to which management accepts this responsibility will determine the success or failure of the entire program.”

They state in Chapter 1—Accident Prevention Organization: “The basic functions of any management are planning and controlling . . . Failure, in too many instances, to give sufficient attention to planning and controlling is largely responsible for high frequency rates.” In Chapter 1, they further point out the need for assignment of responsibility and accountability of management personnel. They state: “Supervisory personnel assigned to the job should confer as soon as practical, review initial planning, discuss any condition changes, and accordingly, alter safety plans. Further, it should be determined that procurement of safety needs has been provided for, that safety policies and procedures applicable to the work are reviewed, and that authority and responsibility have been clarified.” With regard to subcontractors, they point out: “Coordination between the accident prevention activities of the subcontractors and those of the prime contractor is a must, if the objectives of accident frequency reduction and lower costs are to be achieved.”

Safety Inspections

In Chapter 1, they state: "Day-by-day, hour-by-hour, job inspections should be made and a list of violations noted for use and discussion at the next safety meeting of supervisors after corrections have been made. Along with the normal daily surveys of the supervisors, a safety committee should tour the job site to confirm or add to the list of unsafe acts already noted."

e. **Construction Management Association of America**

The Construction Management Association of America gives guidance to construction managers relative to safety management. They point out the following:

- Risk is managed by:

  —Contract agreements.
  —Documentation of the construction activities.

—Your Actions while in the field.
—Close observation of the construction work being performed.
—Schedule, cost, quality, safety.
—Staying one step head of the contractor.

- Proactive Approach

—CM employees trained to identify hazards in the workplace.
—CM addresses safety in pre-job meetings and progress meetings.
—CM addresses safety concerns per the contract.
—Points out safety concerns to the contractor.
—CM provides information to the contractor and owner and advises their employees to keep away from the hazard until correct.

f. **National Safety Council**

Accident Prevention Manual for Industrial Operations:

The National Safety Council is considered by construction safety management professionals as a highly authoritative source for guidance in safety matters. In Chapter 2 of their ACCIDENT PREVENTION MANUAL FOR INDUSTRIAL OPERATIONS, it sets forth guidelines for controlling hazards in the construction industry. It has been available since at least 1969. In their Manual, they point out:

- The importance of insisting upon contractor compliance with all safety and health regulations.
- The need for advanced analyses and planning for safety.
- The need for a preconstruction safety conference.
- The need for periodic safety meetings during which plans are made for anticipating hazards associated with work so that controls can be put in place before the hazard evolves.

Essential to the principles established by the National Safety Council is the principle that all accidents are foreseeable, predictable, avoidable and preventable. Construction safety management should be proactive rather than reactive. That is, plans should be made to predict the hazards and to install the controls before the hazard evolves. This is a proactive approach. It is far more dependable than a reactive approach which would depend upon safety inspection to identify the hazard. Serious injury or death could result before the hazard is identified through safety inspection.

The National Safety Council further points out the importance of "assignment of responsibility" and "accountability" as key elements in a construction safety management program."

Core Safety Materials for the Construction Professional:

A Manual entitled "Core Safety Materials for the Construction Professional" has been prepared by the National Safety Council's Construction Division. In it, it gives guidance regarding the elements of an effective construction site-specific safety plan:

Introduction: An effective safety plan should get its start during the bid process. The owner should require the development of a pre-construction analysis by all successful bidders. The general contractor/project management team should take the lead in the developing process. All subcontractors—both first and second tier subs—should be invited to an initial meeting and encouraged to participate in the process.

Construction Management Responsibility:

a. Plan safety into the project.

    1. Comply with owner's safety requirements and local, state and federal regulations.
    2. Establish minimum safety history requirements (e.g. last five years, EMRs, OSHA inspection history, etc.) for all project contractors.
    3. Investigate, and pre-qualify as acceptable bidders, contractors who meet the pre-determined safety history requirements.
    4. Establish and incorporate into contract documents the requirement for a Project Specific Safety and Health Plan to include:

        a. Construction process plan.
        b. Hazard analysis.
        c. Permit system.
        d. Designated project safety coordinator/administrator.

This document goes on to give guidance with regard to owners, general/prime contractors and subcontractors which is essentially the same as all of the other industry standards and authorities.

g. **Construction Industry Institute**

The Construction Industry Institute is an association of major general contractors/construction managers and major corporations in the United States. The Construction Industry Institute participates with leading universities in the United States. They funded research which resulted in the publication of a document entitled "Managing Subcontractor Safety", Publication 13-1, February 1991. The purpose of the CII Safety Task Force research was to identify the primary means by which general contractors influence the safety performance of their subcontractors . . . The goal was to add to the body of knowledge so that effective measures can be implemented to reduce the cost of accidents.

Conclusions of CII Explained in "Managing Subcontractor Safety"

Task Force research shows that, where subcontractor safety is concerned, the role of project managers is very important. On large and small projects alike, emphasizing safety and providing quality coordination have a favorable impact on the safety of subcontractors. On small projects, subcontractor safety performance also was influenced by the quality of the project management existent on the job and the degree to which workers were dealt with in a humanitarian or personal manner . . . **Since the general contractors have a significant influence on their subcontractors, owners too will have an influence on the safety performance of the general contractor and subcontractor. Thus, it can be inferred from the results of this study that owners also play a major role in construction safety** (emphasis added).

Guidelines for Managing Subcontractor Safety on Construction Projects

The following is a brief summary of the guidelines set forth by CII.

- They point out the importance of selecting subcontractors by evaluating their safety performance when evaluating bids.
- The contract should be detailed relative to how safety will be managed and reported. As a minimum, the scope of work should include requirements for a "Safety Plan", including such information as safety inspection, enforcement, safety staffing, permit required, preemployment testing, substance abuse testing, safety meetings, personal protective equipment required, . . . basic safety training . . .
- Pre-job safety conference to set forth safe procedures, training requirements and a schedule to discuss safety performance and training programs.
- Periodic safety progress reviews between managers and subcontractor safety representatives.

- Managers should conduct their own safety inspections of the subcontractor's work site, and a review of the inspection findings should take place at the periodic meetings.

Safety Rules—Enforcement Procedure

There must be a procedure for enforcing safety rules. This procedure should be written, and should be enforced equally among supervisors, managers, workers and other parties on the site. It should spell out what situations will result in immediate discharge and what actions will be taken on the first, second or third incidents involving violations of a less serious nature.

VIII. U.S. DEPARTMENT OF LABOR, OCCUPATIONAL SAFETY AND HEALTH ADMINISTRATION

OSHA recognizes the need for the general contractor to take reasonable steps to ensure that their work is done safely and in compliance with their regulations by contractor and subcontractor workers.

OSHA Standard Interpretation 1926.32 Addressing Competent Persons at Construction Sites:

OSHA requires that all employers, general contractors, contractors and subcontractors employ OSHA competent personnel to perform safety inspections as part of their safety program. On August 31, 1995, OSHA gave a clarification regarding 1926.32 addressing competent persons at construction sites. The following is excerpted from that interpretation:

> A legal principle relevant is that . . . the general contractor normally has responsibility to assure that the other contractors fulfill their obligations with respect to employee safety which affect the entire site. The general contractor is well suited to obtain abatement of hazards, either through its own resources or through its supervisory role with respect to other contractors. It is therefore reasonable to expect the general contractor to assure compliance with the standards insofar as all employees on the site are affected. **Thus we will hold the general contractor responsible for violations as could reasonably be expected to prevent or abate by reason of its supervisor capacity** (Blount Int'l Ltd., 15 BNA OSHC 1897, 1991–93 Cch OSHD 29, 854 (No. 89-1394, 1992).
>
> On the other hand, the Occupational Safety and Health Review Commission also noted in that decision that the duty imposed on a general contractor is a reasonable one and that the general contractor will not be held liable 'for violations which it could not reasonably be expected to detect or prevent' . . . In addition to whatever responsibility it may have as an

> exposing employer, the general contractor would also share responsibility for those violations by its subcontractors which it could reasonably have protected and had corrected. We would expect general contractors to take the steps necessary to satisfy themselves that subcontractors engage in activities which call for the involvement of competent persons will fulfill that obligation as well as the general inspection obligation imposed by 1926.20(b)(2).

In February of 2009, the United States Court of Appeals for the Eighth Circuit upheld OSHA's right to cite general contractors as controlling employers responsible for compliance with OSHA standards even though their own workers are not exposed to the hazard – Hilda Solis, Secretary of Labor, United States Department of Labor vs. Summit Contractors, Inc., 558 F.3d 815 (8th Cir. 2009). OSHA's enforcement Policy in this regard is set forth in their Multi-Employer Citation Policy—CPL-02-00-124.

OSHA also recognizes the overall responsibility of the contractor at the top in the Code of Federal Regulations.

29CFR1926.16(a) ". . . In no case shall the prime contractor be relieved of overall responsibility for compliance with the requirements of this part for all work to be performed under the contract."

29CFR1926.16(b) ". . . The prime contractor assumes all obligations prescribed as employer obligations under the standards contained in this part, whether or not he contracts any part of the work."

29CFR1926.16(c) ". . . Thus, the prime contractor assumes the entire responsibility under the contract and the subcontractor assumes responsibility with respect to his portion of the work. With respect to subcontracted work, the prime contractor and any subcontractor or subcontractors shall be deemed to have joint responsibility."

29CFR1926.16(d) ". . . Where joint responsibility exists, both the prime contractor and his subcontractor or subcontractors, regardless of tier, shall be considered subject to the enforcement provisions of the Act."

The above OSHA regulations, 1926.16(a) through (d), set forth a philosophy of safety management. This philosophy of safety management guides OSHA's Multi-Employer Citation Policy which considers four types of employers: the Controlling Employer, the Creating Employer, the Correcting Employer and the Exposing Employer. When there is a violation of a particular standard related to a particular hazard, OSHA is required to issue allegations of violations to entities which meet the definition of the four types of employers that is expressed in OSHA's Multi-Employer Citation Policy. OSHA's Multi-Employer Citation Policy requires the controlling employer to exercise reasonable care to prevent and detect violations of OSHA standards. Reasonable care is defined in Multi-Employer Citation Policy CPL 02-00-124, paragraph X.E.4.—Evaluating Reasonable Care:

> In evaluating whether a controlling employer has exercised reasonable care in preventing and discovering violations, consider questions such as whether the controlling employer:
>
> a. Conducted periodic inspections of appropriate frequency (frequency should be based on the factors listed in G.3.);
> b. Implemented an effective system for promptly correcting hazards;
> c. Enforces the other employer's compliance with safety and health requirements with an effective, graduated system of enforcement and follow-up inspections.

With regard to the primary responsibility for implementation of the job site safety program, OSHA is clear in its Basic Instructor Course for Occupational Safety and Health Standards in the Construction Industry. OSHA states the following: "**General contractor has primary responsibility.** The federal safety and health laws now place the primary responsibility for the environmental safety of all personnel on the job squarely on the primary employer, the general contractor. He cannot contract away this responsibility. He must, therefore, insist that the subcontractors become a part of the planning as well as the execution of the job. The fact is that every employer on the construction site is responsible for the safety of his own employees and for the safety of any and all subcontractors working for him. **There is no way, under the Acts, that this responsibility can be contracted away for it is the responsibility under the law and not under the contract** (emphasis added)."

All of the information provided above in this section is simply to show OSHA's understanding of the role and responsibility of the general contractor, contractor and subcontractor. I do not intend to rely on any legal principles, opinions or decisions related to law. My opinions related to OSHA are only whether or not there was a violation of an OSHA standard, including whether or not there was a violation of a standard based on OSHA's Multi-Employer Citation Policy.

The following are the OSHA standards relevant in this case:

29CFR1926.20(b)(1). It shall be the responsibility of the employer to initiate and maintain accident prevention programs as may be necessary to comply with this part.

29CFR1926.20(b)(2). Accident prevention programs shall provide for frequent and regular inspections of the job sites, materials, and equipment to be made by competent persons designated by the employers.

29CFR1926.32(f). Competent person means one who is capable of identifying existing and predictable hazards in the surroundings or work conditions which are unsanitary, hazardous, or dangerous to employees, and who has authorization to take prompt, corrective action to eliminate them.

29CFR1926.21(b)(2). The employer shall instruct each employee in the recognition and avoidance of unsafe conditions and the regulations applicable to his work environment to control or eliminate any hazards or other exposures to illness or injury.

29CFR1926.501(b)(13). Residential construction. Each employee engaged in residential construction activity six feet or more above lower level shall be protected by guardrail systems, safety net systems, or personal fall arrest systems . . .

29CFR1926.503. Training requirements. The following training provisions supplement and clarify the requirements of 1926.21 regarding the hazards addressed in Subpart M of this part.

29CFR1926.503(a)(1). Training program. The employer shall provide a training program for each employee who might be exposed to fall hazards. The program shall enable each employee to recognize the hazard of falling and shall train each employee in the procedures to be followed in order to minimize these hazards.

29CFR1926.503(a)(2). The employer shall assure that each employee has been trained, as necessary, by a competent person qualified in the following areas:

(i) The nature of fall hazards in the work area;
(ii) The correct procedures for erecting, maintaining, disassembling, and inspecting the fall protection systems to be used;

(iii) The use and operation of guardrail systems, personal fall arrest systems, safety net systems, warning line systems, safety monitoring systems, controlled access zones, and other protection to be used;
(iv) The role of each employee in the safety monitoring system when this system is used;
(v) The limitations on the use of mechanical equipment during the performance of roofing work on low-sloped roofs;
(vi) The correct procedure for handling and storage of equipment and materials and the erection of overhead protection;
(vii) The role of employees in fall protection plans;
(viii) The standards contained in this Subpart.

IX. ABC GENERAL CONTRACTORS, INC.'S SAFETY PROGRAM AND POLICY:

Responsibilities of Superintendent:

- Monitor contractor's work to ensure that OSHA standards are complied with
- Hold a pre-job safety conference with contractors
- Hold periodic safety meetings
- Verify that all workers received OSHA-required safety training

X. CONTRACT BETWEEN OWNER AND ABC GENERAL CONTRACTORS, INC.:

Article 10. PROTECTION OF PERSONS AND PROPERTY

10.1. SAFETY PRECAUTIONS AND PROGRAMS. The Contractor shall be responsible for initiating, maintaining and supervising all safety precautions and programs in connection with the performance of the Contract.

10.2. SAFETY OF PERSONS AND PROPERTY

10.2.1. The Contractor shall take reasonable precautions for safety of, and shall provide reasonable protection to prevent damage, injury or loss to:

.1. Employees on the work and other persons who may be affected thereby;

10.2.2. The Contractor shall comply with and give notices required by applicable laws, statutes, ordinances, codes, rules and regulations, and lawful orders of public authorities bearing on safety of persons or property or their protection from damage, injury or loss.

10.2.3. The Contractor shall erect and maintain, as required by existing conditions and performance of the Contract, reasonable safeguards for safety and protection, including posting danger signs and other warnings against hazards, promulgating safety regulations and notifying owners and users of adjacent sites and utilities.

XI. HAZARD ANALYSIS:

The hazard to which Injured Worker was exposed was a fall hazard. The exposure existed because there was no guardrail around the stairway floor opening through which he fell. This exposure was not an isolated incident. Mr. Injured Worker testified in his deposition that in the four other houses prior to this house, there had been no temporary guardrails installed around stairway openings. He testified that the incident stairway had never had a guardrail nor a cover over it since it was created approximately two weeks prior to this incident.

The following is the most important deposition testimony of Superintendent of ABC General Contractors, Inc.:

- Superintendent had no training in OSHA standards nor in workplace safety.
- Superintendent was unaware of the superintendent's safety responsibilities as indicated in the general contractor's safety program.
- General contractor never verified if any of the contractor workers had received OSHA training related to fall protection.
- Superintendent testified that he relies upon the contractors to install guardrails.
- Superintendent does not periodically monitor the job site to ensure that guardrails are installed around stairway openings.
- Superintendent never held a pre-job safety conference with any contractor at this job.
- Superintendent did not have evidence of daily safety inspections being performed at this site by any contractor.
- Superintendent never held any weekly safety meetings with contractors at this site.

It is clear from the above testimony that ABC General Contractors, Inc. did nothing to plan, monitor and ensure that the incident stairway opening was protected by a standard guardrail or cover as required by OSHA.

XII. <u>OPINION/CONCLUSION</u>:

My opinion is based on my training, education and experience in the field of occupational safety and health as well as my review of the documents set forth in Section II. It is my opinion that ABC General Contractors, Inc. violated the principles and practices of construction safety management because they failed to plan, monitor and ensure that the incident stairway opening was protected with a guardrail or cover in compliance with OSHA standards. It is my opinion that ABC General Contractors, Inc. would be considered a controlling employer under OSHA's Multi-Employer Citation Policy. It is my opinion that ABC General Contractors, Inc. violated the aforementioned OSHA violations, its contract with the owner, and its own safety policy.

It is my opinion that the above failures were the cause of this incident.

Index

www.ingramcontent.com/pod-product-compliance
Ingram Content Group UK Ltd.
Pitfield, Milton Keynes, MK11 3LW, UK
UKHW041103150926
475561UK00001BA/19

9 781598 889086